GREAT EASTERN RV TRIPS

Great Eastern RV Trips

A YEAR-ROUND GUIDE TO THE BEST RVING IN THE EAST

Janet Groene and Gordon Groene

RAGGED MOUNTAIN PRESS/MCGRAW-HILL

Camden, Maine • New York • San Francisco • Washington, D.C. • Auckland
Bogotá • Caracas • Lisbon • London • Madrid • Mexico City • Milan • Montréal
New Delhi • San Juan • Singapore • Sydney • Tokyo • Toronto

Also available:
Great Western RV Trips:
A Year-Round Guide to the Best RVing in the West,
Jan Bannan

Ragged Mountain Press
A Division of The *McGraw-Hill* Companies

10 9 8 7 6 5 4 3

Library of Congress Cataloging-in-Publication Data
Groene, Janet.
    Great eastern RV trips : a year-round guide to the best RVing in the East / Janet Groene
  and Gordon Groene.
      p.   cm.
    Includes index.
    ISBN 0-07-134929-4
      1. Automobile travel—East (U.S.)—Guidebooks. 2. Recreational vehicle living—East
  (U.S.)—Guidebooks. 3. East (U.S.)—Guidebooks. I. Groene, Gordon. II. Title.
    GV1024. G94 2000
    917.304'929—dc21

                                                                              99-058718

Questions regarding the content of
this book should be addressed to
Ragged Mountain Press
P.O. Box 220
Camden, ME 04843
http://www.raggedmountainpress.com

Questions regarding the ordering of
this book should be addressed to
The McGraw-Hill Companies
Customer Service Department
P.O. Box 547
Blacklick, OH 43004
Retail customers: 1-800-262-4729
Bookstores: 1-800-722-4726

This book is printed on 60 lb. Finch Opaque
Printed by Quebecor Printing, Fairfield, PA
Design by Paul Uhl, Design Associates
Production by Eugenie Delaney
Production management by Dan Kirchoff
Edited by Tom McCarthy and Shana Harrington
All photographs by Gordon Groene unless otherwise credited

Buicks, Clear Gel, DeLorme, Eagle Brand, Frisbee, Hackers,
Jacuzzi, Sandwich glass, and Tabasco are registered trademarks.

Contents

Introduction

For ten happily homeless years, we lived full-time on the go in the 21-foot (6.4 m), diesel motor home that we still have, using it now for getaways on weekends and long vacation rambles through our favorite haunts. Our year began in southern Florida, where we stored the sailboat that took us to the islands during the cold months. We moved our writing tools, cameras, clothing, and canned goods out of the boat and into the RV and headed north, returning south to the boat in the fall.

One year, combining pleasure travels with a book tour, we followed springtime from Florida to Nova Scotia, doing television appearances and newspaper interviews as the world greened up, latitude by latitude. Of all the pleasures nature provides, few are more energizing than the rush of color and fragrance that is springtime. That year our spring lasted from February through May.

As full-timers we were also able to linger in autumn splendor starting in the far north and moving south with the sun for two or three months. Just as we followed azalea and dogwood festivals on the way north, we followed apple butter stirrings and apple festivals all the way south. With one winter blast, usually in late September or early October, the gaudy colors of Vermont and the Berkshires are blown away, but new spectacles await in southern Ohio, on the Blue Ridge Parkway, and deep into the south, where sourwood and swamp maple trees turn to red neon. Sumac glows, golden rain trees turn to bronze, and dogwoods light up with their red drupes.

Come with us on our north-south-north migrations and on loop tours through the magnificence of North America's eastern mountains, low country, plains, piedmont, and miles of brown sugar shoreline.

Gordon and Janet Groene
jgroene@n-jcenter.com

How to Use This Book

The term *recreational vehicle* means many types of rigs, and we have kept all of them in mind while writing this book. Like many RVers, we began with a tent and moved up to a van before buying our current RV. Ours is a self-contained, single vehicle. We must go everywhere in it, but at 21 feet (6.4 m) it's nimble enough to drive and park in the city and independent enough that we can "boondock,"—that is, survive without hookups—for two or three days without refilling our freshwater tank. However, we happily recognize that the big family of RVers also includes people who have other rigs: a fifth wheeler-plus-pickup truck, a tow car-plus-travel trailer, a class A motor home that may or may not tow a car, a small van, or a pop-top camper. Some of us are self-contained and use campgrounds only for security and social reasons. Others must have the rest rooms and other facilities provided by a campground.

Doing Your Homework

Whether you have a tow car for side trips or must go everywhere in your RV, whether you "dry camp" without facilities or prefer the safety and camaraderie of a campground, this book will work for you only if you do your homework. Maps are provided here only for the most general guidance. By no means do we intend this as a linear tour from here to there. Instead, we assume you'll do as we do, staying in one campsite for several days while making side trips throughout an area.

It's essential that you coordinate this book with the best and most current maps. Our favorites are the Atlas and Gazetteer series published state by state by DeLorme Mapping Company. They are available in bookstores and have latitude and longitude grids for use with a global positioning system (GPS). Although we don't overemphasize GPS in these pages, we use it ourselves as do many RV drivers, boaters, hikers, skiers, and other nature lovers. Navigation by GPS can be done with handheld units or with sophisticated electronic mapping devices that mount on a dashboard. GPS will become increasingly important as more and more geocoded addresses are recorded. The day is not far away when we will be able to find the next campground or gas station by latitude and longitude.

Free maps of states, regions, and many cities are available from the addresses we provide in each chapter's resources section. These resources are gold mines. It's important to allow plenty of time for planning your trip because most resources are so automated, you can't get straight answers by phone or on the Internet. Rather than load this book with details that become outdated quickly, we count on you to get information before you go and to gather more as you travel. In many areas, audio tours are available to lead you every step of the way with directions, sound effects, and invaluable narration.

We highly recommend stopping at the welcome centers found at every major state or provincial border crossing and in major cities. These centers are fountains of free information, free maps, and discount coupons. They also offer such services as free campground reservations, and most have big parking lots, attractive rest rooms, and a drinking fountain.

Because we are writing for all kinds of RVing, we rely on you, the reader, to know what alternate routes will be best for your vehicle, your schedule, and your current weather conditions. There are many good ways to get to most of the destinations we describe. Read about the route with a good map in hand and your own camping goals in mind.

As you enter each new state is a good time to get a highway conditions update. Welcome centers should have this information. In some states this information is also available from a state highway patrol telephone number or CB channel. In any case, we recommend keeping your CB tuned to channel 19 for news of highway problems. If you travel with a cellular phone, note toll-free state highway patrol emergency numbers that are sometimes posted along highways. When you're towing or driving a big rig, you need all the advance warning you can get. Along some highways, signs also announce where to tune your AM radio to get current traffic information.

Just as we assume that you'll have a good map to help plan the routes and side trips in this book, we urge you to buy one of the comprehensive campground guides published by Woodall's or Wheeler's. Each one is about two inches thick and full of information, which is why we don't list campgrounds in this book. We'd have room for little else! We'll get you there. Then it's up to you to decide where to overnight depending on your travel schedule, budget, campsite preferences, and campground discount or membership plans.

Free campground guides are also available from the tourism resources listed at the start of each chapter. A free guide to KOAs (Kampgrounds of America) can be picked up at any KOA campground, and we have found many fine campgrounds just by reading highway billboards. Use all other information in concert with one of the big guides mentioned above. The more complicated your situation (pets, oversize rig, not self-contained, must have modem hookup, require pull-through sites, and so on), the more planning you must do to find the right campsites.

Seeing the Cities

We can't ignore the great cities of the East, but at the same time we realize that some of you want to escape the city and won't venture at all into those we mention. Nor can we tell you all you need to know about tackling New York or Pittsburgh, or even such small cities as Savannah. If you have a car, your travel will be different from the family in a motor home. Even so, most of our city exploring is done by public transportation, on foot, or on tours.

If your campground provides transportation into the city, your situation is different from the family towing a big fifth wheeler and wanting to spend a few hours in downtown Jacksonville, Florida, on their way to a campground near St. Augustine. We recommend that everyone take guided tours, at least for the first day in a new city, to help learn the way around. Finally, don't overlook the pleasures of walking: it's the best way to see historic cities, which were of course designed before motorcars.

Again, do your homework by writing ahead to the resources we provide. They'll send free city maps, sightseeing tips, information on public transportation and tours, and all the other "insider" scoop you need to customize your own trip using the general route we suggest. Each trip isn't carved in stone. We don't expect to tell you where to go, mile by mile, block by block, and hour by hour. RV travel should be spontaneous and flexible. We only hope you'll discover the sites we list—and plenty more besides. If you can find a faster, better way to get there and get around, go for it!

Camping by the Seasons

Even though this book is divided into seasons, most modern RVers consider RV travel a year-round activity. An RV makes the perfect winter home for ski trips and snowmobiling as well as an ideal shelter from the midday summer sun. Just because we describe southern Ohio in autumn or Québec in summer does not mean that you won't have a whale of a vacation in these places at other times of the year.

Despite the heat and humidity, Florida has more visitors in summer than in winter because school is out and families are on the go. Rates go down in much of the state in summer, and waters are calmer for fishing and clearer for diving. And, while temperatures are in the high eighties or low nineties every day, almost every afternoon is cooled by a quick rain shower. Record highs in New York and Boston are higher than those in Miami. Winter is low season in northern Florida and the Dixie states, but golf courses and tennis courts are uncrowded, fish are biting, and many days are warm enough for picnicking in shirtsleeves. Many of our loop tours can be taken any time of year.

How Long Is Long?

In each chapter you'll find a reference to the approximate length of the trip described. Allow for variations of 25 percent or more because we hope you'll be tempted by the side trips we suggest. In fact, we hope that your actual route will resemble a spiral more than a straight piece of string. We aren't too proud to hop on the interstate when it is the quickest way between points of interest. In almost every chapter, we involve an interstate or two, without apology.

As full-timers, we had the luxury of time to linger a month here and six weeks there. The more we stayed and saw, the more we realized we still had to see. Every corner of eastern North America has legends to be learned, people to be met, and natural wonders that may not reveal themselves until the next season, the next full moon, or the next bird migration. Soon after you leave, the same places will be completely different because the fireweed is in bloom or the cotton is ripe or the peach trees are in blossom.

Don't rush things. For people who are lucky enough to pursue the RV life, the highway is home, home is where the heart is, and the heart is wherever you park it tonight.

Choosing a Campground

One of the best things about RV travel is that you're at home anywhere you hit the brakes.

MIDDLETON EVANS, COURTESY MARYLAND TOURISM

Great Falls.

But this can also be a big drawback when night is falling and you don't have a stopping place that is safe, convenient to your route, and equipped with the facilities you need.

If you're self-contained and never use public facilities, you don't care whether the campground's showers are hot and the bathrooms are clean. If your days are spent sightseeing and traveling, you don't need a destination campground with hayrides and a video arcade. If you belong to Thousand Trails, Good Neighbor Club, Good Sam, or Elks, or have a KOA Value Card or a senior citizen pass to national or state campgrounds, your choices will be guided by the discounts due you.

If you're *really* traveling on the cheap and need no facilities, you might even boondock every night. *Travel Centers and Truckstops*, published annually by Interstate America, is an RVers guide to five thousand truck stops in the United States and Canada (see the appendix for more information). Most of the truck stops listed have security and twenty-four-hour access, food, fuel, supplies, and services, but they can be noisy if the truck or RV next door is running a generator.

Here are some points to consider when choosing a campground.

- What is your bottom line? Most rates are for two people and include water and electrical hookups. Additional fees can apply for more people, heat or air conditioning, 50-amp service, sewer or television hookup, holiday weekends, and so on. Government parks usually offer fewer facilities and larger campsites. Private parks offer more activities, more hookups, and smaller sites.
- Do you need a pull-through site? Do you have an extra-long rig? Not all campgrounds can accommodate you.
- Are you fully provisioned, or do you need a campground that has groceries, propane, fuel, bait, ice, and other supplies?
- Do you want a family-oriented place with a playground and activities or a quieter spot frequented mostly by senior citizens?

- Do you travel solo, or do you need a campground where your friends who don't have RVs can join you and stay in a cabin, on-site RV rental, condo, or hotel room?
- Are reservations accepted? Some campgrounds, especially government parks, operate on a first-come, first-served basis. If you're the last one to leave work on Friday afternoon, you could be out of luck.
- What features *must* you have at every campground?

___ Fishing
___ Boating
___ Pets allowed
___ Swimming
___ Hunting
___ Campfires allowed
___ Tennis
___ Golf
___ Motorbikes or ATVs allowed
___ 24-hour in-out privileges
___ Restaurant
___ Square dancing
___ Nearby attractions
___ Health spa/fitness center
___ Handicap access
___ Skiing/sled trails
___ Launch ramp
___ Other

Under *Other*, list your family's favorite offbeat activities, such as waterskiing, scuba diving, skeet shooting, horseback riding, and so on. The more specialized your hobbies or needs are (cave diving, antique hunting, BMX, radio control airplane meets), the fewer campgrounds you will find that are convenient to such activities.

Tips on RV Travel

- Carry at least one day's extra rations in case you are delayed by a breakdown or highway problems.
- Carry a basic tool kit as well as manuals for your vehicle and for all the components of your RV from the toilet to the refrigerator. Also carry any odd-sized tools specific to your rig (see your owner's manual), spare fuses, fan belts, lightbulbs, and fluids, including motor oil. Even if you know absolutely nothing about repairs and maintenance, you'll have on hand the information and spares needed by people who can aid you.
- Make up a vest-pocket telephone book for your RV trip. List your hometown doctors, dentist, and pharmacist, your pet's veterinarian, and neighbors you can call if you need something done at home. Also include numbers for your medical and vehicle insurers and emergency numbers offered by your insurer or RV manufacturer for towing, repairs, and service.
- A ready-made first-aid kit is better than none, but it probably won't contain children's aspirin, sugar-free cough syrup, or some other essential specific to your family needs. Put together a medical kit, depending on your own family needs and the places you are

Trails along Fjord du Saguenay.

FÉDÉRATION TOURISTIQUE DU SAGUENAY–LAC-SAINT-JEAN

going. Before each trip, resupply things that have been used up or are past their expiration dates.

- Campground reservations are essential, especially in the high season, when space is tight, and in the off-season, when many campgrounds are closed.

Reserving a Campsite in National Parks

Contact the park directly to make campsite reservations for that park or make the reservation online at the NPS Reservation Service, <http://reservations.nps.gov/>. Contact individual Canadian provincial parks directly to make campground reservations; call 888-773-8888 for park phone numbers. Some U.S. national and Canadian provincial parks don't accept reservations, instead allocating campsites on a first-come, first-served basis.

Kamping the KOA Way

In addition to RV sites and tent sites, KOAs (Kampgrounds of America) also offer Kamping Kabins, which are bare-bones bunkhouses with no kitchen or bath, and Kamping Kottages, which have a basic bathroom and kitchen, a bedroom with a bunk bed, electricity, heat and air-conditioning, and a living area with a futon sofa that makes up as a double bed. You bring your own sleeping bags, cookware, and all other camping gear. We like the consistency we have found at KOA sites: a swimming pool, activities, a coin laundry, and other features, such as miniature golf, a playground, bicycle or canoe rentals, hayrides, and so on.

Each KOA has its own features, and most KOAs accept pets. Found throughout the United States and Canada and with some sites in Mexico, the chain offers more than seventy-five thousand campsites in hundreds of campgrounds, of which about 90 percent have Kamping Kabins and a growing number have Kamping Kottages.

*KOA
P.O. Box 30558
Billings MT 59114
<http://www.koa.com>*

Take Only Pictures, Leave Nothing But New Friends

RV campers, like motorboaters, snowmobilers, off-roaders, and other motorized sports participants, have an inescapable image problem. There will always be people who believe that only backpackers and canoe paddlers should have access to the outdoors and that the rest of us are polluters with our noise, our exhaust, and our trash. We could point out that we have spent sleepless nights because of tenters with loud laughter, radios, or guitars. We could mention that, for people in wheelchairs, the wilderness is accessible only in an RV. We could even get smug about living for ten years in a space smaller than the average person's bedroom, using only a fraction of the natural resources that it takes to run a house.

Instead, however, we'll appeal to all of our brother and sister campers, whether in tents or RVs, to be better citizens outdoors. Here are some suggestions.

- When checking in at a campground, ask for a site best suited to human occupation under today's conditions. Impact takes a different toll at different times depending on rainfall, the state of any seasonal growth, wildlife migrations or nesting, and fire danger.
- Minimize cooking and trash by planning, precooking, and prepackaging foods.
- Except for safety gear, choose equipment in subtle colors that blend with nature's color scheme.
- Don't play radios outdoors, shout loudly to one another, or do anything to disturb nature's sweet song. Speak and walk quietly. The quieter you are, the more you'll be rewarded with wildlife sightings and sounds.
- Maintain a safe distance between yourself and other hikers so branches released by one person don't snap back and injure the next person in line.
- Walk single file in the center of the trail. Walk in small groups and don't disturb plants, rocks, or other trail surfaces any more than necessary.

How to Use This Book: A Summary

1. Choose a trip from the table of contents. Decide when you'll go and what side trips you want to make. If the trip is a loop, as most of ours are, decide where to begin and end your trip.

2. Contact all of the resources that apply to the trip's chapter, asking for information on campgrounds, sightseeing, and all your special interests, such as birding, fishing, shopping, caving, and so on. Soon your mailbox will fill with tempting brochures, free maps, and invaluable tips. Divide the trip into sections either by the day or by the leg, and sort the brochures into piles or files accordingly. Keep campground information in a separate file.

3. If you're traveling at the height of the season, when campgrounds are crowded, or in the off-season, when some campgrounds are closed, get reservations before you leave home. We prefer not to be locked into too rigid a schedule, though, and may not make reservations at all or may make them on the road only a day or two ahead. If you're self-contained and can drop anchor almost anywhere and if you don't need the kinds of activities that campgrounds offer, you can "wing it" as we do. Well ahead of time, order hard-to-get en-trance tickets, make reservations at special restaurants, and explore discounts. Many communities include discount coupons with their information packets. They're good for restaurants, attractions, and some shops.

4. If you have a mapping program on your computer, work out a couple of itineraries using our route as a guide. If you can take your computer and mapping program along, so much the better.

5. Fine-tune your packing and provisioning for where you are going.

6. Don't forget to take this book with you. It will be as helpful on the highway as it is with advance planning. Read a day or two ahead with an eye toward sightseeing and tourist information centers on your route. Never pass up an official welcome center (but beware of T-shirt shops and tourist traps that call themselves "official" but are anything but).

7. Stay flexible and laugh a lot. If you're delayed by traffic or weather problems, or if you simply decide to spend your entire vacation in one spot rather than soldiering through the entire route we recommend, do it! That's the kind of freedom we all bought RVs for in the first place.

- Don't shortcut the main trail. Rangers have most likely designed the trail this way for a reason, even if it means extra steps for you on switchbacks, stairs, boardwalks, or paving.
- "Clean" rinse water or gray water should be dumped well away from drinking water sources. Use biodegradable cleaning agents. Pour used water down drains where possible. Even clean cooking water could contain salt, which injures plants.
- Use only dead trees for firewood (where allowed), and don't discard anything in the wilderness, even if it's something that will dissolve in the next rain.
- Get the proper permits where required for access to wilderness and private areas.

Spring Trips

Even if you're a year-round RVer, you feel a quickening with the first whiff of warm, humid air. It goes straight to your feet, which start to itch for the gas pedal and for unknown highways. Until school is out, you'll have more roads and campgrounds all to yourself. That could mean the end of May in some areas and late June in others. By the spring-break holidays, attractions begin to come back to life—only on weekends at first except in year-round areas such as Florida and then gradually on more weekends and for longer hours.

The cautious RVer is ready for almost anything in springtime—surprise cold snaps that test your antifreeze, overheated tires during unexpected heat waves, rain-slick roads with icy patches, snowfalls at high altitude, and an unpredictable patchwork of hours at tourist attractions, shops, parks, and restaurants. This is off-season camping at its best, filled with fresh smells and colorful blooms.

*Small Azalea
(Rhododendron albiflorum)*

*Flowering Dogwood
(Cornus florida)*

CHAPTER 1

A Florida-to-Canada Ramble

The Snowbird Follows Springtime

CONTINUE NORTH ON THE NEXT PAGE

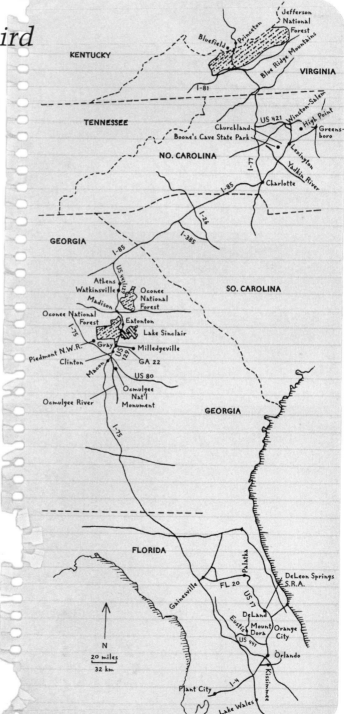

MILEAGE

Approximately 2,000 miles (3,200 km)

RESOURCES

- Canadian Tourism Commission, 550 S. Hope St. 9th Fl., Los Angeles CA 90071, 213-346-2700, or 305 Sea Isle Key, Secaucus NJ 07094, 201-223-1968.
- FLA-USA, 661 East Jefferson St., Tallahassee FL 32301, 888-7FLA-USA (888-735-2872), *http://www.flausa.com.*
- Georgia Department of Industry, Trade & Tourism, P.O. Box 1776, Atlanta GA 30301, 800-VISIT-GA (800-847-4842), *http://www.gomm.com.*
- Pennsylvania Department of Tourism, 800-VISIT PA (800-847-4872), *http://www. visit.state.pa.us.*

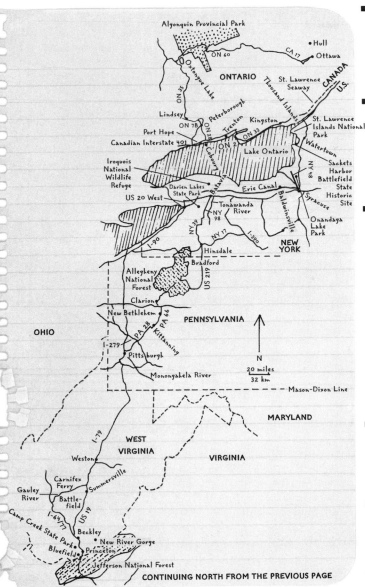

CONTINUING NORTH FROM THE PREVIOUS PAGE

- Southern West Virginia Convention & Visitors Bureau, P.O. Box 1799, Beckley WV 25802, 800-847-4898 or 304-252-2244.
- Syracuse Convention & Visitors Bureau, 572 S. Salina St., Syracuse NY 13202, 800-234-4797 or 315-470-1900, *http://www.syracusecvb. org.*
- Tourism Ontario, 800-ONTARIO (800-668-2746) from Canada or the U.S. 1 Concorde Gate 9th Fl., Toronto ON M3C 3N6, Canada, *http://www.travelinx.com.* Reservations at Ontario provincial parks can be made at 888-ONT-PARK (888-668-7275) and *http://www. OntarioParks. com.* A $9 nonrefundable fee is charged.
- Valleys of the Susquehanna, 210 William St., Williamsport PA 17701. Information on eight counties in central Pennsylvania.
- West Virginia Tourism, State Capitol Complex, Charleston WV 25305, 800-225-5982, *http://www.callwva.com.*
- Winston-Salem Convention & Visitors Bureau, 500 W. Fifth St., Winston-Salem NC 27102, 888-OLD-SALE (888-653-7253) (automated line), *http://www.oldsalem.org.*

Spring's song in the mountains begins with the drip of melting snow that becomes a rushing river, and with drumming rains that coax hyacinths and daffodils out of winter slumber. We RVers are privileged travelers who, months ago, fled the snow for sunnier latitudes. Here in the South, springtime steals in more subtly but no less dramatically. Our goal is to follow its undulating floral waves northward, starting in Central Florida in mid-February and reaching Ottawa, Ontario, by mid-June. One year, our timing was so good that we found fresh strawberries at each new latitude, starting with the harvest in mid-

February at Plant City, Florida, home of the annual Strawberry Festival in February, and ending with wild strawberries in Canada in June.

Go north too quickly and you'll freeze. Travel too slowly and you won't reach your northern goal before school lets out and the roads fill with vacationers. This is off-season travel at its uncrowded best, but it also means that campgrounds may be closed or open only on weekends. Although it's always wise to call ahead, it's essential at this time of year.

Tip:
When making a seasonal migration, it's even more important to be aware of the big picture, weather-wise. Watch the Weather Channel on cable TV, contact <http://www.weather.com>, listen for the radio weather broadcasts, or consult weather maps in the daily paper with an eye to fronts, the jet stream, and long-term trends.

North from Orlando

Our route starts in the Orlando area, where you never realize there has been a winter until live oak forests turn a greener green. Redbud trees blush against blue skies. And the azaleas! This region is known for its morning-glory-size, hot pink Formosa azaleas, the queens of the azalea world. Florida strawberries ripen in February, and you'll see them at roadside stands for half the price of what you'd pay in supermarkets.

Driving through any of the old towns at this latitude—Lake Wales, Kissimmee, Eustis, Mount Dora, Orange City, DeLand— you'll see the azalea show. The older the neighborhood, the more likely that old

Azaleas are a springtime spectacular, starting as early as January in central Florida and moving north with the sun.

homes are surrounded by house-high azaleas in riotous bloom. One of the most spectacular blooms is at DeLeon Springs State Recreation Area north of DeLand on US 17, where centuries-old live oak trees are ringed with azalea bushes as big as Buicks.

From Orlando, take Interstate 4 northeast to DeLand, then US 17 north to reach Palatka by mid-February. Here you'll find Ravine Gardens, a deep and craggy ravine that isn't at all like most Florida terrain. In the 1930s it was planted with thousands of azalea bushes. When they bloom, it's poetry. The annual Azalea Festival may be on while you're here. The festival offers sweet, southern, small-town fun with parades and vittles. After you've had your fill of azaleas, take FL 20 west through Gainesville to Interstate 75. Our route takes us north out of Florida via Interstate 75, with the goal of reaching Macon, Georgia, by about March 20 (see chapter 16 on Okefenokee and coastal Georgia).

Events:
- A Strawberry Festival is held in Plant City, Florida, in February.
- The Daytona 500 is run mid-February at Daytona Beach, Florida.

place among showplaces, covers 18,000 square feet (1,672 sq m) on seven floors and has nineteen hand-carved marble mantels. See it, and as many other of the historic structures as you have time to visit. Ocmulgee National Monument depicts ten thousand years of American Indian history. See a thousand-year-old earth lodge, temple mounds, a funeral mound, and archaeological finds. The park entrance is east of US 80 on Emery Highway: take US 80 east from Macon and follow the signs.

Take US 129 north from Macon toward Gray where, a block west of the highway, you'll find the ghost town of Old Clinton. A bustling frontier town with the look of the New England villages that its residents had come from, Clinton was the fourth largest town in the state by 1820. As you drive its lonely roads, imagine it in 1829 when it had ten stores, four taverns, five law offices, three doctors, a couple of hotels, factories, an academy, and fifty-six homes. When the Civil War began, Clinton was a major center for volunteerism and war materials.

In July 1864, Federal troops en route to Macon plundered the area, and worse was yet to come. By the war's end the town was burned out, ruined economically, and dispirited. It never recovered. Park the RV and walk the ghost town. You'll see the cemetery, where graves date to 1812, and a few homes, some of them built as early as 1810. If you want to come back during Civil War reenactments, write the Old Clinton Historic Society, RFD 5 Box 143, Gray, Georgia 31032, for details.

West of US 129 lie Oconee National Forest and the Piedmont National Wildlife Refuge, but we stay with country roads and take GA 22 into Milledgeville and its antebellum treasures. Park the RV and take one of the trolley tours that run Tuesday and Friday at 10 A.M. and Saturday at 2 P.M. Or stop at the welcome center downtown on West Hancock Street, which is GA 49, to get information, maps, and a southern welcome.

The city was once the state capital, so you can tour the Old Governor's Mansion, the Old State Capitol Building, and a num-

---

> Event:
>
> The annual Azalea Festival in Palatka, Florida, in late February and early March celebrates the season with a parade, the crowning of an Azalea Queen, and mountains of blooms at Ravine Gardens.

Georgia's Antebellum Trail

US 129 from Macon to Athens is a trip through history as well as a natural wonderment that, at this time of year, is a symphony of spring bulbs, flowering shrubs, pansy beds, dogwoods, and the more than 230,000 Yoshino cherry trees that blossom in Macon in time for its Cherry Blossom Festival.

We thought we had seen our share of antebellum homes, but Macon is in a class by itself. Park the RV and take one of the tours, not just because it is hard to navigate the old city in an RV but because tour guides provide invaluable background on the sites you'll see. Founded in 1823 on the Ocmulgee River, Macon became a major cotton port, the "Queen Inland City of the South." With the cotton boom came steamboats and the railroad, and wealthy merchants built mansions each more grand than its neighbor. The Hay House, a show-

---

Maclay State Gardens

From Interstate 75, take a side trip west on Interstate 10 to Tallahassee if you have time to see Maclay State Gardens. If you're early, you'll see the last of the camellias, which bloom through the winter, and the spring blooms are spectacular. Roam the grounds and gardens, tour the home to see how the Maclay family furnished it in the years just before World War II, and have a picnic or a swim. Then head back to Interstate 75, or go north out of Tallahassee on US 319 through historic Thomasville, Georgia.

Lockerly Mansion, on the grounds of the arboretum.

ber of stately mansions. Memory Hill Cemetery dates to 1803. Little River Park offers a boat launch and picnicking. The area's playground is Lake Sinclair, but to avoid the crowds there, take a picnic lunch and spend the day instead at Lockerly Arboretum, a botanical reserve where you can wander pathways lined with shrubs, trees, herbs, and flowers for all seasons. Admission is free, and it's open daily except Sunday. Lockerly, the original mansion on the estate, is beautifully preserved and is sometimes open to the public. There's plenty of parking for RVs.

To continue on Georgia's Antebellum Trail, take US 129 north to Eatonton where you'll see more antebellum homes, pantheons of spring flowers, and a charming little museum devoted to Uncle Remus. North of town off US 441/129, stop to see the strange prehistoric eagle effigy at Rock Eagle Mound, which is thought to be about

five thousand years old. The area has swimming, fishing, boating, and picnic areas.

Continue north on the Antebellum Trail to Madison. Park the RV, pick up a walking tour map at the welcome center on East Jefferson Street downtown, snap the leash on the dog, and stroll through a movie set of antebellum homes and churches. Then proceed up US 441 to Watkinsville. Eagle Tavern, the visitor center here, was opened in 1801 as a stagecoach stop. US 441 takes you to the end of the Antebellum Trail at Athens, in the foothills of the Blue Ridge Mountains. Athens is filled with antebellum structures, including mansions and buildings at the University of Georgia, which was chartered in 1785. Stop at the Convention & Visitors Bureau at 300 North Thomas Street and ask for maps and brochures.

Carolina Bound

Athens's choicest nugget for nature lovers is the State Botanical Garden of Georgia (706-542-1244), a 313-acre preserve that is bursting with spring color in late March. Our route winds east of the madness that is Atlanta, and we continue north on US 441 to Interstate 85 and through South Carolina on a route that skirts the highlands and scoots us across Carolina upcountry toward Charlotte, North Carolina.

Continue on Interstate 85 through thickly populated Charlotte and north

Cowpens National Battlefield

If you want an interesting side trip, head north from Spartanburg on US 221 to Cowpens National Battlefield, which is just over the South Carolina border in North Carolina.

Up to this point, many historic points of interest have been connected with the Civil War, but the Battle of Cowpens took place a century earlier, in the waning months of the Revolution. General Daniel Morgan and his little band of patriots stood fast against the British as though their feet were stuck in tar, earning the Carolinians forever the nickname "tarheels." The battlefield and visitor center are open all year.

The famous double-barreled cannon that defended Athens, Georgia, was a military flop during the Civil War, but it makes a good landmark today.

toward Lexington, which calls itself the Barbecue Capital of the World. Just southwest of the city, Boone's Cave State Park is thought to be on land Daniel Boone's father settled in 1752. A one-room log cabin has been built on the site where the family may have lived. Hike trails that in springtime are a riot of mountain laurel and rhododendron. Fish or canoe the Yadkin River, which is a popular paddling trail. The park doesn't have campsites.

The tri-city area of Winston-Salem, High Point, and Greensboro is a madhouse of highways, but take the time to see Old Salem, in Winston-Salem. From Interstate 85 at Churchland, take US 52 into Winston-Salem and follow the signs: the route to Old Salem is well marked. Built in horse-and-buggy days, Old Salem isn't a place to enter with even a class C motor home, let alone with a trailer under tow. Leave your car or camper at the visitor center on Old Salem Road, and see a village that was settled early in the 1700s, when streams of newcomers crossed the Great Wagon Road, which ran here from Pennsylvania. Among them were a group of Moravians, a religious sect that had its beginnings in Germanic Europe. Take one of the tours on foot or in a horse-drawn carriage for a foray into yesteryear.

Many of Old Salem's hardy eighteenth-century homes are still in excellent repair and are privately owned and occupied. Others operate as they always did as offices and shops, including the historic Winkler's Bakery. In the Single Brothers House, an original Tannenbaum organ still plays. The Fine Arts Center at Salem Academy and College, founded in 1772, holds many special

Event:
On the first Sunday in May, the Ramp Convention in Waynesville, North Carolina (25 miles/40 km west of Asheville), focuses on digging and eating the pungent vegetable. Crafters, music, cloggers, and fun fill the day.

Event:

On Easter, sunrise service in Old Salem, North Carolina, is a Moravian tradition.

events, exhibits, and concerts winter through mid-May. The Museum of Early Southern Decorative Arts has period rooms that faithfully depict Early American life in the southern states. Give it several hours, and stop in the gift shop for fine souvenirs and a package of crisp, paper-thin, buttery Moravian cookies. Admission is $10 adults and $6 children ages 6 to 16.

From Winston-Salem, take US 421 west to join Interstate 77 and a journey northwest through some of the most rugged mountain scenery in the East. In springtime, you'll roll through hillsides dotted with mountain laurel and dogwood as you push through Jefferson National Forest in western Virginia and into West Virginia. If you're a flatlander who is accustomed to breezing along interstates at cruising speed, you'll find the West Virginia Turnpike, which is also Interstate 64/77, a new experience. Dust off your best driving manners if your rig is, like ours, slow on the upgrades.

Entering Bluefield, which takes its name from the blue chicory that carpets the meadows and hillsides, you're already half a mile above sea level, at which we started in Florida. Two Bluefields straddle the state border, one in Virginia and one in West Virginia. On the West Virginia side, see the history of coal mining exhibit in Bluefield's municipal library, Craft Memorial Library, 600 Commerce Street Center. It's open weekday afternoons free.

One of the best free attractions in the East is Tamarack Welcome Center in West Virginia at exit 45 off Interstate 77. The state, eager to sell more locally made goods,

Whitewater rafting in West Virginia is often compared to "a flush and a rush." Here, the New River.

Event:
Wild in the Parks is celebrated in April in all West Virginia State Parks with wildflower hikes and craft festivals. A number of communities also have ramp festivals this month, with a focus on the pungent wild leek (800-CALL-WVA/800-225-5982).

funded this eye-popping building, which looks somewhat like the famous Sydney Opera House in Australia. Find plenty of parking for big rigs, free movies on West Virginia nature and history, a post office, shopping for local crafts, free crafts demonstrations, an art gallery, and a food court managed by the famous Greenbrier resort. The desk staff here are cheerful and knowledgeable about West Virginia, and they'll send you away armed with maps and brochures. Throughout this book, we recommend stopping at state welcome centers, but this one is one of the very best.

West Virginia's rugged mountains abound in campgrounds and great state parks, but most of them require miles of steep, winding driving off the interstate. The closest state park to the highway is Camp Creek State Park (800-225-5982; 304-425-9481) north of Princeton in West Virginia. Take Interstate 77 north from Princeton 13 miles, then follow signs to the park, which is 2 miles (3.2 km) northwest of the exit. Camp, hike, fish, and roam 500 acres of mountain springtime splendor.

Beckley is in the heart of whitewater rafting country. Call West Virginia Tourism for information about rafting the New River or the Gauley River. The season starts March 1, promising the best whitewater in the East. The trip down the New River Gorge, deep in a river-carved canyon past ghost towns that were once thriving mining towns, is unforgettable, and the Gauley provides a screaming run through class 4 and 5 rapids. If you're a mountain

biker, Beckley also offers some of the best biking you'll find on your snowbird trek.

Starting just north of Beckley, US 19 takes you through rugged, rural hill country. From Summersville, turn west on WV 39 to reach Carnifex Ferry Battlefield, the site of a Civil War battle in 1861 in which five thousand troops under General William Rosecrans defeated an undermanned Confederate force. Hike the trails and see the museum; reenactments begin in June and run through the summer. Back on US 19, head north into Weston. The town, now known for its hand-blown glassware, was originally surveyed by the grandfather of Stonewall Jackson, whose namesake state park offers camping, fishing, boating, nature trails rimmed with spring wildflowers, and a museum at Jackson's Mill, where the general worked as a boy. The museum is open Memorial Day to Labor Day.

The precious days of springtime race past as we hurry northward through Morgantown and across the Mason-Dixon Line at the Pennsylvania border. The fastest way to reach our destination of Ontario is to take interstates, which we recommend if the calendar is closing in on you or if your rig is large and cumbersome. Interstate 79 takes you to Erie, Pennsylvania, but later we describe an alternate route that takes back roads through wildly beautiful scenery in Allegheny National Forest (see pages 10–11).

Interstate 79 takes us to Pittsburgh, which is not the gritty steel city of a couple of decades ago. Write to the Greater Pittsburgh Convention & Visitors Bureau, Regional Enterprise Tower, 425 Sixth Av-

Event:
On the first full weekend of each month, Pittsburgh celebrates its Greek Food Festival at St. Nicholas Cathedral, across from the Carnegie Museum. Over Memorial Day weekend, Pittsburgh holds its Folk Festival.

enue, Pittsburgh, Pennsylvania 15219 (800-821-1888), for city maps and directions. For a seagull's view of the city, ride the historic Duquesne Incline for $1 each way (parking is free). It's off Interstate 279 on the south shore of the Monongahela River. If you're driving a motor home, call 412-381-1665 for parking information. Another good way to see the city is aboard the Gateway Clipper Fleet (412-355-7980). Take one of the land tours offered by Gray Line (412-741-2720) or Molly's Trolleys (412-281-2085).

Don't miss the Senator John Heinz Pittsburgh Regional History Center, 1212 Smallman Street (412-454-6000) on the site of an ice company founded in 1898. In pre-refrigeration days, all seven floors of this giant structure were filled with ice that was delivered twice a week to home iceboxes. Now the structure preserves three hundred years of regional history, from a 1790 log house to a 1910 courtyard house representative of the type built for early immigrants to a Happy Days–era ranch home. Pittsburgh is also the home of the Andy Warhol Museum, the Carnegie Science Center, four Carnegie museums, and the Pittsburgh Zoo (one of the nation's major zoo attractions). And of course, the Pittsburgh Pirates will be playing at Three Rivers Stadium as soon as baseball season opens in April. If the kids need a day of fast action, take them to Sandcastle Waterpark, 1000 Sandcastle Drive (412-462-6666),which is open daily after Memorial Day.

Our alternate route, if you have time and an agile rig, is to go north on PA 28

If You Have Time to Linger

If you have time for local exploring, the Finger Lakes area offers a tempting selection. Fish for rainbow trout, take a lake cruise, tour area wineries, and see the Steuben Glass Factory and the Rockwell Museum with its Frederic Remington sculptures at Corning. Then follow Interstate 390 west to Bath, turning east on NY 54 to Hammondsport on Keuka Lake. The Glenn H. Curtiss Museum of Local History there is named for the aviation pioneer and contains local memorabilia as well as a replica of his plane June Bug. Take NY 54A north to NY 364, which takes you to Canandaigua Lake and north along the lake shore into the town of Canandaigua. At Sonnenberg Gardens you can see 50 acres of springtime splendor and tour the Granger Homestead and Carriage Museum. More than fifty carriages and cutters are on view.

From Canandaigua, drive east on US 20 to Geneva to stroll the South Main Street Historic District and see historic homes and shops and the 1894 opera house just east of town overlooking Seneca Lake. Take a guided tour of Rose Hill Mansion, one of the state's grand Greek Revival homes. Furnished in museum-quality Empire pieces, the mansion is open daily starting in May. This area is one of the Empire State's favorite summer playgrounds, so you'll find campsites aplenty in state and private parks. The KOA at Canandaigua (716-398-3582) opens on April 1, and most other parks are open by early or mid-May.

Farther east on US 20 is Seneca Falls, the site of the first Women's Rights Convention in 1848. Today the National Women's Hall of Fame pays tribute to Amelia Bloomer, Susan B. Anthony, Elizabeth Cady Stanton, and other suffragettes. On the south side of town, an observation tower overlooks two locks in the State Barge Canal, which connects Lake Region to the Hudson River and port of New York. The city's historical museum occupies a twenty-three-room Victorian mansion, which is open daily except Sunday. Five miles (8 km) east of town on US 20, Montezuma National Wildlife Refuge is the perfect spot to watch migrations of Canada geese and other birds in springtime.

Stop in Auburn, the largest city in the Finger Lakes region, for supplies and a look at Hoopes Park Flower Gardens, which are splendid in springtime. The home of Harriet Tubman, the escaped slave who rescued hundreds of other slaves via the Underground Railroad, is at 180 South Street. The Seward House, home of William Henry Seward—famous as the nineteenth-century statesman who led the United States to purchase Alaska, known as Seward's Folly—to see historic relics, including Alaskan items. From Auburn, it's a short hop back onto Interstate 90 to get you back on course.

from Pittsburgh along the meandering Allegheny River through Kittanning. In New Bethlehem, turn west on PA 66 to Clarion, then run west on US 322 for a few miles and then turn north again on PA 66, which takes you on a scenery-packed drive through Allegheny National Forest, which has several campgrounds. Whatever travels you make within the forest, plan on joining US 219, which runs north and south on the east border of the forest. Take US 219 north to Bradford, where Crook Farm re-creates the 1850s. The farm opens in May. Bradford is also the home of the Penn-Brad Oil Museum, which has displays showing how the oil boom changed the town. It's open after Memorial Day.

The Empire State

Staying with US 219, cross the state border north of Bradford into New York and take NY 17 east to Hinsdale, then NY 16 north through thrilling scenery. Just past the picnic area below Yorkshire, jog east on NY 39 and then north again on NY 98 toward Batavia. The scenic route follows the Tonawanda River. If you want to stop at Darien Lakes State Park, it's 10 miles (16 km) southwest of Batavia off US 20 West. In the park are hiking, fishing, swimming, and nature watching. Nearby, Darien Lake Theme Park and Camping Resort (716-599-2211) has campsites with hookups plus plenty of razzmatazz, including roller coasters.

Batavia lies where two Indian trails once crossed, a natural choice for a settlement created to sell the more than 3 million acres that belonged to the Holland Land Company. In the Holland Land Office Museum, 131 West Main Street, where deeds were sold, the phrase "doing a land office business" described the brisk trade done here with land-hungry settlers. See Indian artifacts, period furniture and clothing, and reminders of New York's settlement by the Dutch. Northwest of town, the nature lover will find a wealth of waterfowl at the Iroquois National Wildlife Refuge, 15 miles (24 km) northwest of Batavia via NY 63. It's especially recommended during

Early morning and late afternoon are beautiful times to be on the water or camped in a waterfront spot in the Finger Lakes region.

spring migrations, when geese pass by in great honking flocks. The refuge opens mid-March.

From Batavia, Interstate 90 takes you swiftly east past the Finger Lakes to Syracuse. If you have time for a closer look, make a loop tour through historic Cortland, Ithaca, founded 1791, and Watkins Glen State Park. Cornell Plantations in Ithaca are full of bird life and botanical sorcery in the spring. The gorge at Watkins Glen is about 1.5 miles (2.4 km) long, rimmed with 300-foot (91.4-m) cliffs studded with waterfalls; a nightly sound-and-light show plays mid-May through the summer.

Continuing Northward

We're now on Interstate 90, the New York State Thruway. At Syracuse, look into Erie Canal history at the museum and visitor center. You can sign on here for anything from a three-day canal trip to an afternoon excursion. The Discovery Center of Science and Technology is educational fun for kids and adults and, in Onandaga Lake Park, 2½ miles northwest of downtown on Interstate 81 (Liverpool exit), a seventeenth-century French mission has been re-created at Ste. Marie Among the Iroquois. Northwest of Syracuse 12½ miles (20 km) on NY 48 (from town, take Interstate 690) at Baldwinsville, Beaver Lake Nature Center (8477 E. Meed Lake Rd.) has 10 miles (16 km) of trails and boardwalks where you can watch migrating birds as they land on a 200-acre lake for a rest on their way northward. You can also canoe the 560-acre preserve.

When you're finished with Syracuse, head north on Interstate 81, which runs just east of Lake Ontario and its half-dozen lakeside state parks, most of them with camping. West of Watertown, Sackets Harbor (exit at Adams and head west on NY 178 and north on NY 3) is a resort community that begins gearing up for the summer in mid-May. Sackets Harbor Battlefield State Historic Site comprises an 1818 hotel, visitor center, U.S. Navy Yard, the 1850 Commandant's House, and a view of the place where two major sea battles were fought in the War of 1812.

The dime store was invented in Watertown by young Frank Woolworth in 1878. See the town's magnificent marble public library, the history museum, the American Maple Museum, and the Sci-Tech Center with its hands-on fun for children. It's open all year Tuesday to Saturday.

Continue north on Interstate 81, lingering as long as possible in the Thousand Islands area of the St. Lawrence Seaway. Take a cruise from Clayton to Boldt Castle with its amazing boathouse. See the Antique Boat Museum at Clayton, west of Interstate 81 on NY 12E, and the zoo at Alexandria Bay, on NY 12 west of the interstate. Many state parks and St. Lawrence Islands National Park (U.S.) stretch along the seaway for many miles. The Thousand Islands is a major vacation spot for both Americans and Canadians, but the mood in May is one of "insider" discovery because the summer crowds haven't yet arrived.

Springtime in Ontario

You may have been on the road two or three months by now, and still you're in a spring-

Thousand Islands bridge.

THOUSAND ISLANDS BRIDGE AUTHORITY

Event:

In mid-March, many communities celebrate St. Patrick's Day. The Irish Festival in Watertown, New York, is one of the best. Also in mid- to late March is the Central New York Maple Festival at Marathon, 50 miles (80 km) south of Syracuse.

time world of tender new leaves, budding fruit trees, and colorful flowers. Cross the St. Lawrence on the toll bridge on Interstate 81 and head west through tourist towns that are starting to awaken for the season. Our primary road is CA 401, the MacDonald Cartier Freeway, but we'll take as many side trips down to the Lake Ontario waterfront as time allows. The tour boats at Gananoque start running in mid-May, and the local historical museum opens in early June. It's housed in the old Victoria Hotel, built in 1863, and its displays include costumes, Indian and military memorabilia, and Victorian furniture.

Old Fort Henry at Kingston, at the end of the seaway, opens in late May and holds costumed reenactments in season. You're suddenly in the land of the Redcoats, the folks who were on the other side in the bitter War of 1812, when this fort was on constant alert against American invasion. Head southwest from Kingston on ON 33, which takes you to half a dozen provincial parks on Lake Ontario.

Rejoin the MacDonald Cartier Freeway at Trenton and continue the scenic route to Cobourg. Once a busy lake port, it's now a summer vacation center. In its historic Victoria Hall, see a replica of London's Old Bailey courtroom, and an opera house with acoustics so perfect, speakers and musicians could perform without microphones in a preelectronics era.

From Cobourg, take ON 2 to Port Hope and then head north on ON 28 to Peterborough and a choice of provincial parks on the lakes that are part of the Trent-Severn Waterway. We once did the entire waterway by boat, and at every lock saw sightseers enthralled by the process that allows boats to sail up- and downhill. One of the most interesting locks is the lift lock at Peterborough. Join the onlookers.

ON 7B takes you west from Peterborough to Lindsey to meet ON 35 North and a scenic path that leads through lakes and mountain scenery through the western edge of Algonquin Provincial Park. Continue north to Oxtongue Lake, then turn east onto ON 60. This southwestern portion is the most popular part of the park, but most vacationers don't arrive until July. You should have fairly easy going, even with a big rig.

Handy to ON 60 you'll find several trails that take off into the interior of the park. You may see black bear browsing on young leaves of the quaking aspen, and there's always a good chance of seeing moose and wolves in the park. Trout fishing is at its best in early May, before the black flies come out in full force. Watch for returning robins and cedar waxwings. Stay with scenery-rich ON 60, which joins CA 17 and continues east toward Ottawa.

Ottawa was a brawling, muddy outpost when Queen Victoria made it the capital of Canada in the 1850s. The streets were quickly tamed with the addition of the regal Parliament buildings. A greater transformation came in the 1930s with the building of the Art Deco–style Supreme Court. The Royal Canadian Mint is here, and the National Gallery of Canada—which looks as though it is made entirely of glass—is a national showplace. See the Museum of Science and Technology and the Canadian War Museum, where exhibits follow Canada's roles in wars throughout history. Across the river in Hull, Quebec, the Musée Canadien des Civilisations depicts the history of Canada's many native cultures and immigrant groups.

We have now followed springtime north, and all of summer spreads ahead. Go north to the wilderness, east to the Atlantic provinces, west to the prairies, or south to your favorite summering spot.

CHAPTER 2

Illinois and Kentucky
The Land of Lincoln

MILEAGE

Approximately 1,300 miles
(2,080 km)

RESOURCES

- Chicago Office of Tourism, 78 E. Washington St., Chicago IL 60602, 312-744-2400, *http://www.cityofchicago. org/ca/Tourism.*
- Illinois Bureau of Tourism, 222 S. College St., Springfield IL 62706, 800-226-6632, *http://www. enjoyillinois.com.*
- Indiana Division of Tourism, Department of Commerce, 1 N. Capitol St., Indianapolis IN 46204, 800-291-8844 or 317-232-4685, *http://www.state. in.us/tourism.*
- Kentucky Department of State Parks, 500 Mero St. Suite 1100, Frankfort KY 40601, 800-255-PARK (800-255-7275) or 502-546-2172, *http://www.state.ky. us/agencies/parks.*
- Kentucky Department of Travel, 500 Mero St., Frankfort KY 40601, 800-225-TRIP (800-225-8747), *http://www. kentuckytourism.com.*

- Land Between the Lakes, 100 Van Morgan Dr., Golden Pond KY 42211, 270-924-2000, *http://www2.lbl.org/lbl.*
- Louisville & Jefferson County Convention & Visitors Bureau, 400 1st St., Louisville KY 40202, 502-584-2121 or 800-626-5646, *http://www. louisville-visitors.com.*

- Paducah–McCracken County Convention & Visitors Bureau, 128 Broadway, Paducah KY 42001, 800-359-4775 or 270-443-8783, *http://www. paducah-tourism.org.*

South from Chicago

Our trip begins and ends in Chicago, "city of big shoulders" but really not a place to ramble by RV. Still, Chicago has a cornucopia of sightseeing for the RV traveler. If you're camped near the city, take public transportation downtown to see the waterfront, Grant Park (which runs from Randolph Street to McFitridge Drive), and some of the best museums in the nation. The first political convention in the United States was held in Chicago in 1860, at which Abraham Lincoln was made the Republican Party's candidate. He was already dead by 1871 when the infamous Chicago Fire burned most of the city to cinders.

Now we're off to the Land of Lincoln. Interstate 55 takes us south from Chicago to the town of Lincoln, which was surveyed and mapped by Abraham Lincoln in 1833. Just north of the town square, see a faithful replica of the Postville Courthouse (914 8th St.), where Lincoln practiced as a circuit-riding lawyer. Southeast of town (take Interstate 55, exit 123), Edward R. Madigan Railsplitter State Park has picnic tables, woodsy walking trails, a playground, and plenty of the split rail fences that are associated with the young Abe Lincoln. Continue on Interstate 55 to Springfield.

Springfield

Springtime has a special poignancy in this state capital when spring shrubs flower wildly, reminding Lincoln devotees of the poet Walt Whitman's line "when lilacs last in the dooryard bloom'd." The poem tells of Whitman's sadness each spring on the anniversaries of Lincoln's death on April 15, 1865, and his burial in Springfield on May 4. The pink fantasy of redbud trees and the emerging daffodils and narcissus are the first signs of spring here; they're followed by lilacs and fragrant peonies the size of soccer balls in every shade imaginable.

Tip:
When photographing spring wildflowers deep in the woods, it's easier to get a uniform color shot because the light is completely even in the shade. Load a fast film, ASA 200 to 400, use a tripod, and carry a piece of white cardboard or a white umbrella to reflect additional light onto the subject.

Take a boat tour of Chicago's vibrant waterfront.

The house at Jackson and 8th Streets is the only home ever owned by the Great Emancipator. Lincoln and his wife, Mary Todd, bought it in 1844. The house is still filled with family belongings. It was given to the state in 1887 by Robert Todd Lincoln, their only surviving son, and it's surrounded by other homes and buildings that have been restored to their appearances in Lincoln's day. Beginning Memorial Day weekend and continuing through the summer, a sound-and-light show about Lincoln's Springfield years is acted out here.

Tour the Old State Capitol (2nd St. at Capital Avenue), where Lincoln delivered his famous speech describing how "a house divided against itself cannot stand," and see his law office across the street. The old rail station, where Lincoln left for Washington for the last time, is now a museum (Monroe St. between 9th and 10th Sts.). You can also see his towering tomb in Oak Ridge Cemetery (16 blocks north of Old State Capital). The tomb is one of the nation's most visited shrines.

From Springfield, head northwest on IL 97 to Lincoln's New Salem Historical Site, which is 2 miles (3 km) south of Petersburg. At the historical site, the streets look as they did when young Abe came to the village in 1831. We all know the stories of his self-studies and hard work at that time as a shopkeeper, rail splitter, postmaster, and surveyor, as well as of his service in the Black Hawk War. Most of the buildings here have been replicated from original records; one, however—the Ostot Cooper Shop—is an original, built on the site in 1853. The shavings left by the barrel maker at this shop lit the fires that Lincoln studied by. Allow at least a day for wandering the village of homes and shops and viewing the cast of characters that accompanies them. The historical site has campsites,

Southern Illinois Side Trips

Most of southern Illinois is within Shawnee National Forest, with its many campgrounds, miles of hiking trails, countless lakes and rivers for fishing, bridle paths, and wildlife watching. We won't blame you if you quit right here and spend the rest of the summer crisscrossing this wildly beautiful region. You have now driven out of the prairie, with its lush corn and soybean fields, and into the Illinois Ozarks. The going gets steeper and more winding, and state parks come in rapid succession. Sunfish and largemouth bass rise to the bait. Towering cliffs look out over the Ohio River.

From the Marion exit off Interstate 57, turn onto IL 13 and then IL 1 to Cave-in-Rock State Park. There you can walk down a 60-foot (18.3 m) cliff and peer into a cave where river pirates once lay in wait. Fort Defiance State Park on the southernmost point of the state (2 miles/3 km south of Cairo on US 62) marks the site where some of Lincoln's Union troops, under General Ulysses S. Grant's command, left Union territory to invade the Confederacy. In springtime, this entire region is carpeted in spectacular wildflowers.

and private parks are abundant in the Springfield area. Some are open all year.

Continue north on IL 97 across the Sangamon River to Havana, passed through by Lincoln in 1832 on his way home from the Black Hawk War. He returned to Havana often as a circuit-riding lawyer and also as a U.S. senatorial candidate in 1858. The city, which is on the banks of the Illinois River, has a Lincoln monument in a riverfront park off of US 136. Stop to take a stroll and watch boats passing on the river.

Our goal, the Western Kentucky Parkway, is now a day's drive away. Following the back roads, head south on IL 78. Turn west from IL 78 at the hamlet of Virginia onto IL 125; drive to Beardstown and stop at the Lincoln Courtroom and Museum Site. Then continue south on IL 67 through farm country to the Alton area (opposite St. Louis) and take the bypasses that lead to Interstate 64 . Head east on Interstate 64 to pick up Interstate 57, which leads south to

Event:
Springfield celebrates Maple Syrup Time on Saturday and Sunday afternoons from mid-February until early March.

Interstate 24. Enter Kentucky on Interstate 24 South and, at Lake Barkley, turn onto the Western Kentucky Parkway, which leads us to more Lincoln-related sites.

Kentucky Calls

After you cross the river, take one of the exits to Paducah, Kentucky, one of our favorite points along the Ohio River. Walk its old streets to understand the Flood of 1937, one of the most devastating floods in the river's history, and to return to a gentler time of brick streets, gaslights, and friendly shopkeepers. Visit the Museum of the American Quilter's Society (215 Jefferson St.), which houses one of the best quilt collections in the world. See the Market House Museum (South 2nd St. at Broadway St.) and seek out Whitehaven (at exit 7—KY 45—off Interstate 24), an antebellum mansion that also doubles as a visitor center. Pick up a map describing a self-guided driving tour of Paducah, including its dogwood trail if you're here during dogwood bloom in mid-April.

Boat and fish Kentucky and Barkley Lakes.

Paducah is the gateway to the Land Between the Lakes and the state parks that cradle it. From Paducah, take Interstate 24 East to the LBL exit after you cross the Tennessee River. People spend the entire summer in the LBL area, and you may decide to stay, too. You'll find miles of hiking trails, boating, and fishing plus the 170,000-acre peninsula between the two lakes, which is called, appropriately, Land Between the Lakes. Lake Barkley is 118 miles (189 km) long and has more than 1,000 miles (1,600 km) of shoreline; its twin, Kentucky Lake, is about the same size. The area has three major family campgrounds plus launch ramps, picnic grounds, planned programs, a buffalo herd, and a living history farm—Home Place–1850—where costumed "pioneers" go about their daily chores as they would have in the nineteenth century. Admission to Kentucky state parks is free; you'll pay only camping fees.

Leisurely drive the 60 miles (96 km) around Land Between the Lakes; it'll take several hours. There are no commercial facilities on the peninsula, but you'll want to stop to enjoy the scenery, hike some of the 200 miles (320 km) of trails, and scope out the land before tackling the 60-mile (96 km) North-South Hiking Trail.

In addition to the camping at Land Be-

Folks at the Home Place–1850 demonstrate pre–Civil War life.

tween the Lakes, you'll also find campsites at Kenlake State Resort Park and Lake Barkley State Resort Park as well as at private parks throughout the region. Because reservations aren't accepted at Kentucky state parks, it can be hard to find a campsite in summer and on spring weekends.

Lincoln's Boyhood

Follow the Western Kentucky Parkway east through gently rolling country for about 120 miles (192 km). At White Mills, exit onto KY 84 and travel about 20 miles (32 km) east to Hodgenville. Abraham Lincoln was born here on February 12, 1809, at Sinking Spring Farm. When Abe was three, he and his family moved to Knob Creek Farm, 10 miles (16 km) away. You'll find the Abraham Lincoln Birthplace National Historic Site 3 miles (4.8 km) south of Hodgenville on US 31E. The visitor center and the Memorial Building, which contains the log cabin believed to be Lincoln's birthplace, are open and free to the public every day but Christmas.

Go a few miles farther east from Hod-

The Lincoln Cabin is in Lincoln Homestead State Park.

genville on US 31E to Bardstown and then east on the Blue Grass Parkway to KY 555, then south, following signs to Lincoln Homestead State Park. Here you'll see land that was originally settled by Lincoln's grandfather and the home where Nancy Hanks lived while she was courted—successfully—by Abe's father, Thomas Lincoln. There is also a replica of the shop where Thomas did carpentry and blacksmithing. The park doesn't have campsites, but there are picnic tables, a playground, and golf facilities. The exhibits are open May through September. but you can picnic anytime. To continue our journey, return to Bardstown and continue on US 31E/150 into Louisville.

Louisville and the Lincoln Legend

This is a springtime trip, which in Louisville means a month-long schedule of Derby festivals and events culminating in the Kentucky Derby the first Saturday in May. It's the most exciting time of the year to be in this city, the hometown of Muhammad Ali, Tom Cruise, Lionel Hampton, and the Louisville Slugger baseball bat. The city and its surrounding area are a sightseeing bonanza, filled with sophisticated restaurants and endowed with a year-round schedule of sports, concerts, shows, and festivals. Consider a side trip to explore this lively city. For now, however, let's get back to the theme of our trip: the Land of Lincoln.

Abraham Lincoln Birthplace National Historic Site, Hodgenville, Kentucky.

KENTUCKY DEPARTMENT OF TRAVEL DEVELOPMENT

Farmington Historic Home.

Louisville in Spring

In March, Louisville holds its massive Home, Garden, and Remodeling Show, which is a good place to get ideas for furnishing and accessorizing your RV. The fairgrounds in Louisville host an enormous flea market this month and next.

In April, Derby-related events in Louisville include contests, dances, a balloon ascension, a marathon, games, fun, and tomfoolery. Locust Grove, a 55-acre estate with a Georgian mansion (6 miles/10 km north of Louisville on River Rd. to 561 Blankenbaker Ln.), is the scene of a Revolutionary War encampment. The Great Steamboat Race on the Ohio River features the Belle of Louisville, the oldest Mississippi-style stern-wheeler in operation.

The Kentucky Derby is run the first Saturday in May in Louisville. Later in the month, a Square Dance Festival takes over the Exposition Center at the fairgrounds and, at the end of the month, a reggae festival plays downtown.

Farmington Historic Home, at the junction of Interstate 264 and US 150, was built in 1810 by John and Lucy Speed from a design by Thomas Jefferson. The house is a Federal-style masterpiece with octagonal rooms, a hidden staircase, and all the features desired by a wealthy family of the times. The Speeds made their fortune from their 552-acre hemp farm in an era when riverboats carried the nation's commerce (hemp ropes were an essential boating basic). Joshua Speed, John and Lucy's son, had gone west to seek his fortune and had roomed with the young Abe Lincoln for three years. In 1841, Lincoln visited his close friend Joshua and Joshua's family for three weeks here at Farmington. Stop here to see Lincoln memorabilia and a remarkable home, which was lived in until the 1950s. A small admission is charged. An annual March event, Mary Todd's Favorite Tea Party at Farmington offers the chance to sample the Lincolns' favorite teas and cookies.

And Back to Illinois

Head west from Louisville on Interstate 64 across the Ohio River and turn north onto IN 66 at Carefree, Indiana, to see Marengo Cave. Travel west on IN 64 from Marengo to reach the state parks and campsites around Patoka Lake. From the Patoka Lake area, drive west on IN 164 to Jasper and then south on US 231. Just after you cross Interstate 64 is the Lincoln Boyhood National Memorial, then Lincoln State Park, which is the site of the Lincoln family farm between 1816 and 1830. Abe's mother, Nancy Hanks Lincoln, died when she was thirty-four and Abe was nine; she is buried here.

See the video at the visitor center and tour the log cabins and farm buildings, where interpretive characters carry on everyday life of the 1820s. The state park has a 58-acre lake, campsites, motor-free boating, and the outdoor musical *Young Abe Lincoln*, which runs June through August. The farm opens in mid-April. Indiana has another truly important Lincoln site,

Chicago's Water Tower is one of the few structures that survived the Great Fire of 1871.

but it's at Fort Wayne, well out of reach on this loop tour. Keep in mind for a future trip that the Lincoln Museum in Fort Wayne claims to have the largest collection of Lincoln memorabilia in the world.

Our next wayside is Danville, Illinois. Travel west on Interstate 64 to US 41 and then head north on US 41 to Interstate 74. Go west on Interstate 74 to Danville. In Danville, visit the mansion at 116 North Gilbert Street. This house was built in 1855 by Dr. William Fithian, who hosted Abraham Lincoln here on September 21, 1858. Popular legend has it that Lincoln addressed a crowd from the balcony. The house is now the Vermilion County Museum, with a carriage house and an herb garden on the property. Camping is available at Kickapoo State Park (4 miles/6 km west of Danville off Interstate 74)—which has fishing, canoeing, hiking trails, and horseback riding—or in Forest Glen Preserve, southeast of town on US 150 in Westville. At Forest Glen, climb the observation tower overlooking the Vermilion River.

Continue west on Interstate 74 to Champaign-Urbana and then drive southwest on Interstate 72 to Decatur, where the Lincolns arrived in 1830 and homesteaded on the Sangamon River. Lincoln Trail Homestead State Park (10 miles west of Decatur on US 36 or Interstate 27, then south on County Road 27 at Mt. Zion) covers 162 original acres and commemorates the Lincoln era. Camping is available at this state park and at Spitler Woods State Natural Area southeast of town on US 36 as well as at commercial campgrounds throughout the region.

You're now an easy half day's drive from greater Chicago, where our trip began. Take the direct route on interstates or set your GPS on Chicago and work your way there on the grid of arrow-straight roads that run east to west and north to south through farm country. As you near the confluence of the Illinois and Kankakee Rivers, choose from the abundant wildlife refuges, parks, and green spaces for your last night on the loose before reentering the metropolitan maze.

CHAPTER 3

The Southern Appalachians
Mansions, Magnolias, and Moon Pies

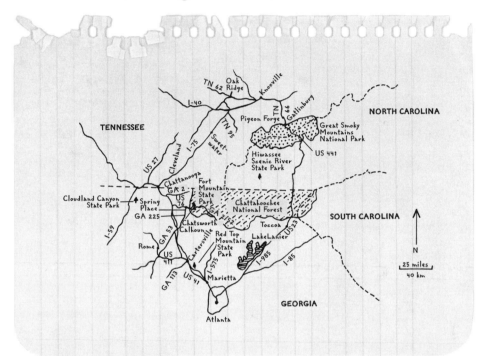

MILEAGE

Approximately 500 miles (800 km)

RESOURCES

- Atlanta Convention & Visitors Bureau, 233 Peachtree St., Atlanta GA 30303, 800-ATLANTA (800-285-2682) or 404-521-6600, *http://www.atlanta.com*
- Blue Ridge Parkway, 400 BB&T Bldg., 1 Pack Sq., Asheville NC 28801, 828-271-4779.
- Chattanooga Area Convention & Visitors Bureau, 2 Broad St., Chattanooga TN 37402, 800-322-3344, *http://www.chattanooga.net/cvb*.
- Gatlinburg Department of Tourism, Visitor Services, 234 Airport Rd., Gatlinburg TN 37738, 800-267-7088, *http://www.gatlinburg-tennessee.com*.
- Georgia Tourism Division, 285 Peachtree Center Ave., P.O. Box 1776, Atlanta GA 30303, 800-VISIT-GA (800-847-4842) or 404-656-3590, *http://www.itt.state.ga.us* or *www.georgia.org*.
- Great Smoky Mountains National Park, Gatlinburg TN 37738, 423-436-1200.
- Knoxville Convention & Visitors Bureau, 601 W. Summit Hill Suite 200B, Knoxville TN 30902, 800-727-8045.
- Marietta Visitors Bureau, 4 Depot St., Marietta GA 30060, 800-451-3480, *http://www.mariettasquare.com*.
- North Carolina State Tourism, 301 N. Wilmington St., Raleigh NC 27601, 800-847-4862.
- Tennessee Department of Tourist Development, 320 6th Ave. N., Rachel Jackson Bldg., Nashville TN 37243, 800-Go2TENN (800-462-8366) or 615-741-2159.

Springtime in Atlanta

The center of a wheel with interstate spokes converging from all directions, Atlanta has been a transportation center since before the Civil War, when it was a rail hub. That made it a war prize, resulting in the burning of Atlanta made so memorable by *Gone with the Wind*. While you're here, read the book again or see the movie.

Atlanta is a tangle of highways with some of the worst crowding in the country, so plan your trip carefully with the help of a good map. We usually stay at a campground within walking distance of MARTA (Atlanta's public transportation system) so we can readily enjoy downtown activities. The High Museum of Arts is one of the best art museums in the south, and Atlanta Botanical Garden is spectacular in springtime. Atlanta is also home to CNN headquarters, which offers behind-the-scenes tours. You'll see how television shows are put together and will probably recognize some of your favorite news announcers. Tours last about forty-five minutes and leave every hour on the hour.

Springtime in Atlanta

On the Tuesday before Ash Wednesday, Atlanta has a traditional Mardi Gras parade.

In mid-February Atlanta Botanical Gardens hosts its Camellia Show.

On St. Patrick's Day, big parades take to the streets of downtown Atlanta and Buckhead.

The Daffodil Show is held in late March at Atlanta Botanical Gardens.

From late March to late April, Callaway Gardens holds its Celebration of Spring.

The sunrise service on Easter at Stone Mountain is held at daybreak in one of nature's most spectacular cathedrals.

In mid-April Atlanta's Dogwood Festival is an art show, street fair, and hot-air balloon extravaganza.

Don't miss the Cyclorama (800 Cherokee Ave., S.E.) in Grant Park, a 400-feet-wide (121.9 m) painting that is both an interesting record of the Battle of Atlanta and an artistic tour de force. It was painted on linen in 1886 by fifteen artists and is one of

ATLANTA CONVENTION & VISITORS BUREAU

Atlanta was burned during the Civil War, but today the city is mightier than ever. These Civil War–era cannons contrast with the city's twenty-first-century skyline.

only a handful of such works in the world.

The Atlanta Preservation Center (404-876-2040) offers a variety of walking tours. One tour features the Fox Theater District; the restored Fox Theater is one of the nation's best examples of the extravagant movie palaces built during Hollywood's golden years. It's almost as big as Radio City Music Hall in New York City, and its theater organ is one of the largest in the world. Other tours are offered of historic Oakland Cemetery, where Margaret Mitchell, author of *Gone with the Wind*, is buried; Druid Hills, where the fictional Miss Daisy of *Driving Miss Daisy* lived; Sweet Auburn, with its African-American history; the state capitol; Underground Atlanta; and the historic downtown.

End your day at Underground Atlanta, a delightful shopping, dining, and entertaining complex that almost never sleeps. If you're lucky, you'll spot the Zero Mile Post, where the massive Atlanta railroad system began in the early 1800s.

Georgia's rhododendron are a springtime specialty.

Marietta

Leaving Atlanta on Interstate 75 North, you head into kudzu country, where the aggressive and fast-growing vine covers everything in its path with a shroud of green.

One of our favorite places, Marietta (an hour north of Atlanta off Interstate 75) has more than two hundred homes that are at least a century old as well as four National Register Historic Districts. Stop at the visitor center for maps of self-guided walking and driving tours, including a 17-mile (27.2 km) Civil War trail. Before leaving the town square, stroll its perimeter to see smart restaurants, shops, galleries, and the old courthouse. Locals call it Glover Park after the first mayor, who donated the land to the city before the Civil War. Ask directions from here to the old post office that now houses the Marietta–Cobb County Museum of Art.

Take US 41 or Interstate 75 3 miles (4.8 km) northwest of Marietta to Kennesaw Mountain National Battlefield Park, which still contains 11 miles (17.6 km) of original earthworks. When General William Sherman's army of a hundred thousand was marching toward Atlanta, two fierce battles raged here at Kolb's Farm. The 2-mile (3.2 km) hiking trail is a self-guided nature and history walk. Other trails are 5, 10, and 16 miles (8, 16, and 25.6 km) long. In springtime, azaleas and dogwood put on a boffo show, which is soon followed by a rapture of rhododendron. The park doesn't have camping, but private and U.S. Corps of Engineers campgrounds are nearby.

While you're in Marietta, rent the Disney movie *The Great Locomotive Chase*. This true-life Civil War drama started in Marietta, where you can see the hotel, the old Kennesaw House, at which the spies

For More Information

Georgia Welcome Centers are found where major interstates enter the state from Tennessee, Florida, South Carolina, and Alabama and on US 280 in Plains.

The Etowah Indian Mounds in northwest Georgia were built by pre-Columbian Indians.

began their adventure. The hotel, where conspirator James Andrews stayed before the raid, is now the Marietta Museum of History. The story ends in Chattanooga, where the conspirators, who were caught and hanged, are buried. You can see their gravestone, topped with a locomotive, when you reach Chattanooga.

Six miles (9.6 km) north of Marietta on US 41 (this minor road runs more or less parallel to Interstate 75) find Big Shanty Museum, home of the locomotive *General*. This is the actual engine captured by a group of Union spies who hoped to damage the tracks between here and Chattanooga, cutting off a vital Confederate supply line. In a thrill-a-minute chase depicted in *The Great Locomotive Chase*, the Yankees were captured and, for a time, the Reb railroad was saved. The story comes alive in the museum here, which contains period artifacts, including personal items that belonged to the soldiers who participated. It's open daily except major holidays.

Continuing north on Interstate 75, slip

out of the Civil War mood for as long as you can and enjoy the swimming, boating, fishing, and hiking at Red Top Mountain State Park, which is 2 miles (3.2 km) east of Interstate 75 south of Carters Mill. The park's name comes from its rusty red soil, rich in iron. Along the trails you'll see remnants of old iron mines. Lying to the northeast, the main body of Chattahoochee National Forest is filled with state parks, rushing rapids, historic towns, and touristy fun that we'll see on our return trip. For now, head instead into another strip of the forest that lies north of Rome. Near Cartersville, head southwest on GA 113, watching for signs to the Etowah Indian Mounds, some of the oldest Indian ceremonial mounds in the East. The Etowah tribe that lived here around A.D. 1000 to 1500 numbered several thousand.

Take GA 113 east to pick up US 411 into Rome, the home of magnificent Berry College. Visitors are welcome to tour the 26,000-acre campus and see the museum, the original Berry plantation house, the art gallery, the formal gardens, and miles of nature trails, which in springtime are lined with blooming trees, shrubs, and wildflowers. It's all a tribute to Martha Berry, who founded a school for poor mountain children and ended up with this showplace, which is almost completely self-sufficient. Don't miss the gift shop, where many of the handmade goods were crafted by students who are required to learn a marketable skill in addition to their formal degrees.

In Rome, the cityscape is crowned by the Old Town Clock, built in 1871 atop the 104-foot (31.7 m) water tower located atop one of Rome's seven hills. One story is that the city was not named for Rome, Italy, but was just one of several names thrown into a hat. Don't tell that to the Italian government, which gave the city a statue of Romulus and Remus in 1929. The statue is still in front of City Hall.

Chieftains Museum (north of Rome off US 27) was the home of an important Cherokee leader, Major Ridge. Ridge was a businessman and slave owner who created a comfortable mansion here in the wilds of north Georgia.

When gold was discovered in north

Chieftains Museum.

Georgia, the push was on to force the Cherokees off their lands, resulting in the tragedy we now call the Trail of Tears. This story is best told at New Echota. Follow GA 53 from Rome to Calhoun. New Echota is northeast of Calhoun on GA 225 half a mile (0.8 km) east of Interstate 75. Once a Cherokee village with homes, a school, a courthouse, and a newspaper, New Echota was destroyed by Federal troops when the Cherokees were forced to leave their homeland. During restoration of the community by the state of Georgia, a century after the Trail of Tears, the movable type used in the printing press was discovered deep in a well. It isn't known whether it was thrown there by a scornful farmer or hidden there for safekeeping. Today, park rangers will print a broadsheet in Cherokee on the recovered press while you watch.

After visiting New Echota, plan to spend the night at Fort Mountain State Park. Take GA 225 north from Calhoun and at Spring Place go east to Chatsworth, where GA 2/52 leads to the park. The park is awesome in springtime when the wild dogwoods and mountain laurel bloom. The mountain may really have been a fort cen-

turies ago, or perhaps the snaking, 855-foot (260.6 m) wall was built for ceremonial reasons by unknown tribes. It's obviously made by human hands, but its origins re-

One of the restored buildings at New Echota.

main a mystery. Swim, fish, and hike miles of trails through springtime splendor and then make your way back to Interstate 75 via US 76.

Two sightseeing blockbusters lie just south of Chattanooga, Tennessee. Cloudland Canyon State Park (east of the Trenton exit off Interstate 59) is next to heaven on the western edge of Lookout Mountain (8 miles/12.2 km east of Chatsworth on TN 52). Hike craggy trails that take you to breathtaking views of waterfalls, canyons, and the gorge cut by Sitton Gulch Creek. Camp here for as long as you can spare. It isn't far from here to Chickamauga and Chattanooga National Military Park (take GA 2E, from Interstate 75 southeast of Chattanooga).

Chickamauga and Chattanooga National Military Park

Bruised bodies and bloodied pride were still fresh in the minds of Georgians and Tennesseans twenty-five years after the Civil War when two generals, one Union and one Confederate, decided to meet here for a barbecue. The year was 1890: townfolk gathered, and dialogue began about the two victories that had been won here, one by the North and one by the South. It was not only the first, frail beginning of healing, but it was also the start of accurate historic record keeping. Both sides reported exactly where they had been, what they had done, and when. This site is said to be the most accurately chronicled battle site of the war.

See the museum and the film, and take the self-guided driving tour. Stop as often as you can to read markers, photograph the impressive monuments, and hike back into the woods to imagine the land as it was in the midst of battle. The battlefield , which covers 8,100 acres, straddles the Georgia-Tennessee border.

Chattanooga Shines

One of our favorite hangouts in Chattanooga is Choo-Choo (1400 Market St.), an architectural prizewinner of a railroad terminal that has been turned into a complex featuring a hotel, entertainment, shopping, and restaurants. On Friday and Saturday evenings starting at the end of April, live concerts play in the outdoor gardens. Spend an afternoon and evening here.

Save a day to take the children to the Creative Discovery Museum (101 W. 2nd St.), which has a year-round schedule of activities and displays, and to the Tennessee Aquarium (1 Broad St.), which is endlessly entertaining for all ages. The largest freshwater aquarium in the world, it's open every day except Thanksgiving and Christmas.

Take a ride on the Tennessee Valley Railroad (take the Jersey Pike exit from Interstate 75), which starts running in late March. You can bring a picnic or eat in the deli at the Grand Junction Station; call the Chattanooga Area Convention & Visitors Bureau (CACVB) for rail reservations. A number of state parks in the Chattanooga area offer camping; good private campgrounds are also abundant. Calling itself "next door to outdoors," Chattanooga is also the gateway to Cherokee National Forest, Nantahala National Forest, and rafting on the Hiwassee River as well as houseboating in the Grand Canyon of the Tennessee River.

We've made it up Lookout Mountain in our RV, so you can too, although we don't recommend making the climb if you're towing a trailer. The view of the river and city is a hazy dream, and the dogwoods in springtime are unforgettable. It's more fun to take the Lookout Mountain Incline Railway, the steepest passenger railway in the world; call CACVB for reservations. Inside Lookout Mountain Caverns, you'll see Ruby Falls, a 145-foot (44.2 m) cataract that is totally underground.

If you've driven any secondary highway in the South, you've seen signs advising you to "See Rock City." Seeing Rock City, which is located on Lookout Mountain, has become trendy. The souvenirs are silly and fun, the birdhouses are practical, and the attraction itself is worth a visit, especially in springtime when the flower beds are a riot of color. A natural rock sculpture garden, Rock City blooms in spring with cherry trees, azaleas, nandina, spirea, lilacs, wild ginger, black-eyed susans, lily of the valley, and much more.

A Tale of Two Cities

We're headed for Oak Ridge and Knoxville. For quick and easy running, take Interstate 75, with an overnight at Hiwassee State Scenic River north of Cleveland or a stop at Sweetwater to take a glass-bottom boat tour at Lost Sea Caverns. The skeleton of a prehistoric jaguar was found here in 1939. Continue on Interstate 75 to Interstate 40 and then travel west one exit to take TN 95 into Oak Ridge. From here, TN 62 leads into Knoxville.

When the "atomic city" of Oak Ridge was founded early in World War II, it was so secret that it didn't appear on maps. Elaborate cover-ups had to be created while a city grew here in the heavily forested wilderness to support scientists who had to be supplied with housing, food, and equipment for producing uranium 235. Now visitors are welcome to visit the American Museum of Science and Energy, the graphite reactor built in 1943, and the Children's Museum of Oak Ridge. The site offers science history for serious scholars and a nostalgic look at the wartime United States for the lay audience.

The city of Knoxville, founded on the frontier in 1786, was a battleground during the Civil War and is now a gateway to the tourism tomfoolery that surrounds Gatlinburg and Pigeon Forge. It still retains much of its "aw-shucks" southern manner, though. The downtown has become an art colony, and the surrounding country roads are a haven for artisans and crafters. See the Knoxville Museum of Art, take the children to the East Tennessee Discovery Center in Chilhowee Park, and check out

such historic points as White's Fort (205 E. Hill Ave.), which is the original pioneer house built in 1786; Governor Blount's Mansion, which dates to 1792; the pink marble Ramsey House northeast of town on Thorngrove Pike, and the Armstrong-Lockett House (2728 Kingston Pike) with its historic furnishings and terraced gardens.

Frosting on the Cake

Ready now for some fun after all the serious history and nature watching? From Knoxville, head east on Interstate 40 and then south on TN 66 (which becomes US 441) to Pigeon Forge for country music, country food, and country crafts. This is the playground of the mountains, still uncrowded in springtime when the wildflowers are at their best and all the tourist attractions are still fresh and eager to please. Do it all: Dollywood with its forty live shows and thirty-one rides, which include a roller coaster, the Comedy Barn, Carbo's Police Museum, the Country Tonight Theater, the Dixie Stampede, and the Elvis Museum, said to be the largest private collection of Elvis memorabilia in the world. Whitewater rafting in the area begins in March.

Proceed south on US 441 to Gatlinburg, our gateway to Great Smoky Mountains National Park. Campsites are available in the park itself, but the most developed campgrounds are in Gatlinburg, many of them on the trolley route that shuttles visitors around the community. Start at Sugarlands Visitor Center, which has park information, exhibits, and a video program. Ask rangers for advice about your travels in the mountains according to the type of vehicle you have. Cades Cove, which is 25 miles (40 km) west of Sugarlands, is a picture-book hamlet that shows how the original mountaineers lived.

The national park is threaded with miles of hiking trails that are at their most beautiful in late spring, when rhododendron bloom, and in the fall, when the hardwoods turn brilliant red and yellow. The land is a geological marvel, with mountains that rise to 6,642 feet (2,024 m) at Cling-

Event:
In Knoxville, the Dogwood Festival in late April is one of the largest in the south, with 60 miles (96 km) of self-guided driving trails.

About the Blue Ridge Parkway

Offering one of the most breathtaking drives in the nation, the Blue Ridge Parkway is a 470-mile (752 km) route that follows the crest of the Blue Ridge Mountains from Shenandoah National Park in Virginia south to Great Smoky Mountains National Park. The speed limit is 45 miles an hour, which is a good thing for large rigs. This is not a route to take for speed; it's for sightseeing. We don't recommend arriving before May 1 because few campgrounds are open, days can be cold, and the occasional late-season snow can make the roads slippery. The springtime spectacular that blooms at lower altitudes in March and April doesn't arrive at this altitude until early May.

The whole trip requires about sixteen hours of driving, but we recommend giving it a week or more, allowing time to stop at all eleven visitor centers, take guided walks, explore the many hiking trails, photograph waterfalls, see living history programs, and attend evening talks. Fish mountain streams for brook trout, rainbows, and brown trout, and fish Bass Lake for bass and bluegills. At Mabry Mill, see early American exhibits including a water-powered gristmill and a blacksmith shop. Along the route you'll find local crafters selling such mountain specialties as whimmy-diddles, dulcimers, and jaw harps.

Don't let your provisions and gas reserves fall too low along this route, especially in the off-season. The road is busiest in October, when leaf peepers are here to see 81,000 acres of forest fireworks, and in June, when the rhododendron bloom.

whitetail deer. Cottontail rabbits are found everywhere, from the lowest to the highest elevations.

Tip:
Between May 15 and October 31, camping reservations are required in Great Smoky Mountains National Park, and you can stay no longer than seven days. Call 800-365-CAMP (800-365-2267). A Tennessee or North Carolina fishing license can be used in the park regardless of state borders. Brook trout are protected, and even possession of these endangered fish is prohibited.

Peregrine falcons, river otters, and red wolves have been reintroduced here. Coyotes are native to the park, and beavers and muskrat make homes along the streams. Rattlesnakes and copperheads are among the park's snake population, and there are salamanders galore. For the nature lover, there is no end to the pleasures that will be seen here day and night in all seasons.

When you're ready to return to Atlanta, take US 441, which bisects the park on a wildly winding, climbing route through a corner of North Carolina and into northern Georgia, where you can explore the eastern parts of Chattahoochee National Forest. The forest has half a dozen state parks with campgrounds and endless hiking trails, waterfalls, and trout streams. Stay on US 441 (which becomes US 23) with a stop to see Tallulah Falls and Toccoa Falls and perhaps an overnight at Lake Lanier and its islands (exit at Flowery Branch and follow signs). Return to Atlanta on Interstate 985.

mans Dome, 6,593 feet (2,010 m) at Mt. LeConte, and 5,048 feet (1,539 m) at Newfound Gap. Set out on the trails with your nature identification books and begin checking off trees, wildflowers, and birds.

Look for green-winged teal, great egret, great blue heron, pelicans, bald eagles, grouse, and owls. As summer approaches, you might spot a ruby-throated hummingbird feeding on cardinal flowers along a rocky creek. Wild turkeys are occasionally seen. With luck you'll also spot wild boar, black bear, elk, bobcat, fox, and

Event:
If you're in Helen, Georgia, in mid-April, do the Volksmarch, a forest walk with 3K, 10K, and 20K options. Also in mid-April is the World Championship Gold Panning Competition in nearby Dahlonega.

Historic Tennessee and Mississippi
Tracking the Natchez Trace

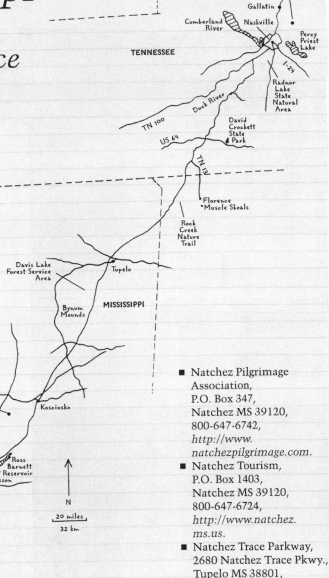

MILEAGE
Natchez Trace Parkway is 407 miles (651.2 km) long, plus optional side trips.

RESOURCES
- Mississippi Tourism Division, P.O. Box 849, Jackson MS 39205, 601-359-3297, *http:www. visitmississippi.org.*
- Nashville Convention & Visitors Bureau, 161 4th Ave. N., Nashville TN 37219, 800-657-6910 or 615-259-4700.

- Natchez Pilgrimage Association, P.O. Box 347, Natchez MS 39120, 800-647-6742, *http://www. natchezpilgrimage.com.*
- Natchez Tourism, P.O. Box 1403, Natchez MS 39120, 800-647-6724, *http://www.natchez. ms.us.*
- Natchez Trace Parkway, 2680 Natchez Trace Pkwy., Tupelo MS 38801, 800-305-7417.
- Tennessee Department of Tourist Development, 320 6th Ave. N., Nashville TN 37243, 800-GO2TENN (800-462-8366) or 615-741-2159.

A Well-Worn Path

For centuries before the first European settlers began following the trade route we now call the Natchez Trace, the trail was beaten deep into the soil by Choctaws and Cherokees and by other tribes before them. Before that, the trail likely was followed by migrating herds of buffalo and deer. When French traders arrived in the 1700s, they found that a web of well-worn trails already existed between Nashville, Tennessee, and Natchez, Mississippi. The route was used by early British explorers and by early flatboaters, who floated their goods down the Mississippi River and then made their way back north by foot, horseback, or wagon via the Natchez Trace Parkway.

Settlements sprang up along the route. The Federal government appropriated funds to improve the road so mail could pass along it. Soon the Trace streamed with peddlers and settlers, adventurers, and ne'er-do-wells who lay in wait in forest shadows, ready to rob the unwary. Goods moved south by flatboat to feed ever-growing populations downriver. However, when steamboats made it possible to go upriver by boat instead of by taking the long, hazardous land route, the Trace's glory days stopped almost as suddenly as they had begun. The road lay forgotten until the 1930s, when it was made a parkway managed by the National Park Service. Today's route laces back and forth across the original route, sometimes covering it and sometimes following the deeply rutted tunnels through thick forest that were the original Trace.

Natchez

The city of Natchez has an enchantment all its own, and we never tire of visiting here. Springtime brings azaleas and other spring flowers as well as the annual Pilgrimage, held spring and fall. Many of the city's grand old mansions are open to the public all year, but during Pilgrimage, a time when many more private homes and gardens are opened by their owners, visitors come by the busload. Nowhere does the grandeur of the old plantation South shine more brilliantly than in Natchez, where at least fifty mansions survived the Civil War and dozens more homes of architectural or historical significance have also been preserved. The homes were built with the fortunes made here when cotton was king and steamboats carried this white gold to mills in the industrialized North.

Spend as long in the city as you can spare, touring old homes and imagining how families lived here in the days of Rhett and Scarlett. Then, for a look at another layer of local history, see the Grand Village

With luck, you'll see the magnificent *American Queen* in your travels along the Mississippi River.

Event:

Pilgrimage in Natchez lasts an entire month, from early March through early April.

(400 Jefferson Davis Blvd.) of the Natchez Indians.

Our trip up the Trace starts where the route crosses US 61. Natchez State Park has campsites and a network of old plantation roads, which are now used for horseback riding and ATVs. At many points along the Trace you'll find markers, roadside rest areas, exhibits, and marked nature trails. Take your time so you don't miss anything. At Emerald Mound on the Natchez Trace Parkway, 12 miles (19.2 km) northeast of Natchez, you'll find an 18-acre Indian mound built by the Mississippian culture about 1250–1600 A.D. It's the second largest such mound in the United States. It took centuries to heap basketful upon basketful of earth to create flattop mounds for ceremonial purposes. When De Soto came this way in the 1500s, he reported that such mounds were still in use.

Tip:
Open to the public, Melrose Estate (601-446-5790) is an antebellum home within Natchez National Historical Park. Tour the house and grounds and fish from the banks of the pond.

Stop at Loess Bluff Nature Area to see Ice Age deposits of rich soil pushed here from far away by a massive glacier. Pass the Mount Locust Inn, one of the old traveler inns, which has been restored along the Trace. Our next stop is the Bullen Creek Nature Trail through a forest of hardwoods. At Magnum Site, see grave sites where Indian artifacts were found. Cross Bayou Pierre, and you'll find a campground at Rocky Springs. Keep an eye out for original sections of the Trace, and walk along them to get a sense of the old flatboaters and their long journeys back northward.

The Trace leads through Jackson, Mississippi, where you can tour the State Capitol building at 400 High Street, built in beaux-arts style, and the Governor's Mansion, built in 1842 and furnished with priceless antiques. Don't miss the mansion's gardens. At their zenith in springtime, they are a showplace of gazebos and flowering shrubs covering an entire city block. Also grand at this time of year are Mynell Gardens, a 5-acre showplace garden with a historic house that is also open to the public. See the Old Capitol (Capitol St. at State St.),

Wisteria, a woody vine that produces clusters of sweet-smelling blooms, is the South's answer to the lilac.

built in 1839, museums, the zoo, and an original battle site at Battlefield Park.

Just north of Jackson, the Ross Barnett Reservoir has a marina, a boat launch, and picnic sites. Created by damming the Pearl River, the lake is 43 miles (68.8 km) long and is a favorite for fishing, waterskiing, and camping. Returning to your trip up the Trace, stop at the Mississippi Crafts Center to see demonstrations of basket making,

Event:

In Jackson, Mississippi, a rodeo is held the second week in February, and the Mississippi State Horse Show is held in April.

weaving, carving, and other native skills and then stop at five-hundred-year-old Indian burial mounds, and take the nature trail through Cypress Swamp.

The Trace passes Kosciusko, an altered spelling of the name of the man the town honors, General Thaddeus Koscioszko. A freethinking Polish general who came to fight in the American War for Independence, he was a hero in the Revolution and then returned home to fight for Polish independence. West of town at Goodman (exit 146 off Interstate 55), just west of the Trace, Holmes County State Park has lakes for fishing and boating, nature trails, an archery range, and campsites. If you continue north on the Trace without stopping off at the park, you'll soon come to Jeff Busby, which has campsites, a store, and the only gas station on the Trace.

As you continue north on the Natchez Trace Parkway, you'll see vestiges of the old Trace time and again. Stop at Bynum Mounds, the site of a prehistoric Indian village and burial mounds, and at Davis Lake Forest Service Area, which has campsites, swimming, and boating. Just south of Tupelo, see the site of a Chickasaw Indian village, which has exhibits and a marked trail.

Because parkway headquarters are at Tupelo, it's a good place to review the big picture. At the Natchez Trace Parkway Visitor Center, see a museum and interpretive center and an audiovisual program. The visitor center is 5 miles north of town at the junction of the parkway and US 45 Business.

Resuming your trip north on the Trace,

A Stop at Tupelo

If you want to stop off in Tupelo, see Elvis Presley Park and Birthplace, where Elvis lived until he was three years old. The park offers camping, boating, fishing, and swimming. West of town in the Tupelo Museum, see NASA equipment used in the Apollo program, Elvis memorabilia, a replica of a Western Union telegraph office, and Civil War and Indian mementos. Camping can be found west of town at Trace State Park off MS 6 and east of town at Tombigbee State Park, also off MS 6.

you'll see a trailhead that leads to an unnamed cave. Take the short hike before resuming the route. Next, stop at Bear Creek Mound, an Indian ceremonial mound. Watch for the trail marker designating the path to the highest point on the parkway in Alabama. Staying with the Trace, you're in Alabama only briefly. Stop at the well-marked site where a Chickasaw chieftain operated an inn for early travelers. Muscle Shoals, Florence, and other Alabama tourism treasures are nearby, so consider making them a side trip if time allows.

Next you'll find a boat launch and picnic tables at Colbert Ferry. Then stop at the Rock Creek Nature Trail, which leads to a sweet-water spring, and stop again near TN 13, where sections of the original Trace are clearly visible. After the Trace crosses US 64, watch for a 2.5-mile (4 km) loop drive over the original Trace. The stretch of US 64 between the Tennessee River and Interstate 24, is wildly scenic, so consider making a side trip if you have plenty of time. David Crockett State Park (west of Lawrenceburg off US 64) has campsites. Crockett operated a gristmill here along Shoal Creek. The highly developed park has a water-powered mill, restaurant, dinner theater, swimming pool, and lighted tennis courts. In summer, concerts play the amphitheater.

Meanwhile, back on the Natchez Trace, we head north to the Meriwether Lewis Site, the burial site of the famous explorer. The site has a campground and hiking trails. Continuing toward Nashville, pass an old tobacco barn and, near the Duck River, a home that was built in 1818. The parkway ends southwest of Nashville. Continue into the city on TN 100.

Nashville: Music City

Suddenly we're back in a big city of highways and pizzazz and some of the most exciting sightseeing in the South. Again, we recommend plugging into a tour or two to help get your bearings before you tackle the city on your own. Gray Line does motor coach tours, and there are specialized tours by coach as well as a choice of two historical walking tours. Take one of the boat excursions on the Cumberland River, keeping in mind the river's importance in city history. Write ahead for brochures that describe self-guided walking tours, so you can fill in the blanks after taking the guided tours.

The most appealing sites for children will likely be the Cumberland Science Museum with its hands-on exhibits, the Country Music Hall of Fame because it has something for everyone, the Nashville Toy Museum, and the Nashville Zoo. At Grassmere Wildlife Park, you'll see native animals, including bison. Dragon Park (3777 Nolensville Rd.) is a playground with a big dragon, sidewalks for skating, and plenty of playground equipment and picnic tables. During the full moon, take a family nature hike or canoe cruise at Radnor Lake State Natural Area, which you reach by driving 7 miles (11.2 km) south on US 31, then west on Otter Creek Road for 1½ miles (2.4 km).

On a walking tour of downtown Nashville, peek into Union Station (Broadway at 10th Ave.), a stone masterpiece built in Romanesque Revival style, and stop at the main post office with its superb art deco interior. Downtown on the river, Riverfront Park is a good place to sit on terraced steps and watch the boats go by, catch a riverboat for a historical tour or a dinner cruise, or tour Fort Nashborough (1st Ave. N. at Church St.), which is built on the original site of the original fort. In summer, concerts are held in the amphitheater; see if anything is playing during your springtime visit.

Shop in the Arcade, a glass-roofed mall typical of the arcades built in the early 1900s, which is located between 4th and 5th Avenues north of Church Street. This mall dates to 1903. Bicentennial Mall, on the other hand, is an outdoor greenspace; walk its pathways through a boulder garden and view exhibits that give you a short course in Tennessee history. The Presbyterian Church at 5th Avenue and Church Street dates to 1851. It's designed in a distinctive Egyptian style. Take a look at the lobby of the Hermitage Hotel at 231 6th Avenue North. It's a fine example of beaux-arts architecture. Shop the downtown farmer's market, which has fresh produce, restaurants, and take-outs.

For Country Music Fans Only

If you're a country music fan, you've found the Holy Grail in Nashville. Start your pilgrimage at Ryman Auditorium at 116 5th Avenue North downtown. Built in 1892, the auditorium hosted performances by John Philip Sousa, Mae West, and Charlie Chaplin and has come into the modern era with performances by Bruce Springsteen and James Brown. Opera and symphonies played here. Caruso sang from its stage, and Billy Sunday preached. Edward Strauss led the Vienna Orchestra, and Anna Pavlova danced. Still, the old tabernacle is best known as the former home of the Grand Ole Opry. For fifty years, all America tuned in to radio broadcasts beamed from here.

Now restored to its original grandeur, the Ryman (615-871-5027) is open daily 8:30 A.M. to 4 P.M. for tours. Admission is $6. Step on the stage where William Jennings Bryan orated and Hank Williams Sr., Patsy Cline, and Loretta Lynn sang. On display in the museum are exhibits and memorabilia from the auditorium's rich history. It's still a venue for big-name concerts and shows and is said to have the best acoustics this side of Carnegie Hall. If you're driving your RV, use the parking lot at Third and Gay Streets. It's only a couple of blocks from the Ryman, where a high rig won't fit under the entry arch.

An entire industry is built around Nashville's music, as we learned when we overnighted at the Opryland KOA (800-KOA-7789/800-562-7789). One of several resort campgrounds that focus on country music, the Opryland KOA has its own concerts as well as shuttles to the many music halls in the area. The Holiday–Nashville Travel Park (615-889-4225) also has concerts on site and runs tours to other country music attractions.

You can spend an entire season here going to country music shows and theaters. Nashville Night Life Theater and Nashville Palace have breakfast concerts, dozens of other concerts that twang into the wee hours, and many live broadcasts and taping sessions.

Nashville can be as highbrow as it is country. The Cheekwood Museum of Art (1200 Forrest Park Dr.), housed in a fine

Event:
In Nashville, Tin Pan South is the annual get-together of the Nashville Songwriter Association International.

mansion, has collections of silver, porcelain, sculpture, and American art. Fisk University's Aaron Douglass Gallery (Jackson St. and 17th Ave. N.) is known for its African and African-American collections. The university's Carl Van Vechten Gallery, which occupies a Victorian gymnasium at D.B. Tood Boulevard and 17th Avenue North, has works by modernists including Georgia O'Keeffe. The Parthenon in Centennial Park (West End Ave. and 25th Ave. N.) is a full-size replica of the original structure in Greece. It was built as a temporary plaster building for the Tennessee Centennial in 1897, but locals loved it so much, it was re-built in the 1920s as a permanent art museum. It has some copies of Elgin marbles, American works, and an enormous sculpture of Athena. In the park itself, rent a paddleboat, see a steam engine and a fighter plane, and browse the memorial statues. The Tennessee State Museum in the James K. Polk Office Building (505 Deaderick St.) has a good collection of historical arts and artifacts. Admission is free; it's closed Sunday and Monday.

For Civil War history, see the Lotz House Museum in Franklin (south of Nashville off Interstate 65). The home was built in 1858 and stands near the site of the Battle of Franklin. Wounded from both sides were sheltered here. If you're a Civil War reenactor, the gift shop carries a good supply of reproductions for use in soldiering.

North of Nashville is the zoo as well as, at Hendersonville, Historic Rock Castle, a house that dates to the 1780s. Mansker's Station Frontier Life Center in Goodlettsville, 15 miles (24 km) northeast of Nashville, was founded in 1779 near a salt lick where hunters came to find game for meat and pelts. Tour the house, built in 1785, and see tools

and furnishings used by early settlers. The Hermitage, found on the east side of town, was the home of Andrew Jackson and his wife, Rachel, from 1804 until their deaths in 1845 and 1828, respectively. It's been carefully restored to its 1830s appearance. The complex includes another historic home, Tulip Grove; two original log cabins; and a church that Jackson built for his wife in 1823. If you read up on the turbulent history of the times, the love Andrew and Rachel had for each other, and the scandals that surrounded them, the displays of the couple's belongings become even more meaningful.

On the south side of town, see Travellers' Rest, a home built in 1799. The furnishings are original and include rare portraits of Rachel and Andrew Jackson. On the west side of town, Belle Meade is a grand plantation with a Greek Revival mansion, stables, a carriage house, and guides in period costume. While you're in the area, stroll the 55-acre Cheekwood, a botanical marvel of spring wildflowers, bulbs, flowering shrubs, and herbs. There's also a Japanese garden as well as a manor house that dates to the 1920s. Have lunch in the Pineapple Room.

Bledsoe Creek State Park in Gallatin, 25 miles (40 km) northeast of the city off TN 25, has a lake for fishing and boating, launch ramps, and hiking trails through woodlands where some of the area's first white settlers stalked game. Long Hunter State Park (take the Hermitage exit east of downtown) has day activities only, but it's on massive Percy Priest Lake with its excellent hiking, swimming, picnicking, fishing, and boating. If you need handicap access, take the wheelchair-accessible trail. Nashville is surrounded by convenient state parks with campsites, and its choice of private campsites and resort campgrounds is superb.

Nashville Speedway is a NASCAR track that opens in April. Auto racing can also be found at Highland Rim Speedway in Greenbrier, 20 miles (32 km) north of Nashville. The city's baseball team is the Nashville Sounds, an AAA farm team for the Chicago White Sox. Play starts in April, and the scoreboard is in the shape of a guitar. Music City USA? You'd better believe it!

CHAPTER 5

The Call of the Carolinas
Tidewater, Piedmont, and Pine Hills

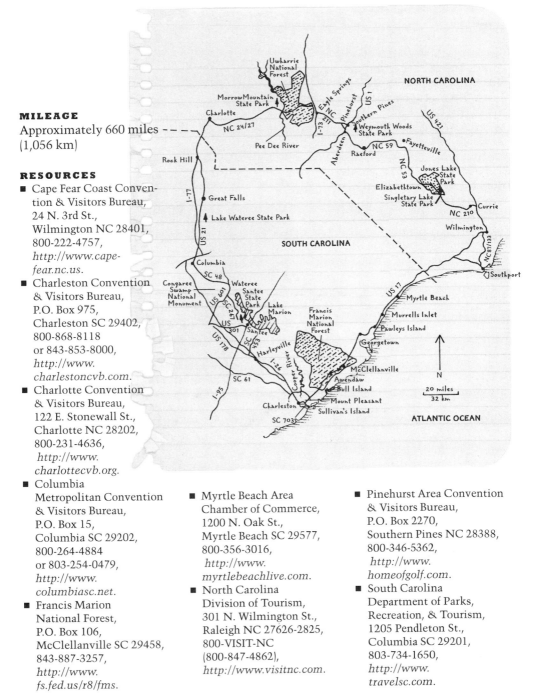

MILEAGE

Approximately 660 miles (1,056 km)

RESOURCES

- Cape Fear Coast Convention & Visitors Bureau, 24 N. 3rd St., Wilmington NC 28401, 800-222-4757, *http://www.cape-fear.nc.us.*
- Charleston Convention & Visitors Bureau, P.O. Box 975, Charleston SC 29402, 800-868-8118 or 843-853-8000, *http://www.charlestoncvb.com.*
- Charlotte Convention & Visitors Bureau, 122 E. Stonewall St., Charlotte NC 28202, 800-231-4636, *http://www.charlottecvb.org.*
- Columbia Metropolitan Convention & Visitors Bureau, P.O. Box 15, Columbia SC 29202, 800-264-4884 or 803-254-0479, *http://www.columbiasc.net.*
- Francis Marion National Forest, P.O. Box 106, McClellanville SC 29458, 843-887-3257, *http://www.fs.fed.us/r8/fms.*

- Myrtle Beach Area Chamber of Commerce, 1200 N. Oak St., Myrtle Beach SC 29577, 800-356-3016, *http://www.myrtlebeachlive.com.*
- North Carolina Division of Tourism, 301 N. Wilmington St., Raleigh NC 27626-2825, 800-VISIT-NC (800-847-4862), *http://www.visitnc.com.*

- Pinehurst Area Convention & Visitors Bureau, P.O. Box 2270, Southern Pines NC 28388, 800-346-5362, *http://www.homeofgolf.com.*
- South Carolina Department of Parks, Recreation, & Tourism, 1205 Pendleton St., Columbia SC 29201, 803-734-1650, *http://www.travelsc.com.*

Charlotte's Tourism Treasures

Our loop begins and ends in Charlotte, North Carolina, a tourist favorite, where visitors can choose from a long menu of sightseeing and sports. Spend a day at Paramount's Carowinds theme park with its thrill rides, shows, and fun. It opens in late March but should still be uncrowded during your spring visit. Call 704-588-2600 for ticket information. Tour the Charlotte Motor Speedway and stay for a race if one is scheduled. Take a tour aboard the Adams Stage Coach (704-537-5342), which takes up to six people over a 6-mile (9.6 km) route past historic points and interesting architecture, or with City Tours of Charlotte (888-488-0578 or 704-535-6518), which has motor coaches. Day Trippin' in the Carolinas is a driving-walking tour packed with fascinating facts. You'll see miles of streets canopied with willow oaks, a city trademark. Stock up on fresh Carolina produce at the Farmer's Market on Yorkmount Road. It opens mid-March and runs Tuesday through Saturday.

Tip:
Among races at Charlotte Motor Speedway is the NASCAR Coca Cola 600, which is said to be second in attendance only to the Indianapolis 500. RV camping is permitted in the infield, so get your name on the waiting list by calling 704-455-3200. It may be several years before your turn comes.

The oldest home in Mecklenburg County is the Hezekiah Alexander Homesite, which you can see in East Charlotte. It was built in 1774 and occupied until the 1940s. Alexander was a crusty Scot, one of the signers of the Mecklenberg Declaration of Independence in 1775. Alexander and his fellow Carolinians declared their freedom from British rule more than a year before the United States issued its own Declaration of Independence.

Head out of Charlotte southbound on Interstate 77 and at Rock Hill, South Carolina, take US 21 South for a pretty drive closer to the Catawba River. At Great Falls, stop for a picnic overlooking the water.

Kings Mountain National Military Park

Take a side trip to Blacksburg, South Carolina, which is west of Charlotte off Interstate 85 and is the location of Kings Mountain National Military Park with its Revolutionary War sites. More than a thousand of the King's men were downed here by the Patriots, effectively ending British domination of the Carolinas. See the audiovisual presentation, walk the 2.5-mile (4 km) battlefield trail, and hike the 16-mile (25.6 km) trail through springtime splendor.

There's good fishing all along the river and dam sites here as well as at Lake Wateree State Park. US 21 brings you into Columbia, the state capital, with its wide boulevards and stately mansions. See the State House with its blue granite columns, the First Baptist Church dating to 1860, museums and mansions, and Riverfront Park, where an old canal site has been turned into a maze of trails for hiking and biking. Consider parking your RV and taking a guided city tour to get your bearings before venturing out on your own.

Leave Columbia on SC 48, which takes you to Congaree Swamp National Monument, 20 miles (32 km) southeast of the city. This 22,000-acre preserve has monster trees, some with trunks 20 feet (6.1 m) around, and a great variety of flora and fauna. Walk the boardwalk and 18 miles (28.8 km) of trails and take a self-guided canoe trip through the swamp. Ranger-led nature walks are offered Saturday afternoons at 1:30 P.M.

Continue east to US 601 at Wateree. Head south on US 601 to pick up SC 267, which runs south along Lake Marion. Stop for fishing at Santee State Park. At Santee, hop on Interstate 95 South and, a few exits later, take Interstate 26 heading southeast toward Charleston. Francis Beidler Forest, your next stop, can be entered only from the southwest via secondary roads, so take the Harleyville exit off Interstate 26, turn south (right) on SC 453 to US 178, turn left through Harleyville, following the signs. Four Holes Swamp, a sanctuary, is home to stands of ancient bald cypress trees, tupelo gum, and water oaks, which shelter 44 species of mammals and 140 species of birds.

In spring, freshened with winter rains, the swamp is a flowing river. Walk the loop trail and boardwalk, which covers 1.5 miles (2.4 km) from the visitor center. If you want to canoe the sanctuary's 60 miles (96 km) of water trails or take a night walk, arrangements must be made with the manager (843-462-2150). American history tells of General Francis Marion, the famous Swamp Fox of the Revolutionary War. It was here that he hid out, venturing out to stage guerrilla raids against the British. When you're ready to leave, return to Interstate 26, which leads you quickly to Charleston.

Charleston

By late January crocus are already peeking through the warming soil, and springtime arrives with a rush in February when hyacinths, star magnolias, wisteria, and winter jessamine bloom. March and early April are a climax of dogwoods, azaleas, Cherokee roses, red maples, snowdrops, and sweet flags, and by early May the cannas, mimosa, white lilies, and saucer-sized magnolias are in full bloom. All this and history too. Charleston is one of America's most captivating cities.

Almost the entire history of American architecture can be seen in Charleston in just a few days. The French Huguenot Church on Church Street is a fine example of Gothic Revival, the Colonel John Ashe House is an Italianate treasure, and the Settile House on Green Street is just one of many Victorian masterpieces. The John Lining House on Broad Street represents a fine example of Colonial style, 1690 to 1740, the Miles Brewton House on King Street is a Georgian, and the Nathaniel Russell House on Meeting Street is a superb Federal-style building. An example of Classic Revival is the Beth Elohhim Synagogue on Hasell Street. Stroll through 350 years of history as you walk street after street of preserved and restored structures.

Start your sightseeing with a guided tour, which is the most economical way to get into several historic properties as well as

the best way to see many of the sites. Streets are narrow and often one-way, so this isn't a city to tackle in a motor home. As you enter town on US 17 or Interstate 26, you'll see a visitor welcome center at the Meeting Street exit. Park here and get the lowdown on tour options, including horse-drawn carriage, aerial, hot air balloon, motor, walking, and water tours, the last of which gives an entirely different view of the Low Country. (Fort Sumter, where the Civil War began, can be reached only by boat.) From the visitor center, DASH (the Downtown Area Shuttle) can get you to most of the city's points of interest and parking garages. Buy a pass for one, three, or thirty days.

While you're in town, see the Gibbes Museum of Art with its fine collection of miniatures, the Nathaniel Russell House with its stunning staircase, and the Old Exchange and Provost Dungeon where pirates and Indians were jailed in the days of old Charles Towne. It's open daily except Sunday. At the Old Charleston Joggling Board Company, see this ages-old alternative to the porch swing. In addition to the many historic buildings that are open to the public, private homes here are a streetscape of

---

Springtime in Charleston

In February, Charleston is the scene of the Lowcountry Blues Bash with more than fifty acts at ten venues over ten days.

The Southeastern Wildlife Exposition, also held in February, is the largest show of its kind. It features crafts, paintings, sculpture, and carvings representing wildlife.

Mid-March to mid-April, the Historic Charleston Foundation sponsors its annual Festival of Houses and Gardens. Private homes are opened for tours to raise funds for restoration projects.

Also in April, Charleston holds its Lowcountry Cajun Festival with zydeco music, crawfish eating, and family fun.

Late in April, the Blessing of the Fleet in Charleston Harbor is held followed by music and feasting.

The Spoleto Festival in late May through mid-June is one of the South's major cultural events, featuring world-renowned artists in dance, opera, music, and theater.

history. We enjoy simply walking up one street and down the next while imagining that it is the eighteenth century.

Outside the city, see Drayton Hall, built in 1742 in Georgian Palladian style. It's the only plantation house on the Ashley River that survived the Civil War fully intact. Nine miles (14.4 km) northwest of Charleston on SC 61, the house is open March through October. Tours are given on the hour. Magnolia Plantation and Gardens (10 miles/16 km northwest of the city on SC 61) features 500 acres of wetlands, trails, cypress trees reflected in pools of dark waters, 900 varieties of camellias, 250 varieties of azaleas, and an herb garden. Walk the boardwalk and climb the observation tower to view the birds and alligators. Fourteen miles (22.4 km) northwest of the city on SC 61 is Middleton Place, which was originally a guest wing of a plantation house burned by Union troops during the Civil War. This wing survived and became the family home. It's furnished to show how planters lived between 1714 and 1865.

At Patriots Point in Mount Pleasant, just across the Cooper River Bridge from Charleston, see the world's first nuclear-powered merchant ship, the *Savannah*; the World War II destroyer *Laffey*; the diesel submarine *Clamagore*; and the aircraft carrier *Yorktown*. The ships are open daily; admission is charged. Also in Mount Pleasant off Route 17 is Boone Hall Plantation, once the largest pecan plantation in the world. See the avenue of oaks as well as nine original slave cabins.

Take SC 703 south out of Mount Pleasant to Sullivan's Island, home of the Caw Caw Interpretive Center, a 643-acre park

Once endangered, the pelican has made a comeback since the banning of DDT.

with 8 miles (12.8 km) of nature trails and boardwalks through its cypress swamp, oak forest, and salt and fresh water wetlands. While on Sullivan's Island, also visit Fort Moultrie, which is open every day. The structure began as a log fort during the American Revolution, and the great Seminole chief Osceola is buried just outside its main portal. Return to the mainland on SC 703 and find Coleman Blvd. Turn right to reach US 17.

The South Carolina Coast

We now head north on US 17. Watch for roadside stands where you can shop for sweetgrass baskets. Weaving skills were brought to the Carolinas from West Africa by slaves, who kept the traditional motifs alive. Today the baskets made in this tradition are collectibles that increase in value as they age. Francis Marion National Forest is on your left as you travel north on US 17; to your right is the Atlantic Ocean.

Take the ferry to Cape Romain National Wildlife Refuge's Bull Island, which opens March 1. Six miles (9.6 km) long, the island is a refuge for such endangered species as the red wolf, the American Bald eagle, and the loggerhead sea turtle. Hike 16 miles (25.6 km) of trails through a maritime forest and explore Boneyard Beach and its wrecks. At Awendaw, stop at the Sewee Visitor & Environment Education Center, which has live birds of prey, a red wolf education area, and hands-on displays explaining the ecosystems of the region.

In Francis Marion National Forest you'll find 250,000 acres of outdoor recreation: camping, boat ramps, fish ponds, rifle ranges, hiking trails, horse and motorcycle trails, and picnic areas. When the spring wildflowers are in bloom, it's heaven. A few miles farther north at McClellanville, catch the ferry to Raccoon Key in Cape Romain National Wildlife Refuge. Probe into saltwater creeks and walk sun-warmed beaches. (For information on both the Bull Creek ferry and the Raccoon Key ferry, call Coastal Expeditions, Inc., at 843-881-4582.)

The stretch of US 17 you're now traveling was settled centuries ago by rice

Myrtle Beach—the Branson of the East, Nashville with beaches—features the Carolina Opry.

planters. Hopsewee Plantation (12 miles/ 19.2 km south of Georgetown) is a 1740s rice farm that was the birthplace of a signer of the Declaration of Independence, Thomas Lynch Jr. Beginning in March, it's open Tuesday through Friday. Nearby, Hampton Plantation State Park has an unfurnished mansion that dates to the mid-1700s, possibly as early as 1735. It was visited by George Washington in 1791. In Georgetown, see Prince George Winyah Episcopal Church, which was founded in 1721. Then visit the Rice Museum and learn the importance of this crop from colonial days to the present.

Between Pawleys Island and Murrells Inlet, stop at Brookgreen Gardens to take a trail ride on horseback, kayak the creeks behind Springfield Plantation, walk the forest with a naturalist, stroll one of the South's most striking sculpture gardens, see the banks of the Waccamaw River where Laurel Hill Plantation once stood, and take a two-hour cruise past Sandy Island to see eighteenth- and nineteenth-century plantation houses.

BEACHES CALL

Continue north on US 17 through a springtime seascape of beaches, seabirds, creamy surf, and plenty of places to shop, eat, and sightsee. We depart for now from nature watching and history hunting to get into a party mood. Myrtle Beach calls itself the golf capital of the world, so if you're a golfer, go no farther. Play hundreds of holes at almost one hundred championship golf courses here. A good place to begin is Tee Time Central (800-344-5590 or <http://www.mbn.com>).

Myrtle Beach's Camping World is the place to get parts and spares. This popular playground city also has campgrounds galore, including a big KOA (800-255-7614), and several resorts, including Ocean Lakes Family Campground (800-722-1451). Ocean Lakes is on the ocean and has an Olympic-sized outdoor pool, an indoor pool, and telephone hookups with free local calls. If you're ready for city lights after days of historic plantations and nature watching, bust out now to see the Dixie Stampede Dinner and Show, Hard Rock Cafe, Planet Hollywood, All-Star Cafe, NASCAR Cafe, House of Blues, a Salute to Elvis at Eddie Miles Theater, Broadway shows, Medieval Times Dinner and Tournament, live shows at the Alabama Theater, and country music at the Carolina Opry.

Dance to oldies at Studebaker's. Shop

massive malls, factory outlets, Basketville, and the shopping-dining-entertainment complex at Barefoot Landing. The Myrtle Beach Pavilion Amusement Park opens mid-March with thrill rides, shops, games, dining, and a boardwalk. Myrtle Waves Water Park also opens mid-March with splashy rides for all ages. Play miniature golf, drive bumper cars at the Grand Prix, see an IMAX movie at Discovery Theater, and go to the zoo, the aquarium, and Alligator Adventure.

Myrtle Beach also has its educational side. Take a cruise aboard the Hurricane Fleet to see how shrimp are netted. Go deep-sea fishing and sea kayaking down the Waccamaw River through Heritage Preserve or paddle through the salt marshes out to Bird Island. See the art museum.

Our next waypoint is Wilmington, North Carolina. From Southport, take NC 87/133 into Wilmington and along the way pass Orton Plantation, which in springtime is a botanical bonanza of azaleas, camellias, pansy beds in all colors, pink and white dogwood, and fruit trees in blossom. As the days grow warmer, rhododendron bloom followed by crape myrtle and oleander. Construction on the plantation house, which can be seen from the outside but is privately occupied, was begun in 1735. Don't miss the bird watching at Orton Pond, a watering hole for anhinga, osprey, and red-cockaded woodpeckers.

Fishing in the Cape Fear–Wilmington area, which has fresh, salt, and brackish water, is some of the best in the east. Find a home base in the area and spend several days here fishing, lazing, or sightseeing.

On the Way to Wilmington

En route to Wilmington, North Carolina, leave US 17 whenever the seaside calls to drive down secondary roads to places such as Sunset Beach, Holden Beach, and Caswell Beach. The historic village of Southport (east of US 17 via NC 211) is a walking city. Spanish sailors first discovered the area as early as 1521 when it was already a major Indian settlement. European settlement goes back to the 1700s, so your rubbernecking stroll will take you past ancient churches, homes, and cemeteries. From Riverside Park, you can see both Bald Head Lighthouse and Oak Island Lighthouse. Nearby Fort Johnson was founded in 1745.

Wilmington calls for a guided tour at first so you don't miss the gossip and legends. Tours are available on foot or by trolley, horse-drawn carriage, and boat. We recommend taking at least one tour each on land and water. Airplane and seaplane flight-seeing tours out of the airport are also a good way to see the Cape Fear area with its beaches and many silvery inlets.

On your tours you'll see historic homes and churches, gardens, museums, and a must-see, the battleship *North Carolina*. Visitors can see the museum, sick bay, engine room, galley, decks, and guns of this World War II ship. Visit Fort Fisher State Recreation Site (take SC 421 south from Wilmington) where a fort finally fell to Union forces in 1865. Its last ocean port now lost, the Confederacy was close to the end. Much of the original fort has been reclaimed by the sea, but the earthworks are still interesting. An audiovisual presentation tells the story of the battles here.

Leaving Wilmington northbound on US 421, turn left on NC 210, which takes you to Moores Creek National Battlefield near Currie. Stop at the visitor center to hear the story of the 1776 battle in which Carolina Loyalists fought the Patriots, who wanted independence for the United States. The British sympathizers and their gold were captured, ending British hopes to defeat the revolutionaries by invading from the south. The site is open all year and has picnic tables.

Event:

Myrtle Beach holds its big stamp show in February. March brings the annual doll show and sale and a weeklong Canadian-American Days Festival. At Myrtle Beach State Park, nature lovers meet one day in April for bird watching and another day for a forest walk.

From Currie, continue west on NC 210 and intercept SC 53 through Elizabethtown. You'll find two back-to-back state parks along the way, Singletary and Jones Lake, which in springtime are coming alive with skittering squirrels, greening trees, timid wildflowers, and hungry fish. Continue on NC 53 through Fayetteville. Fort Bragg, which is the home of the 82nd Airborne Division War Memorial Museum and the John F. Kennedy Special Warfare Museum, lies on the west edge of Fayetteville. Stop for a visit or skirt the fort by taking NC 59 west to Raeford and then picking up NC 211 northwest to Aberdeen and US 1 north into Southern Pines, another mecca for golfers and the center of North Carolina's sandhill country.

If you're a golfer, you're in the heart of some of the South's most historic golfing, the Pine Hills region. Play the legendary Pinehurst Resort and Country Club as well as scores of other courses nearby. Pinehurst was founded late in the nineteenth century as a health resort. Park in the big lot as you enter the village of Pinehurst and take off on foot on narrow streets to see the tight-knit settlement where wealthy northerners once came for winter sunshine. Before the village's founding, the area was a wasteland of cut timber. It was transformed by the planting of thousands of trees from all over the world, lavish gardens, and flowering shrubs. Dine at a sidewalk café, shop smart boutiques, see the old theater and the newly restored Holly Inn, and enjoy the park-like setting of this planned community.

The Lowdown on Low Country Cuisine

People from Britain and the continent settled the Low Country and were joined by slaves from Africa and the West Indies, Spanish Jews, French Huguenots, Portuguese fishermen, and Yankee carpetbaggers. Each group of settlers brought its own imprint and long traditions to the kitchen, but much of the cuisine was formed from what was available. Chief among the abundant, native foods were succulent fish and shellfish as well as rice, an important crop from the time of earliest settlers. Popular legend has it that Carolina Low Country rice was so good, it was sent to the Orient for use on emperors' tables. The area's long growing season meant an abundance of yams, peanuts, benne seeds, blackeye peas, and other southern staples—including bourbon, the whiskey that was invented in young America. Pecans and peaches thrived, and apples arrived from the Carolina highlands. You'll dine well in the Low Country.

The Pine Hills region has antiquing, a pottery trail that includes historic Jugtown Pottery, country restaurants, forgotten hamlets, and—well, this won't be for everyone—the Taxidermy Hall of Fame. Weymouth Center in Southern Pines is a Georgian-style mansion built in the 1920s, which is filled with literary memorabilia. Drive 3 miles (4.8 km) southeast from Southern Pines on Indiana Avenue, then turn north on Fort Bragy Road to reach Weymouth Woods State Park (Sandhills Nature Preserve), where you will find 571 acres of spring wildflowers, creeks, a beaver pond, and more than 4 miles (6.4 km) of nature trails.

NC 211 takes you west from Southern Pines to Eagle Springs. From here, jog north briefly on Interstate 73 and go west at the next exit on NC 24/27 through the center of Uwharrie National Forest. At the forest's western edge along the Pee Dee River, Morrow Mountain State Park has fishing, hiking, and nature watching. From here it is a short ride back via NC 24 to Charlotte, where our Carolinas adventure began.

Events:
- Early in April, Wilmington holds its North Carolina Azalea Festival with garden tours, a parade, and pageants.
- On the second Saturday in April, the Stoneybook Steeplechase Races are held in Southern Pines. Also in mid-April the Southern Pines Garden Club has its tour of homes and gardens.

Summer Trips

By summer your RV is in its best fighting trim, all filled and emptied, lubed and prettied, and provisioned for serious mile-making. Most campers go to maximum travel with minimum maintenance now to take advantage of a season that, in Canada and the Northeast, may only last for three months or less. You don't want to miss anything, yet you're already thinking about getting Up There and back before the snow flies.

This is the season to take the RV to the beach—to the water's edge in many places—and use it as a private cabana. Host a family reunion at a campground that has campsites, tent sites, and cabins or condos to accommodate everyone. Escape the heat in the mountains. Or do the contrarian thing by going to Florida, where it is "off" season, and discover the sailing, scuba diving, fishing, and snorkeling that are best in summer. With the kids out of school, give your RV trip an educational theme by visiting Civil War sites or driving the Natchez Trace. Camp college towns to help a high-schooler decide where to go to college. These are the months you've worked for all year.

*Southern Magnolia
(Magnolia grandiflora)*

MARYLAND OFFICE OF TOURISM

IRVING ECO-CENTRE LA DUNE DE BOUCTOUCHE

MUNAUTE URBAINE DE QUEBEC

ANDRÉ F. BOULIANE, COURTESY OFFICE DU TOURISME ET DES CONGRES DE LA COM-

MIDDLETON EVANS

CHAPTER 6

A Ride 'Round Chesapeake Bay
Feast on Seafood and Seascapes

MILEAGE
Approximately 800 miles
(1,280 km)

RESOURCES

- Colonial Williamsburg Foundation, P.O. Box 1776, Williamsburg VA 23187, 800-361-6571, *http://www.history.org.*
- Maryland Office of Tourism, 217 E. Redwood St., Baltimore MD 21202, 800-MDISFUN (800-634-7386) or 800-543-1036, *http://www.mdisfun.org.*
- Norfolk Convention & Visitors Bureau, 232 E. Main St., Norfolk VA 23510, 800-368-3097 or 757-664-6620, *http:www.norfolkcvb.com.*
- Petersburg Visitors Center, 425 Cockade Alley, Petersburg VA 23803, 800-368-3595, *http://www.petersburg-va.org.*
- Richmond Convention & Visitors Bureau, 550 E. Marshall St., Richmond VA 23219, 800-370-9004, *http://www.richmondva.org.*
- Virginia Potomac Gateway Welcome Center, 3540 James Madison Pkwy., King George VA 22485, 800-453-6167 (or 800-336-3078) or 540-663-3205, *http://www. northernneck.org.*
- Virginia Tourism Corporation, 901 E. Byrd St., Richmond VA 23219, 800-253-2767, *http://www.virginia.org.*

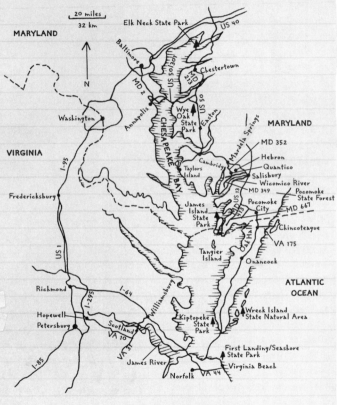

Cradle of the Confederacy

Head south from Baltimore, Maryland, or Washington, D.C., into rolling hills where some of our nation's most important historic dramas were played out: Fredericksburg, Richmond, and Petersburg, Virginia. Interstate 95 is the quick way to travel, but US 1 parallels it for slower, more scenic travel.

In the Fredericksburg area, visit Chancellorsville Battlefield, Fredericksburg Battlefield, Spotsylvania

Take a Side Trip or Two

From Fredericksburg, you can make a loop to the east on VA 218 to Caledon State Natural Area. Continue on VA 218 (which becomes VA 205) to Oak Grove, and pick up VA 3, which takes you to George Washington Birthplace National Monument, Westmoreland State Park, and the birthplace of Robert E. Lee. Or, head southwest on VA 208 to sprawling, 13,000-acre Lake Anna with its 200 miles (320 km) of meandering shoreline, thirty species of fish, families of deer, wild turkey, and waterfowl as well as Lake Anna State Park with its 9 miles (14.4 km) of hiking trails and interpretive programs.

Court House Battlefield, and Wilderness Battlefield, which was the site of the first battle between Robert E. Lee and Ulysses S. Grant. All of the battlefields are open daily and are well marked by highway signs. The first three have visitor centers with audiovisual shows and exhibits.

Visit the Fredericksburg Area Museum, 803 Princess Anne Street, which has exhibits from prehistoric times to the present. See an old medical office—Hugh Mercer Apothecary Shop at 1020 Carolina Street—dating to the eighteenth century, the James Monroe Museum and Library (508 Charles St.), and many historic homes, including the Mary Washington House (1200 Charles St.), Rising Sun Tavern (1306 Carolina St.), and Kenmore (1201 Washington Ave.), an eighteenth-century house.

Much of the sightseeing in this area centers around Civil War history, which is especially poignant here where the last, desperate battles played out. Richmond fell, and the surrender was signed at Appomattox.

On to Richmond

Interstate 95 or US 1 brings you to historic Richmond, capital of the Confederacy and today a tourism bonanza for all ages. It's the home of the Virginia Historical Society museum, Paramount's Kings Dominion theme park (home of the world's first linear, suspended roller coaster), the Museum and White House of the Confederacy, the Federal Reserve Bank Money Museum, the Virginia Aviation Museum, a zoo with white tigers, a historic downtown, and a long list of mansions, more museums, and sightseeing pluses. The Executive Mansion here is the nation's oldest governor's mansion in continuous use. Dating to 1813, it underwent a massive renovation in 1999.

Tip:

The best way to see historic Richmond is with Historic Richmond Tours (707 E. Franklin St., 804-780-0107). You'll travel by van with a knowledgeable guide. The company also sells a Downtown Block Ticket that, for one price, buys admission to many historic sites you can tour on your own.

Richmond is also one of the few cities that offers whitewater rafting right through town. Or, take one of the eight- to ten-passenger bateaus that ply the canals leading to the James River. The canals were chartered by George Washington in 1784. You can see the riverfront in miniature at the Nature Center at Maymont, a historical estate-turned-park at Hampton St. and Pennsylvania Ave., which has a three-dimensional model of the James River. The city's riverfront is in the process of becoming a showplace of walkways, hotels, shops, and restaurants.

From Richmond, continue your journey on Interstate 95 toward Petersburg.

Two Civil War Trails

Two scenic driving tours follow Virginia Civil War trails, one following Grant's campaign and another retracing Lee's Retreat. For maps and brochures of these routes, call 888-CIVIL WAR (888-248-4592). For a free brochure describing a driving tour that follows George Washington's footsteps through central Virginia, call 888-828-4787 or write George Washington Trail, P.O. Box 110, Mount Vernon VA 22121.

For More Information

Roadside Welcome Centers are on Interstate 95, Interstate 85, and Interstate 77 at the Virginia–North Carolina line; Interstate 77, Interstate 64, and Interstate 81 near the Virginia–West Virginia line; Interstate 81 at the Virginia-Tennessee line; US 13 near the Virginia-Maryland line; Interstate 66 between US 29 and VA 234, and Interstate 95 between US 17 and VA 3.

Stop at Pamplin Historical Park, which is just off Interstate 95/85, to see Civil War battles come to life. The park has a furnished plantation home, a virtual battle, and interpretive characters who act as soldiers and civilians of the 1860s. Petersburg, like Richmond, has a good choice of museums and mansions, including the Trapezium House (Market and High Sts.), built in 1817, and the Centre Hill Mansion (Center Hill Ct.), built in 1823.

When you're finished touring Petersburg, retrace your path north on Interstate 95 to the Hopewell exit and pick up VA 10 to Surry, where VA 31 takes you to Scotland at the edge of the James River. Catch the free ferry to Williamsburg from here. For departure times, call 800-VA-FERRY (800-823-3779), or just show up. Waits are rarely more than half an hour, and no reservations are taken. Rigs shorter than 14.5 feet (4.4 m) can be accommodated. When you land, you'll be in one of the nation's tourism hot spots.

Tip:

For a brochure on Virginia travel for people with disabilities, call 800-742-3935 or TDD/TTD 804-371-0327.

Colonial Williamsburg and the Tidewater

Colonial Williamsburg (CW) is a 173-acre living museum that can take a lifetime to cover. Once the capital of America under British rule, CW has been restored to its eighteenth-century roots, complete with stores, taverns, acres of gardens and green spaces, a courthouse complete with stocks where the naughty were punished, and a glittering Governor's Palace.

Still part of the Colonial Williamsburg Foundation but 7 miles (11.2 km) southeast of Colonial Williamsburg, on the James River, is Carter's Grove, a plantation with an eighteenth-century mansion that's been restored to its appearance when the Rockefellers lived in it in the 1930s. If you plan to visit both places, be sure to get a combination admission ticket.

Williamsburg's variety of sights and activities is enough to bring your trip to a stop. The Williamsburg KOA (757-565-2907 or 800-KOA-1733/800-562-1733), runs a free shuttle to CW so you can park your rig and forget about it.

A swirl of activities goes on all year at CW, from lessons and meetings to the singing of Christmas carols. Interpretive characters in costume sweep the streets, make soapbox speeches, serve meals, and otherwise live as if King George were still on his throne. Many of the homes are privately owned and occupied by people who love the time-warp atmosphere, decorating

The Colonial Capitol in Colonial Williamsburg.

Visitors to Colonial Williamsburg revel in the atmosphere of days gone by.

Event:
Something special is going on every day at Colonial Williamsburg. Request a schedule before you go, and plug into local life for as long as you can spare. As a "resident" rather than a day-tripper, you can attend seminars, demonstrations, courses, and other forms of entertainment.

houses in season as the original occupants would have done and sometimes even taking to the streets in colonial garb. The more you can lose yourself in the historical game, the more fun you'll have. Mention television or Velcro, and these folks won't know what you're talking about.

Tip:
If you are over sixty-five or under sixteen, you won't need a fishing license to tap into one of the nation's most lush fisheries, the waters of Virginia. Bluefish run May through November, and you're also likely to catch croaker, flounder, drum, and Spanish mackerel. No matter where you camp along this route, you're never far from lively fishing in fresh, brackish, or salt water.

Busch Gardens Williamsburg is a blockbuster theme park that's open daily all summer. Jamestown Settlement depicts life in America's first permanent English colony. Sherwood Forest Plantation, the home of President John Tyler, is open to visitors but is still the private residence of the president's grandson.

Event:
Harborfest is held the first full weekend in June in Norfolk with fireworks, seafood, boat races, and ship tours.

Leaving Williamsburg, follow Interstate 64 to Hampton Roads, an area that includes Newport News, Hampton, Norfolk, and Portsmouth. Take the Poquoson exit and head east to bird-watch at Plum Tree Island National Wildlife Refuge, swim off windswept beaches, beach-comb fabulous Virginia Beach (where you can also see the Virginia Marine Science Museum), and stroll the edge of the Atlantic at First Landing/Seashore State Park.

At 1 Waterside Drive, Nauticus, the National Maritime Center in Norfolk, is a must for nature lovers. More than 150 exhibits, including computers and videos, introduce you to the science of the sea. Kids will love the touch pool, where they can pet a shark. Nature lovers will also enjoy Norfolk Botanical Garden (on Azalea Garden Road, adjacent to the airport), which you can tour on foot or by boat or tram. Visit the Chrysler Museum of Art (245 W.

Olney Rd.), one of the nation's top museums. Tour historic homes and museums, see the impressive Douglas MacArthur Memorial (Bank St. and Hall Ave.), ride the pedestrian ferry across the Elizabeth River to Portsmouth, and take a free tour of the Norfolk Naval Base. A good way to see Norfolk's historic downtown is on the Norfolk Trolley Tour (757-640-6300).

Leave Norfolk northbound on US 13. You'll immediately come to the Chesapeake Bay Bridge-Tunnel,` one of the world's great engineering marvels, a magic

The Chesapeake Bay Bridge-Tunnel.

carpet that takes you over and under the water until suddenly you're on the fabled Eastern Shore with its islands, villages frozen in time, picturesque lighthouses, shipwrecks, and the famous wild ponies of Assateague. RVs are permitted on the bridge-tunnel, provided you turn off the propane at the tank. The fare for a car is $10, and prices go up according to how many axles you have. A car towing a two-axle trailer pays $16; three axles, $19.

The southern tip of the barrier island forms the Eastern Shore National Wildlife Refuge, where an elevated platform lets you walk a wildlife trail past a World War II bunker. Look for herons, ducks, turtles, butterflies, songbirds, and hawks. Sightings are especially good at the pond at the visitor center. As you drive north, pull over

Event:
The Boardwalk Art Show is held in Virginia Beach in June.

Great Dismal Swamp

If you want to see the Great Dismal Swamp National Wildlife Refuge, it's south of Norfolk on US 17 just north of the North Carolina border. The name isn't fair (although there are plenty of voracious mosquitoes). Far from dismal, the swamp is a 106,000-acre wildlife wonderland roamed by bears, foxes, bobcats, and deer, and it has a big population of migrating birds. Hiking access is from Washington Ditch, south of Suffolk.

often to bird-watch, sightsee, fish at the pier or at the southernmost pull off, look for dolphins and ships, and have a snack at one of the rustic restaurants. Just north of the crossing, Kiptopeke State Park is also an excellent bird watching post.

While on the Eastern Shore, roam lonely beaches to discover ancient seashell deposits, salt flats filled with denizens of the salt marshes, dunes, sea oats, and nesting birds. Take a sightseeing cruise to Tangier

The anhinga, or snake bird, must dry its wings between fishing expeditions.

Crab pots stand at the ready on a Smith Island dock.

Island from the ferry dock at Onancock. Tangier Island, which lies in the Bay, is the soft-shell-crab capital of the world. Residents here still speak with an old-time Elizabethan accent.

When you return from the island, continue north on US 13. At Oak Hall, visit the world's largest decorative duck decoy factory. Feast your fill of fresh fish, oysters, clams, and crab in rustic local restaurants. A mile north of Oak Hall, pick up VA 175

For the Birds

Birding on the Chesapeake Bay Bridge is unequaled for quantity and quality. About three hundred species have been sighted here including some birds that are found nowhere else in Virginia. If you're a serious birder, arrange in advance for a permit to stop and bird-watch on four manmade islands along the bridge-tunnel route. For more information, write to the Chesapeake Bay Bridge and Tunnel District, 32386 Lankford Highway, Box 111, Cape Charles VA 23310, or call 757-331-2960.

to Chincoteague, where you can see the Oyster and Maritime Museum and the Refuge Waterfowl Museum. Each July, wild ponies swim from Assateague Island to Chincoteague, where they are auctioned. From the wildly beautiful sands of the barrier islands, look for seabirds and dolphins. Keep an eye out for the rare Delmarva squirrel, which is sometimes seen in remote corners of the Eastern Shore.

Marvelous Maryland

US 13 takes you into Maryland. Because this trip focuses on the Chesapeake Bay, we'll resist the temptation to go east to the beaches and barrier islands and instead will head west from Pocomoke City on MD 667 to James Island State Park, a 3,147-acre peninsula, which is almost entirely surrounded by the Bay. On warm summer nights, the sweet smell of the salt sea is intoxicating.

From the state park, continue north on MD 413 to join MD 13. MD 13 leads into Salisbury, the uncrowned capital of the

Relive horse and buggy days in historic Chestertown.

Delmarva Peninsula, an area where Maryland is bordered by Delaware and Virginia (Del-Mar-Va). See the Ward Museum of Wildfowl Art (909 S. Schumaker Dr.), which has some of the best decoys in the world, and visit the 12-acre Salisbury Zoological Park (755 S. Park Dr.). Leave the area by heading west along the Wicomico River on MD 349, turn north on MD 352 to Quantico and MD 352 to Hebron, and then head west on US 50, where you'll find a picnic area at Mardela Springs. Cross the Nanticoke River, keeping a sharp eye out for the birds that inhabit the wildlife management areas on both sides of US 50. Stop to fish the Choptank River at piers just east of Cambridge. Stop in Cambridge itself. The Visitor Information Center at the bridge

> ### Take the Scenic Route
>
> *For a scenic side trip, take MD 33 west, stop at the Chesapeake Bay Maritime Museum, and then continue through pretty farm country to Tilghman. From this narrow finger of land, you'll have water views on both sides.*

has current local maps and campground information.

Southwest of Cambridge at Taylors Island on MD 16, Tideland Park (410-397-3473) is a good place to overnight while you explore this lovely area. The park is open through November. See Old Trinity Church, built in the late 1600s and still home to an active congregation, as well as Spocott Mill, a replica of an original mill. You'll also see a restored schoolhouse and miller's cottage. This corner of Dorchester County is the home of the 17,000-acre Blackwater National Wildlife Refuge (410-

Event:
Cambridge holds a colorful Sailboat Regatta in July.

228-2677), so the bird watching is superior. Stop at the refuge's visitor center at 2145 Key Wallace Drive, Cambridge, for maps that show a scenic drive, an observation tower, and hiking trails.

Point north from Cambridge again on US 50 toward Easton, stopping at Third Haven Meeting House, which was built by Quakers in the 1680s and is one of the oldest frame churches in the nation. The Historical Society of Talbot County, housed in an 1810 Federal-style townhouse, is open daily except Monday.

From Easton head north on US 50 through lovely tidewater scenery. You'll pass Wye Oak State Park, where a 450-year-old white oak stands 95 feet (29 m) tall and has a trunk 21 feet (6.4 m) in circumference. This tree is said to be the largest white oak in the United States. The park's old mill, which still produces cornmeal, dates to the 1670s. Flour from here was sent to George Washington and his hungry troops at Valley Forge. The park also has picnic sites, a shop where you can buy freshly ground grains for tomorrow's pan-

cakes, and a restored church dating to 1721.

From here, US 50/301 can take you back across the toll bridge to Annapolis and Baltimore, with a stop at Sandy Point State Park if you'd like. Or, continue north on MD 213 through the beautiful countryside of Queen Annes County. Stop in Chestertown to see the art galleries and the stately old homes built before the Revolution. Common lore has it that local citizens had their own rebellion by throwing a shipment of English tea into the Chester River rather than paying the hated tax. Every Memorial Day weekend, the caper is reenacted.

Stay with scenic MD 213 to wend your way northward, taking your time to stop at charming villages, the Old Bohemia Church (built in 1704), and the demonstration forest at Elk Neck, where more than 3,000 acres shelter wildlife, food plots, experimental plots, and other forestry. At the far end of the peninsula, Elk Neck State Park has trails, fishing, boats for rent, and hardwood forests buzzing with birds and wildlife. From here, it's an easy return to Baltimore via Interstate 95 or US 40.

CHAPTER 7

Canada's Magnificent Maritimes
The Atlantic Provinces

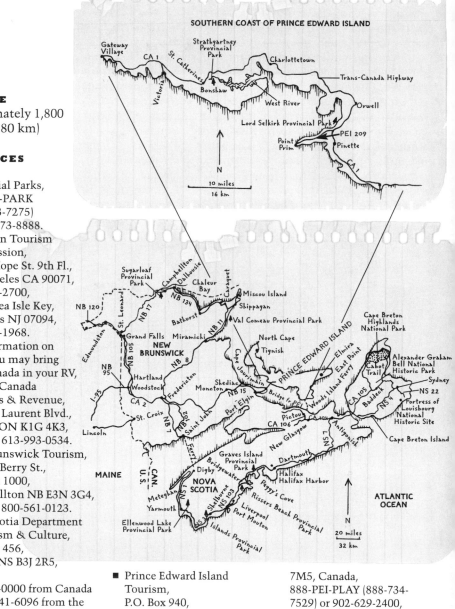

MILEAGE
Approximately 1,800
miles (2,880 km)

RESOURCES
- Canada
  Provincial Parks,
  800-213-PARK
  (800-213-7275)
  or 888-773-8888.
- Canadian Tourism
  Commission,
  550 S. Hope St. 9th Fl.,
  Los Angeles CA 90071,
  213-346-2700,
  or 305 Sea Isle Key,
  Secaucus NJ 07094,
  201-223-1968.
  For information on
  what you may bring
  into Canada in your RV,
  contact Canada
  Customs & Revenue,
  2265 St. Laurent Blvd.,
  Ottawa ON K1G 4K3,
  Canada, 613-993-0534.
- New Brunswick Tourism,
  26 Rose Berry St.,
  P.O. Box 1000,
  Campbellton NB E3N 3G4,
  Canada, 800-561-0123.
- Nova Scotia Department
  of Tourism & Culture,
  P.O. Box 456,
  Halifax NS B3J 2R5,
  Canada,
  800-565-0000 from Canada
  or 800-341-6096 from the
  United States.
- Prince Edward Island
  Tourism,
  P.O. Box 940,
  Charlottetown PEI C1A
  7M5, Canada,
  888-PEI-PLAY (888-734-
  7529) or 902-629-2400,
  http://www.peiplay.com.

52

Across the Border

Canada's summers are short and the visitor's time may be even shorter, so we suggest that you enter the country from Maine on Interstate 95, which leads you near Fredericton, New Brunswick, and return by ferry out of Yarmouth, Nova Scotia, to either Portland or Bar Harbor, Maine. You'll have a good variety of sightseeing plus the pleasure of the sea trip. From eastern Canada, call Prince of Fundy Cruises (800-565-7900) for ferry information.

Get used to seeing everything written in both English and French, which is disconcerting at first. Even more disconcerting is being surrounded by Francophones who can't—or won't—speak English. It happens, we are told, but our own experiences in Canada have all been pleasant ones. We are willing to have a jolly good try at speaking any local language, and folks have always responded in kind.

New/Nouveau Brunswick

The first European settlers on this Canadian coast, discovered in 1534 by Jacques Cartier, were the French, who soon established

> ### The Shining Saint John River
>
> *The Saint John is an important recreation resource. Entering Canada from Houlton, Maine, where Interstate 95 becomes NB 95, you can begin your trip by heading south along NB 540 toward Kirkland for hiking and nature watching at North Lake and Spednic Lake Provincial Parks.*

a trading post at the mouth of the Saint John River. The province's name honors the Braunschweigers (Brunswicks) of Germany, whose royal family sat on the English throne. During the Revolution, Americans who wanted to remain under English rule fled here. Another huge influx of newcomers occurred during the potato famine of the 1840s, which drove hundreds of thousands of Irish off their farms. English is still the predominant language, but you'll hear a lot of French, including the ancient "Valley French" spoken along the Saint John River Valley.

Our master plan is to take the scenic route encircling 2,690-foot (819.9 m) Mount Carleton, the highest point in the

Puffins can be seen along the New Brunswick coastline.

NEW BRUNSWICK TOURISM

Canada Day

Canada Day is celebrated on July 1. If you can find a hometown celebration near you, bring a maple leaf flag to wave and enjoy the holiday with your northern neighbors.

Event:
In July, join the Bon Ami Festival Get Together for feasting and folk ways in Dalhousie, New Brunswick.

province. We'll ramble through timeless villages, along bold seacoasts, and finally back to Fredericton.

From NB 95 and the Woodstock area, go north on CA 2. At Hartland, see the longest covered bridge in the world. CA 2 takes you north along the Saint John River to Grand Falls or, if you prefer a more stop-and-start route through small towns, take NB 105. This is potato country, and fields that are left fallow are covered with wildflowers. At the annual Potato Festival at Grand Falls, one of the largest waterfalls in the East, boats are covered with flowers and sent crashing over the falls. Grand Falls is a popular spot for tourists and has a good choice of campgrounds. Take a day to hike the trails through the rugged river gorge.

Continue north to Edmundston to see the botanical gardens as well as Les Jardins Provincial Park with its kiddy rides. Edmundston is the terminus of Le Petit Temis, an 81-mile (129.6 km) rails-to-trails route for biking and hiking. Walk it as far as you care to. Then drive NB 120 into the kingdom of Madawaska. A thumb of land that juts out of Canada into Maine, the Republic of Madawaska has its own flag, its own French patois, and a whale of a festival in midsummer with folksinging, dancing, and lumberjack contests.

From Madawaska, retrace your route south to St. Leonard, where scenic NB 17 takes off northeast toward Chaleur Bay. When you reach the bay at Dalhousie and Cambellton, you're in lands settled by English, Scots, and Acadians. The Babel of language is fun to hear. See Sugarloaf Provincial Park (off NB 17 west of Campbellton), go salmon fishing on the rivers and bays, and shop for local crafts and arts. Continue on NB 134 along the dramatic coastline with its views of Chaleur Bay, keeping an eye out for a ghost ship that is said to sail the bay, until you reach Bathurst. Most campgrounds in the area are open early May to late September.

NEW BRUNSWICK TOURISM

Take a break from the road to sea kayak the spectacular New Brunswick coast.

Event:
Late in July and extending into August, Edmunston, New Brunswick holds La Faire Brayonne, the largest French-language festival east of Québec. Sample Brayonne foods, crafts, and culture at this annual celebration.

Mount Carleton Provincial Park

If you want to venture into Mount Carleton Provincial Park while driving to Chaleur Bay, take NB 180 east from Five Fingers. The nature watching and hiking in this park offer the rawboned backcountry at its best.

From Bathurst, follow NB 11 along the coast to enjoy the scenery. You won't win any speed contests because you'll be tempted to stop often and get out the camera. At Caraquet, shop the art galleries and spend a day at Village Historique Acadien on Boulevard Saint-Pierre, a living history settlement where "settlers" reenact nineteenth-century Acadian life. Caraquet is one of four New Brunswick cities where you'll find a Day Adventure Centre, which sells a variety of packages of admission and rides tickets.

Event:
In Caraquet, New Brunswick, Le Festival Acadien celebrates Acadian culture and includes a Blessing of the Fleet.

Continue on scenic NB 11 south along the coast, with a stop at Val Comeau Provincial Park for nature walks and awesome views of the Gulf of St. Lawrence. About 40 miles (64 km) farther on NB 11 is Miramichi, famed for its salmon fishing. There's a good choice of outfitters, so here's the chance to fill your freezer with good eating for the next week or so. Head south-

Islands in the Sun

If you drive out NB 113 from Caraquet to Shippagan, you'll find a fishing village and a museum devoted to fishing and boating. If it's warm enough, take the bridge to Miscou Island for a swim off beaches that seem to be at the edge of the world.

west out of Miramichi on NB 8 toward Fredericton. You'll follow a scenic highway with plenty of places to pull off, picnic, and get acquainted with small-town folks.

Fredericton offers shopping, nightlife, dining, and other big-town pleasures as well as important sightseeing points, which include Christ Church Cathedral, a Gothic masterpiece completed in 1853, and Beaverbrook Art Gallery, where Lord Beaverbrook's personal collection boasts works by Dali and Gainesborough. Portraits by Joshua Reynolds are on display in

Can You Say "Kouchibouguac"?

Rather than turning toward Miramichi, stay with NB 11 if you want to make a side trip to Kouchibouguac National Park. The park's 92 square miles (238 sq km) of wilderness offer hiking, fishing, deserted beaches, and nature watching.

For another pleasing side trip, you could continue on NB 11 south to Shediak, which calls itself the Lobster Capital of the World. The town holds a Lobster Festival in July with a parade, contests, arts and crafts, and feasting on luscious lobster. July is a wonderful time to be here as well as at Parlee Beach Provincial Park nearby. The park's waters, warmed by the tides of the Northumberland Strait, are the least icy you'll find up here.

the Legislative Building, which also has a very rare copy of the Domesday Book, an eleventh-century survey of English landholdings ordered by William the Conqueror. At the Military Compound, where reenactments are staged in summer, tour a museum with relics from the city's past. Take a walking tour with a costumed guide, or rent a canoe to paddle the Nashwaak. Campsites are abundant in provincial parks and at several private campgrounds, but because this is peak season, be sure to call ahead for reservations.

Saint John

From Fredericton, take NB 102 south along the river for a slow, winding, scenic ap-

NEW BRUNSWICK TOURISM

Melvin's Beach, St. Martins, New Brunswick.

proach to Saint John (for a faster trip, take NB 7). Samuel Champlain visited the Saint John area in 1604 and—as was customary for Catholic explorers—named it for a saint. Saint John's growth really began, however, in the late 1700s with the arrival of three thousand Loyalists from New York and New England. These forbears are remembered in July at Loyalist Days with a reenactment of their landing at the riverfront.

While in Saint John, take one of the walking tours and shop the Old City Mar-

ket, which dates to 1876. The city has museums, a zoo, and a nature center, and it's a favorite spot to watch the tidal bore, which occurs when massive tides in the Bay of Fundy rise and push the Saint John River back upriver accompanied by a symphony of soft sea sounds. From Saint John, take the ferry to Digby, Nova Scotia, where new adventures await. Call 800-561-0123 for information, directions, and schedules.

Tip:
At any Visitor Information Centre, pick up the forms required to get a refund of the 7 percent Goods and Services Tax paid on every purchase in Canada. As a nonresident, you pay it at time of purchase but file later for the rebate. It's essential that you save all receipts.
For further information, call Revenue Canada at 902-432-5608.

Event:
In August, Saint John, New Brunswick, hosts its annual Festival by the Sea with three hundred entertainers and one hundred performances over nine days.

Nova Scotia

Long before hardy Scots arrived and named this place "New Scotland," it was home to the Micmac Indians, whom evidence suggests were visited by seafaring Vikings. The Vikings probably came here to gather wood for treeless Greenland. French settlers arrived in 1605 and named the area Acadia, but when King James gave great land grants here to his Scottish subjects, Nova Scotia it became. The French were expelled in 1755, but their story continues in chapter 19 because some of the Acadians of Canada became the Cajuns of Louisiana.

We love the Scottish accents here where many people continue to speak Gaelic. You'll also hear French, of course. When the Acadians were permitted to return to Nova Scotia after 1783, many found that their homes and farms had already been taken over by new settlers, so many of the Acadians and their French ways went to New Brunswick. The largest Acadian colony on Nova Scotia today is on what is called French Shore, between Digby and Yarmouth. Stop in Digby to stroll the docks, enjoy the fishing village ambience, and gorge on Digby Chicks, which are tangy, plump, smoked herring.

Inland Side Trip

Kejimkujik National Park lies about 40 miles (64 km) inland from Nova Scotia's eastern coast and NS 103. From Liverpool, take NS 8, which cuts across the entire peninsula. The national park merits a visit for hiking, fishing, and canoeing narrow streams that thread through the green forests. Sportsmen come here to hunt moose and fish for trout; summer visitors can pan for gold. It's a perfect spot for serious hiking and paddling in the outback.

Farther up the coast, pass the seaside adjunct of Kejimkujik National Park at Port Mouton. Stop at the visitor center and enjoy the scenery. Stay with the coastline on NS 103 past Rissers Beach Provincial Park and go into Bridgewater for shopping and an hour at the museums. You'll see the last of what were once seven mills along the LaHave River.

Legendary Lunenberg

From Bridgewater, take NS 3 east to Lunenberg, a fishing and boat-building town, which is as picturesque as a movie set. The famous schooner Bluenose *was built here as well as the ship filmed in* Mutiny on the Bounty. *The visitor center on Blockhouse Hill is a good place to pick up maps and brochures; it also has campsites.*

From Digby travel south on NS 1, where a string of picture-postcard villages straggles the coast back to back, most of them centered around a church and its high spire. At Meteghan, hike to the natural cave, said to have been a transfer point for booze during U.S. Prohibition. Almost every seaport in Canada has a Prohibition story, and all of the stories make for good listening. In Yarmouth, pick up NS 3. Just east of Yarmouth, stop at Ellenwood Lake Provincial Park for fishing and nature walks.

Staying with NS 3, hug the coastline. NS 3 joins 103 for the trip up the east coast. Along what is known as the Lighthouse Route, stop often to gaze out over the open Atlantic and imagine the time early in World War II when this was a killing fields for merchant ships that had little protection against German submarines. The story is told in Farley Mowat's *Grey Seas Under*. It makes a good read at any time, but especially while you're here where the heroism can still be felt. The Islands Provincial Park near Shelburne has nature trails and awesome scenery.

The roads get busier as the route nears Graves Island Provincial Park. Follow NS 333 for a brief visit to the artist colony of Peggy's Cove. It's easy to see how an artist could spend a lifetime here, never wanting for beautiful scenes to paint or photograph.

Returning to NS 103 and continuing on to Dartmouth and Halifax, get a taste of city life after all of your seaside rambles. At the Shearwater Aviation Museum, 13 Bonaventure Street in Shearwater, see displays that depict Canada's maritime aviation history. The Black Culture Centre (1149 Main St., Dartmouth) is an interesting look at black history, which goes back more than three hundred years in this area. Learn about the seas through displays and an audiovisual show at the Bedford Oceanographic Institute, Shannon Park, Dartmouth. Halifax also has an aviation museum, a 17-acre Victorian formal garden, and the Maritime Museum of the Atlantic (1675 Lower Water Dr.). The *Titanic* exhibits at the Maritime Museum are outstanding, and you can also learn about the Halifax Explosion, which happened in 1917 when a World War I munitions ship exploded in the city's harbor. Windows were shattered 100 miles (160 km) away, more than two thousand people were killed instantly, and pieces of wreckage were found many miles away.

Spend a day at the Halifax Citadel National Historic Site, where soldiers in kilts drill, play bagpipes, and reenact nineteenth-century barracks life. The audiovisual presentation, which lasts almost an hour, is first-rate entertainment. Have lunch at the nineteenth-century restaurant, where you can get a bowl of soldier's stew. It tastes better than it sounds.

Leaving Halifax on NS 7, you'll follow the beautiful eastern shore of Nova Scotia and then turn inland, still following NS 7 through eye-popping scenery, to Antigonish. Campgrounds and provincial parks are found all along this popular tourist trail. The season is short and intense, so reservations are always recommended.

From Antigonish, take CA 104 across the Straits of Canso onto Cape Breton Island. The road becomes CA 105. Our sightseeing goal is the town of Baddeck, where Alexander Graham Bell lived for the last

Island Ferry

The seventy-five-minute ferry ride to Prince Edward Island from Pictou runs every seventy-five minutes from mid-May through most of December. Call 888-249-SAIL (888-249-7245) for more information. The toll bridge at Gateway Village (888-437-6565) is always open.

thirty-five years of his life. More than just the inventor of the telephone, he was a hero who worked with the deaf. It was he who recommended "Miracle Worker" Anne Sullivan to the family of blind, deaf Helen Keller. At the Bell Home on Chebucto Street, see exhibits on Bell's many experiments in communications, aviation, deaf education, hydrofoils, and much more. On Sundays, kids make and fly kites here to learn about aerodynamics. Don't miss the view from the gardens on the rooftop of the Bell Home.

Baddeck is also the beginning and end of the Cabot Trail, a 185-mile (296 km) loop. Drive the trail around the edge of the island for one of the most beautiful tours of the trip. The road is steep and slow going in many spots; there aren't a lot of passing lanes, so stay alert for traffic behind you. When we find we're creating a bottleneck here, we pull over and enjoy the scenery while impatient drivers speed on by. At Cape Breton's northern edge is Cape Breton Highlands National Park, a good spot to spend several days hiking mild or rugged trails.

From the national park, take CA 105 south to Sydney and then pick up NS 22 southeast for 23 miles (36.8 km) to Fortress of Louisbourg National Historic Site. Park your vehicle, enter the grounds, and you're suddenly in the 1740s. More than just the fort, Fortress of Louisbourg is an entire reconstructed French city of homes and buildings where costumed "townfolk" go about their daily lives, serve food, run the government, argue politics, and totally round out the experience for awed visitors. You'll need an entire day here, so overnight before and after in one of the private or provincial parks. Return to Sydney and

Exploring Cape Breton

Using Cape Breton Highlands National Park as a base, head over to Cape St. Lawrence and the very northernmost point of the cape. Go salmon fishing in the Cheticamp River. Take a whale-watching cruise or simply stop along the Atlantic coast, train your spotting scope at the sea, and hope for a sighting. At Ingonish, swim in the ocean or in a freshwater lake that is just a short walk away from the sea.

head southwest on NS 4, which takes us back to Antigonish.

From Antigonish, follow CA 104 west and, at New Glasgow, watch for CA 106 to Pictou. Our next waypoint is Prince Edward Island, which can be reached by ferry from Pictou. There's also a toll bridge that crosses to the island from Cape Jourimain, east of Moncton, but it's more fun to go over by ferry and return on the bridge.

Prince Edward Island

Perhaps it's just imagination, but Prince Edward Island, the beloved vacation spot called PEI, has its own magical glow much like that we felt at the Isle of Skye in Scotland. It could be the enduring popularity of *Anne of Green Gables*, the book, film, and musical set here. Thousands of people each year visit the grave of the book's author, Lucy Maud Montgomery, in Cavendish Cemetery here.

Prince Edward Island has more than fifty campgrounds as well as fifteen golf courses, including the Links at Crowbush Cove, rated among North America's top ten. Take sailing excursions, go sea kayaking, try one of a hundred trout fishing holes, take a seal-watching cruise, and much more. At any visitor center, ask for the Passport to Heritage, which describes the historic sites and museums and includes information on their hours and admissions. Ask about the Ship-to-Shore Day Tour in

Anne of Green Gables

Of the 800,000 visitors who come to Prince Edward Island yearly, more than half visit Green Gables House. Some even choose to be married in the parlor of Anne of Green Gables Museum, where the story's author, Lucy Maud Montgomery, also was married. More than half a million copies of the novel Anne of Green Gables are sold every year, and more than 140 countries broadcast television programming connected with the red-haired orphan described by Mark Twain as the "dearest and most moving and most delightful child in fiction." If you don't know who she is, read the book and you'll be smitten too.

the Wellington–Mont Carmel area for a look at Acadian music and festivals.

Driving distance from East Point to North Cape, at opposite tips of the island arc, is 170 miles (272 km), so you can easily rack up hundreds of miles here on

Biking is big on Prince Edward Island.

coastal roads, country lanes, and sightseeing loops. Along the way, find campgrounds, provincial parks, visitor centers, quaint villages, places to eat and shop, and sightseeing. If you'd rather see the island by bicycle, ride the old railroad right-of-way along Sentier Trail, which runs from Elmira, just west of East Point, to Tignish, just south of North Cape. A serious biker can make the trip in a couple of days; duffers will want three or four days.

From the Wood Islands Ferry Terminal and Wood Islands Provincial Park, head west on the CA 1 through Pinette, then turn left on PEI 209 toward Point Prim to see the lighthouse, which is the island's oldest, and Polly Cemetery. The cemetery's name comes from the name of the ship that brought early settlers to the island. Many of the settlers are buried here. If you can be in town on a Tuesday evening, make reservations at the Point Prim Chowder House for an evening of seafood and fiddle music.

This is the quieter side of the island, well away from tourist centers, so take time to ride bicycles on country lanes and walk windblown shores. Lord Selkirk Provincial Park, which is just off the Trans-Canada Highway on your return from Point Prim, offers nature trails and a nine-hole golf course. The highway then leads to Orwell, where you can see the nineteenth-century homestead of writer-doctor-teacher-soldier Sir Andrew Macphail. Something is always going on in the complex, especially in summer, so take a workshop in Celtic dance, eat in the restaurant, and tour the home and grounds. Every Monday evening, "Hold On To the Haggis" is an evening of music and entertainment. On Wednesday, Orwell Corner Historic Village showcases talented local singers and musicians. On Thursdays, there's Irish set dancing and an evening of fiddling at the Macphail Homestead. When leaving Orwell, stay with CA 1 into Charlottetown.

CHARLOTTETOWN

Charlottetown is a lively city by PEI standards, but to the visitor this quaint capital is a stride back in time. See Province House National Historic Site (Richmont St.), which dates to the 1860s, visit St. Dunstan's Basilica (45 Great George St.) with its three copper spires, shop the Farmer's Market for fresh produce and ethnic foods, and dine in a good choice of Lebanese, Chinese, and Italian restaurants. Take an afternoon break at a sidewalk café or brewpub, and hang out at the harbor in Confederation Landing Park at Queen and Grafton Streets.

Stroll in the formal Victorian gardens at Ardgowan National Historic Site (2 Palmers Ln.). Visit Beaconsfield Historic House (2 Kent St.), which was built in 1877 and is one of the island's most impressive mansions. It's open daily in summer. Guides will show you the nursery, gallery, and typical Victorian double parlor. Pick up your "Anne"-related souvenirs and collectibles at the Anne of Green Gables Store on Queen Street. The building is a restored brick "mercantile" on historic Victoria Row.

Leave Charlottetown and head south-

> **Event:**
> Mid-June to early October the Charlottetown Festival on Prince Edward Island features plays and musicals. *Anne of Green Gables, The Musical,* runs until September.

> **Event:**
> In June, the Moncton Jazz Festival plays in Moncton, New Brunswick.

west on CA 1 to Strathgartney Provincial Park. Continue on to St. Catherines, where you can rent a canoe and paddle with the West River's tides into the Bonshaw Hills. Call ahead (902-675-2035) to make sure your trip coincides with the tides, which are formidable. At Bonshaw, south of St. Catherines on CA 1, the Car Life Museum has more than twenty vehicles including a 1959 Cadillac owned by Elvis Presley, a 1914 tractor, and an 1898 steam car. The museum is open every day.

Continue west on CA 1 to Victoria. Park and stroll the old streets past pretty homes, tearooms, and shops. Then, before leaving the island on the 9-mile (14.4 km) Confederation Bridge, stop at the Official Island Store gift shop at Gateway Village. You will have barely tasted the beauty, expanse, seaside views, and inland glories of Prince Edward Island. If time allows you to continue touring the island, this shop is also the official welcome center where you can get maps and guidance for further touring.

Crossing the bridge brings you back to New Brunswick. At Port Elgin, turn right on NB 15 to Moncton. Keep track of the tidal clock, or ask locally about a good place to view the tidal bore. The quickest way to Fredericton is CA 2. Continue on CA 2 past Fredericton to Woodstock, and then take NB 95 to the border, where the road becomes Interstate 95 in Maine. For a more scenic drive, take CA 2 from Fredericton and, at Long Creek, take NB 4 to St. Croix on the Maine border, where it becomes ME 6. Just past Lincoln, rejoin Interstate 95.

No matter which route you choose, don't miss Kings Landing Historic Settlement, which is 23 miles (36.8 km) west of Fredericton on CA 2. Spend an entire day in this living history museum, where daily life goes on as it did when British sympathizers from the United States settled here in 1783.

CHAPTER 8

Historic Québec
Drive Your RV to Francophone Canada

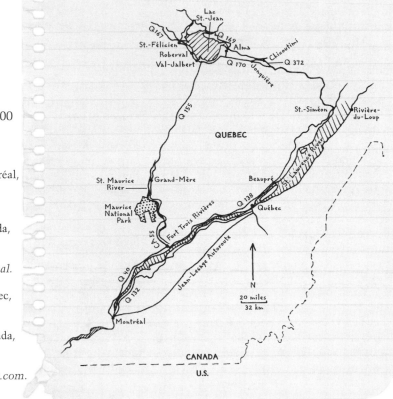

MILEAGE
Approximately 600
miles (960 km)

RESOURCES
- Tourisme Montréal,
  1555 Peel St.
  Suite 600,
  Montréal PQ
  H3A 3L8, Canada,
  800-363-7777,
  *http://www.
  tourism-montreal.
  org.*
- Tourisme Québec,
  C.P. 979,
  Montréal PQ
  H3C 2W3, Canada,
  800-363-7777,
  *http://www.
  bonjour-quebec.com.*

Montréal: *Vive la Différence!*

No other place in North America is quite
like Québec, which contains Montréal, the
second-largest French-speaking city in the
world, second only to Paris. You can't drive
your RV to France, but you can wheel into
Québec just as easily as you could drive to
Indiana or Delaware. Our loop begins and
ends in Montréal, but the culture shock hits
well before you get here. The French have a
long, proud history in Canada, and they
aren't about to let you forget it. Relax and
join Québec's citizens in celebrating French
language and culture, and you'll have one of
the most exotic "foreign" vacations to be

found in North America. In exchange for
battling the language barrier, you'll learn
some French, get some experience with the
metric system, and dine more regally than
ever before in your life.

Choose a campground near enough to
Montréal to offer public transportation or
pick-up service by one of the tour companies. We don't recommend venturing into
the city in an RV or even in a car. Traffic is
bad, roads are narrow, and parking is impossible. The public transportation is excellent, so there is no reason to drive in and
fumble around on your own. Unless you're
fluent in French, make sure any guided

61

tours you sign up for are in English so you can get the most from you travel experience. Take one or two tours by boat, bus, or on foot. You'll soon feel at home and able to take off on your own to see the city's chief sightseeing treasures. Don't rush it. The national pastime here is to enjoy sidewalk cafés and parks, a coffee or an aperitif, people watching, and the good life.

The Musée des Beaux-Arts de Montréal has superb permanent collections, and it's a good bet that a world-class visiting collection or two will be on view. The museum is open daily except Monday, free to the public. If you're into modern art, the Musée d'Art Contemporain is on the Plâce des Arts. The Musée McFord d'Histoire Canadienne focuses on the history of the people of Canada, and the Musée d'Histoire Naturelle Redpath has collections of native rocks, stuffed birds and animals, and fossils. Underground Montréal is an enormous shopping and dining complex, free from weather worries. This is an ideal place to spend a rainy day or to wait out a hot spell.

Vieux-Montréal is the core of the old city. It is located on lands that were occupied by Indians when Jacques Cartier landed here, at the confluence of the St. Lawrence and Ottawa Rivers, in 1535. Permanent settlement began a century later. See the Plâce d'Armes with its fountain and statuary, the Notre-Dame Basilica with its stunning altar and reredos, and Saint-Sulpice Seminary, which was built in 1685. The city's oldest building, it is still home to the Sulpicians, who were the city's first missionaries. The city hall, Hôtel de Ville, is a fine example of Second Empire architecture. The Château Ramezay, a museum which dates to 1705, is open daily except Monday.

See Saint-Joseph's Oratory, an enor-

> **Event:**
> In early July, musicians from twenty countries perform every kind of jazz at the Montréal International Jazz Festival. From mid-June to late July, the annual Fireworks Competition lights up the city's sky.

mous church on Mont-Royal, and Mary Queen of the World Cathedral, which is a replica one-third the size of St. Peter's in Rome. The city's botanical park is the third largest in the world, after London and Berlin, and has 180 acres of florals and greenery as well as the Insectarium, which houses 250,000 specimens.

North from Montréal

There is no easy way to get out of the Montréal megalopolis, but Sunday morning is a good time to tackle the Autoroute de la Rive Nord (CA 40), which follows the north shore of the St. Lawrence River. It meets CA 55 at Fort Trois Rivières, which is the site of the original fort and is not to be confused with the bustling industrial city of Trois Rivières on the south side of the St. Lawrence. Head north on scenery-rich CA 55 along the St. Maurice River. It becomes CA 155 when it crosses to follow the east side of the river. What is the third river of the *trois*? There isn't one, but the islands may have made the original explorers think that three rivers came together here. The name stuck.

Maurice National Park (take the Grand-Mère exit from CA 155) is a tapestry of woods and water. Drive the parkway that threads through the park. Fish for brook trout and northern pike, hike short and medium-length trails, canoe, and swim Lake Edouard. It's more crowded than some of the more remote lakes, but it has facilities and supervision. The park is one of southern Canada's most beautiful, and exploring here could fill a happy summer.

> **Event:**
> In mid-August, more than 150 hot air balloons rise above the St.-Jean-sur-Richelieu region south of Montréal.

Events:
- From late June to the first of August, the largest classical music festival in Canada, Festival International de Lanaudière, plays in Joliette.
- June 24 is the feast day of Québec's patron saint, St.-Jean Batiste.

However, the restless RVer moves on, following the long, lovely PQ (for Province Québec highway) 155 all the way to Lac St.-Jean at the end of the Saguenay River. Turn left on PQ 167.

Pass through Val-Jalbert, a former ghost town where you'll find a revitalized settlement with shops, galleries, and restaurants in the original buildings. Moving on, visit Roberval, which was founded in 1855 and has a museum of history and aquatics. Also see the grandly modern Our Lady of Roberval Church with its coppery shine and white steeple. Take a moonlight cruise on

the lake and river. Continue on PQ 167 to St.-Félicien, and then turn right on PQ 169, which will take you all the way around the lake.

Eat your fill of blueberries, which are harvested in this area by the ton. In some places, you can pick your own. Fish for trout, freshwater salmon, pike, and doré. Go sea kayaking and canoeing.

Tip:
Seeing the Saguenay Fjord from the water will add an entirely new dimension to your trip. The waters are bracketed by cliffs that rise as high as 1,500 feet (457.2 m). Excursion boats operate out of Chicoutimi and Tadoussac.

Just south of Alma, pick up PQ 170, which heads east along the Saguenay. Our scenic drive continues through Jonquière and Chicoutimi. (Leave PQ 170 at Jonquière and follow PQ 372 to Chicoutimi.) Take every chance to get out and look over the Saguenay with its dramatic bluffs and to take boat excursions. At Chicoutimi, tour the old pulp mill, which was built in the

FÉDÉRATION TOURISTIQUE DU SAGUENAY-LAC-ST-JEAN

The roads overlooking Lac St.-Jean are ideal for bicycling.

Fjord du Saguenay.

1890s. Take in the local museums and the Cathedral of St. Francis Xavier, and have an afternoon of fun at Chicoutimi Road Safety Village with its observation tower, miniature cars, train, and simulators.

Leaving Chicoutimi, follow PQ 170, which meets the St. Lawrence again at St.-Siméon, a good place to stop at the overlook and have a picnic while you watch ferries sail across to Rivière-du-Loup. Now head west on PQ 138 for more scenic views as you drive toward the city of Québec. At Beaupré, you may want to make a religious visit—or just a sightseeing one—to the Basilica of Sainte-Anne-de-Beaupré. More than 1.5 million faithful come here each year to pray to the saint, who is believed to perform miracles. You'll see stacks of their discarded crutches and braces inside the church.

Québec City

Campgrounds abound on both sides of the St. Lawrence as we approach Québec City. Again, choose a campground that is handy to public transportation or a pick-up point

for one of the bus tours. We don't recommend going into the city in your own vehicle. With food and wine this good, it's best to have a designated driver.

The French established a fur trading post in 1608 at the place they called *Kebec,* an Indian word meaning "where the river narrows." Located on an imposing promontory above the river, it was the perfect place to fortify; thus, La Citadelle is a star-shaped fort overlooking the city from the top of Cap Diamant. Château Frontenac, a hotel that looks like a European castle, dominates the city. Think of the city as a series of three walking tours—Upper Town, Lower Town, and the military sites—and take an English-language guided tour for each if possible.

A visit to military sites starts with the imposing, three-quarter-mile wall. Europe has walled cities but, except for Québec, walled cities are almost unknown in North America today. See the Citadel (La Citadelle), the powder magazine, and the Royal 22nd Regiment Museum. Walk the ramparts of the wall for views of the city. Pass an idle afternoon at Battlefields Park on the Plain of Abraham—entrances to the park are along the Grand-Alleé overlooking the St. Lawrence River from the Citadel to Gilmour Hill. Today the park is a pleasant greenspace for picnicking and walking, but in 1759 it was the scene of a battle in which the English defeated the French and changed Canada's history. In the Musée du Québec, see exhibits that go back to the city's earliest history.

Take another day to tour Lower Town,

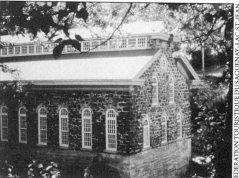

The historic pulp mill at Chicoutimi.

TOURISME QUÉBEC

People take to the streets during the Québec Annual Summer festival.

where the original settlement was built. Tall, narrow buildings are squeezed together on narrow streets. On Plâce Royale, see Our Lady of Victory Church, which was founded in battle and rebuilt after it was destroyed in the battle of 1759. Plâce Royale is also the place to get visitor information and hook up with a walking tour. View the exhibits at Maison Chevalier, the Museum of Civilization, and Le Vieux Port, which is a busy waterfront shopping, dining, and entertainment center. A farmer's market can be found here most days in summer, and

If You're Headed Back to Maine

A third choice for your return from Québec if you're feeling footloose and fancy free is to skip Montréal and take PQ 73 and PQ 173 south from Québec along the Chaudiere River, through scenic hills and small towns. Just past St.-Georges, head south on PQ 204 to visit Mont-Mégantic Provincial Park. From the park, head south to Notre-Dame-des-Bois and join PQ 212 east to enter Maine on ME 27 just north of Stratton.

Event:
In Québec City, musicians, acrobats, comedians and dancers perform at the Du Maurier Summer Festival. For two weeks in late July and early August, the fireworks and pyro-musical extravaganzas of Le Grand Feux Lot—Québec illuminate the city, accompanied by four days of the New France Celebration in early August.

you can spend hours in boutiques, galleries, and sidewalk cafés.

Your third tour should be in Upper Town, starting at the Plâce des Armes. See Holy Trinity Anglican Cathedral, built in 1804, and the Basilica Notre Dame de Québec, where construction was started in 1647. A museum in Québec Seminary, which is open only on guided tours, features local and overseas works.

The slow, scenic route back to Montréal follows the south bank of the St. Lawrence River along PQ 132; a quicker way is to take the Jean-Lesage Autoroute.

CHAPTER 9

Inviting Michigan
A Mackinac Odyssey

MILEAGE
Approximately 700 miles
(1,120 km)

RESOURCES
- Holland Area Convention & Visitors Bureau, 76 E. 8th St., Holland MI 49423, 800-506-1299, *http://www.holland.org.*
- Mackinac Island Chamber of Commerce, P.O. Box 451, Mackinac Island MI 49757, 800-454-5227, *http://www.mackinac.com.* or *http://www. mackinacisland.org.*
- Mackinaw Area Tourist Bureau, P.O. Box 160, Mackinaw City MI 49701, 800-666-0160, *http://www. mackinawcity.com.*
- Michigan Parks & Recreation Bureau, Department of Natural Resources, 318 N. Capitol, Suite 12, P.O. Box 30257, Lansing MI 48933, 517-483-4277.
- Michigan State Parks, 800-44PARKS (800-447-2757) or *http://www.dnr.state. mi.us* for camping reservations at all parks.
- Travel Michigan, Victor Office Center 2nd Fl., 201 N. Washington Sq., P.O. Box 30226, Lansing MI 48909, 800-543-2937 or 517-373-0670, *http://www.michigan.org.*

- Traverse City Convention & Visitors Bureau, 101 W. Grandview Pkwy., Traverse City MI 49684, 800-TRAVERS (800-872-8377), 231-947-1120, or 231-947-3134, *http://www. tcvisitor.com.*

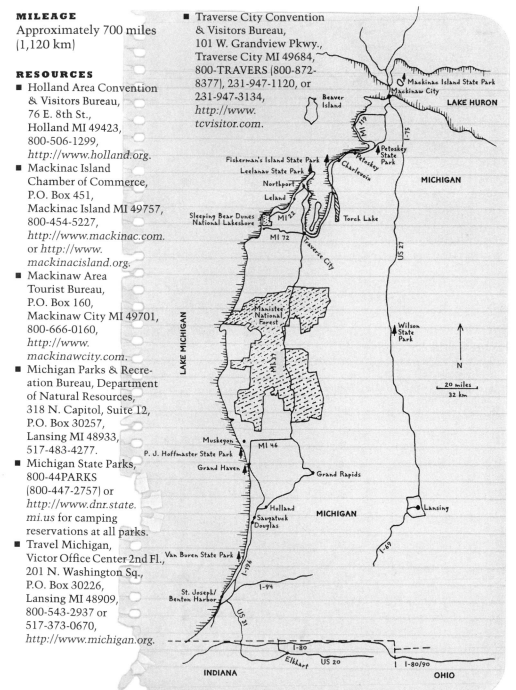

Start from Square One

Pick up your new RV at Elkhart, Indiana, which for many RVers is square one, the place where the great adventure begins. Head west on Interstate 80, and take the US 31 North exit. At St. Joseph–Benton Harbor, take the Interstate 94 bypass (unless you're here early enough to attend St. Joseph's Blossom Festival, which is held late April to early May), and bear left on Interstate 196 along the shore of Lake Michigan. Traffic begins to get less daunting now as you cross the Paw Paw River and stop to fish, hike, and swim at Van Buren State Park (exit shortly before South Haven). Campsites abound in this popular tourist area.

When we lived in Illinois and bought our first van camper, Michigan was a magnet we couldn't resist. It continues to have irresistible appeal all year. Saugatuck, which is off Interstate 196 (look for the Saugatuck-Douglas exits), and its twin city, Douglas (both are at the mouth of the Kalamazoo River), have been artist colonies for more than a century. Outstanding artists have summer homes here, and art shows run through the summer in town and at Ox-Bow, an art colony that was established here by the Art Institute of Chicago in 1914.

Weekends can be crowded and touristy in summer, so spend weekends camping and hiking the outback and do the town during the week. Take a boat excursion on Lake Michigan or the Kalamazoo River. Go fishing for coho, lake trout, perch, walleye, or chinook salmon with one of the many expert guides. Swim off the brown-sugar beaches. Shop trendy boutiques and galleries, and dine indoors or out at chic cafés. Tour the SS *Keewatin* Marine Museum, housed in a passenger steamer that was a part of the Canadian Pacific Railroad sys-

> **Event:**
> Lake Bluff Art Fair, held mid-July in St. Joseph, is one of the state's major art shows. On the third weekend of July, St. Joseph's Venetian Festival features boat parades, fireworks, concerts, contests, food booths, and a sand castle building contest.

tem at the turn of the twentieth century.

Explore the softly sculpted sand dunes, which change with each visit. In summer they're a haven for wildflowers, but the sands themselves are the real story. Midway through the nineteenth century, this area was a major lumbering center. A community called Singapore hummed with sawmills and became such a population center that it had its own post office and paper money. After the Chicago Fire, when the demand for timber for rebuilding the city reached fever pitch, the big trees of this area were felled to the last stump.

> **Tip:**
> Michigan is accessible year-round for RV travel, so come again in winter for the downhill skiing, cross-country skiing, snowmobiling, and ice fishing. Many private campgrounds and about a third of the state park campgrounds are open all year.

When Lake Michigan storms howled ashore after this, there were no trees to tame the winds and no roots to hold the sand. Within a few years, lands that were once covered with lush forests became a dune-filled desert and, with each new storm, the remains of Singapore were buried deeper in the shifting sands. Today the town is just a memory. There's no camping at Saugatuck Dunes State Park, but it is the perfect place to hike lonely trails that lead to Mount Baldy with its see-forever views.

> **Event:**
> On the last weekend of July, Harbor Days at Saugatuck feature family fun and a Venetian boat parade.

MICHIGAN TRAVEL BUREAU

De Zwaan, in Holland's Windmill Island Municipal Park.

Continue north on Interstate 196. Stop at Holland, which was settled in 1847 by Dutch immigrants fleeing religious prejudice in their homeland. The town continues to trade on its Dutch roots. Tourists arrive by the busload during Tulip Time Festival in May, but Holland is beautiful with flowers throughout the summer. When the tulips are finished, gardens light up with daylilies and annuals in every hue. Tour De Klomp Wooden Shoe and Delft Factory. See an authentic, working windmill known as De Zwaan. The windmill is in Windmill Island Municipal Park (7th and Lincoln Sts.), which has a shop where you can buy whole wheat flour produced by the eighteenth-century mill that was brought

here by special arrangement with the Netherlandish government.

Visit the Holland Museum, Cappon House with its original furniture and millwork, and Dutch Village (1 mile/1.6 km northeast of town on US 31), where an entire nineteenth-century Dutch village has been re-created. The village's shops, restaurants, and gardens cover 15 acres. Also stop by the beach at Holland State Park on Lake Michigan, 7 miles (11.2 km) west, off US 31.

Continue up the Lake Michigan shore on US 31, with stops at some of the many parks along the way. You'll cross the Grand River that flows down from Grand Rapids and then go through Grand Haven, an old lakefront resort where you can stroll the boardwalk, see the fountain's light-and-music spectacle, and attend waterfront band concerts on Wednesday evenings in July and August. Campsites at Grand Haven State Park (231-798-3711) are convenient to activities in town and at the beach, but they aren't the place for a back-country retreat.

We now approach Muskegon, which lies at the southwest edge of Manistee National Forest. A busy, lumber center, the city has miles of public waterfront. Get acquainted by riding the trolley, which stops at the major tourist attractions. See the USS *Silversides*, a submarine that served in the Pacific in World War II, sank twenty-three enemy ships, and rescued American aviators who went down during air strikes against Japan. The submarine is at 1346 Bluff Street near Père Marquette Park. At the Hackley & Hume Historic Site (472 and 484 W. Webster Ave.), tour two mansions built by wealthy lumbermen at the height of Victorian excess. See elaborate millwork,

Event:

Holland's famous Tulip Time Festival in early- or mid-May features parades, Dutch food, breathtaking gardens, and nearly two thousand klompen (wooden shoe) dancers.

stained glass windows, carved mantels, and extravagant furnishings. Downtown on Morris Avenue, an Indian burial ground dates to 1750.

Muskegon's amusement water parks are open all summer. At the art museum, see works by such great painters as Winslow Homer and Andrew Wyeth. Learn the story of the city's brawling, lumbering past at the Muskegon County Museum. Even if you're not camping the state parks here, visit them for nature walks, beaches, boating, sailboarding, and bird watching. Head south on Henry Street to Pontaluna Road, then west to Lake Harbor Road to reach the Gillette Nature Center at P. J. Hoffmaster State Park—it's a good place to learn about local flora and fauna.

You could stay with the coastline now, stopping at state parks, but we recommend taking MI 46 east from Muskegon and then going north on MI 37 through the lovely green heart of Manistee National Forest with its birch and oak, basswood and sugar maple. Fish streams and ponds. Hike miles of trails. Photograph wildflowers. Listen to birdsong, and let the forest sounds sing you to sleep. Scenic MI 37 takes you into Traverse City.

Traverse City

French trappers from Québec visited this sheltered area on the Grand Traverse Bay in the seventeenth century, but the first settlers, Presbyterian missionaries, arrived in 1839. A fifty-room hotel opened in 1873, charging $2 a night. Today Traverse City is the cherry-growing center of the state and the capital of a year-round tourism region that includes Interlochen, home of a National Music Camp and summertime concerts. Three stables offer horseback riding, and a couple of Indian-owned casinos hum with games of chance. The fall color is spectacular and the area offers plenty of skiing, ice fishing, and snowmobiling in the winter, so consider coming back in other seasons.

As part of your summer visit, play a

The orchards around Traverse City produce abundant cherries.

TRAVEL MICHIGAN

dozen golf courses. Go to the zoo, home to native animals including coyote and bison. See what's playing at the City Opera House, a Victorian masterpiece built in 1891. The area has several historical museums including, at Northwestern Michigan College, the Dennos Museum Center with one of the largest Inuit collections in the country, sculpture, and a hands-on gallery for children.

Hop aboard the tall ship *Malabar* for picnic or sunset sails of West Grand Traverse Bay, or take a catamaran sail by moonlight. Ride the Grand Traverse Dinner Train. Hike the Sand Lakes Quiet Area. All motorized vehicles are banned here, so you can peacefully hike 10 miles (16 km) of trails from one fishing lake to the next. Bicycle or skate Traverse Area Recreation Trail (TART), a 9.7-mile (15.5 km) trail, or the Leelanau Trail, which follows an old rail bed. Ask locally about mountain biking. Although it isn't permitted on national

---

Sleeping Bear Dunes National Lakeshore

Head west from Traverse City on MI 72 to explore this coastal region. Eons ago, the inexorable crawl of mighty glaciers scraped the area, depositing seeds and sands that they pushed before them. Learn about this 71,000-acre preserve at the visitor center at Empire. The name comes from an Indian legend of a mother bear who tried to swim across from the Wisconsin shore with her cubs to escape a forest fire. Too tired to keep up, the cubs fell behind, and the mother bear went to the highest bluff on the Michigan shore to watch for them. Today she is the highest dune, the 460-foot (140.2 m) Sleeping Bear, and her cubs are the two Manitou Islands offshore.

You can drive a 7-mile (11.2 km) loop through the dunes, take day trips to the Manitou Islands by boat, climb the South Manitou Lighthouse for a spectacular view, hike self-guided trails, and visit Sleeping Bear Maritime Museum. Canoe the Crystal and Platte Rivers. Walk lonely beaches, watching for buffalo berries and beach peas. Shop at boutique wineries to buy rare local wines by the case.

The Old Mission Peninsula

On your trip up US 31, we recommend taking a detour on MI 37 (20 miles/32 km each way) up to Old Mission to see the lighthouse, which was built in 1870. According to a sign posted here, you're now at the forty-fifth parallel, halfway between the North Pole and the Equator. The 400-acre park here has hiking trails through abandoned orchards. On the way back to US 31, stop at Elzer's Farm Market for fruit and vegetables.

---

park lands, the area offers plenty of challenging rides for serious cyclists.

This is farm and orchard country, so never pass up a farmer's market. West of town on MI 72, Gallagher's Farm Market spills over with fresh peaches, cherries, apricots, and apples in season. Continue west on MI 72 and turn north on MI 22 to drive completely around the Leelanau Peninsula. Stop often along the way to fish for brown trout and steelhead. Pass through Leland and Northport on the way to Cat Head Point and Leelanau State Park and then travel south through Suttons Bay. Pick up US 31 again when you get back to Traverse City.

The drive along Grand Traverse Bay is beautiful. The route rides a thin finger of land edged to the west by the bay and to the east by Torch Lake, which measures more than 300 feet (91.4 m) at its deepest point. Just south of Charlevoix on US 31, Fishermans Island State Park has woods, dunes, and miles of lakeshore. Hike, picnic, and look for Petoskey stones (which are actually fossilized coral). At Charlevoix, take a two-hour cruise aboard the schooner *Appledore*. Take the ferry to Beaver Island (616-547-2311) to learn about the bizarre Mormon kingdom that ruled here for a time. Go fishing, or buy fresh fish right off the boats at the docks. Or, rent a bike at the docks and explore the island, which is 13 miles by 6 miles (20.8 by 9.6 km).

The section from Charlevoix to Petoskey on US 31 is one of Michigan's most scenic routes. When the railroad came to

Event:

Petoskey holds its Art in the Park festival mid-July. On the second weekend of July, costumed characters reenact life as it was when Petoskey was a French trading post.

Petoskey in the 1870s, tourists weren't far behind, and the city filled with big, wood hotels that burned down almost as quickly as they were built. Fortunately, brick became a popular building material, and the grand, brick Perry Hotel still stands. This is a city for strolling, shopping, people watching, and dining. Walk through the historic Gaslight Shopping District. The highway goes through the center of town, but you can walk under it through a tunnel to the parks at the waterfront. Visit the Little Traverse History Museum to see historic photos and a collection of materials connected with Ernest Hemingway, whose family vacationed at Walloon Lake when he was a child. After Hemingway was injured in World War I, he came to Petoskey to recuperate.

Petoskey Stones

Not stones at all but fossilized coral that lived here 300 million years ago, Petoskey Stones are covered with small rings that can be seen more clearly when wet.

If you're up for hiking and biking, the Top of Michigan Trail leaves town for a 10-mile (16 km) trip around the bay. The entire trail covers 12 miles (19.2 km) from Charlevoix to Mackinaw City. Northeast of town on MI 119, Petoskey State Park has campsites, great fishing, and a mile of sandy beach where you might find Petoskey Stones.

If you are pressed for time, US 31 takes you to Interstate 75 and Mackinaw City. If the day is fine and you can spare the time, follow MI 119, which leaves US 31 just past

Bay View and rejoins US 31 just south of the Mackinac Bridge. The road is narrow and winding and isn't recommended for big rigs—especially if a gale is blowing—but it is one of the most scenic drives in the state as it makes its way through a canopy of trees that form a green cathedral.

Mackinaw City

This point at the top of the Lower Peninsula has been a strategic outpost since Indian times. The French established a trading post here in 1681 and built Fort Michilimackinac early in the 1700s. The fort changed hands twice during the French and Indian War. Today it's a busy, touristy, com-

MICHIGAN TRAVEL BUREAU

The Mackinac Bridge is one of the longest suspension bridges in the world.

TRAVEL MICHIGAN

Grand Hotel, Mackinac Island.

mercial city with blockbuster attractions that aren't to be missed. Colonial Michilimackinac re-creates life here in the French and British eras of the eighteenth century. Archaeological research goes on and artifacts are on display from hundreds of years of history while you see living history: cooking crafts, social occasions, and military drills. Kids eat up this delightful history lesson. You can buy a combination ticket that also gets you into Fort Mackinac on Mackinac Island.

Drive 3 miles (4.8 km) southeast of Mackinaw City on US 23 to reach Old Mill Creek State Park, on the site of a lumber mill that was established in the late 1700s. See the working sawmill, the beaver pond,

and an audiovisual presentation. Hike the trails, which lead to some of the area's best views of the Straits of Mackinac. Visit Teyson's Woodland Indian Museum, which is located over the cafeteria on North Huron Street. Exhibits describe local Indian history and the lumber era.

Admission to the Mackinac Bridge Museum, which is upstairs at 231 East Central Street, is free. Learn how this engineering marvel was created. The idea of building a bridge across the Straits of Mackinac had been a dream for years, but spanning 5 miles (8 km) of powerful Lake Michigan was a fearsome project. One of the world's largest suspension bridges, the Mackinac Bridge opened in 1957 and turned a lengthy ferry ride into a ten-minute joyride. The middle of the bridge rises 199 feet (60.7 m) above the water.

The Mackinaw City area has private campgrounds including a KOA (800-KOA-1738/800-562-1738) and campsites at Wilderness State Park (231-436-5381), which has 16 miles (25.6 km) of hiking

Event:
Mackinaw City's Kite Festival is held the third weekend in June. On Labor Day, hordes of people walk across the Mackinac Bridge.

trails and 26 miles (41.6 km) of shoreline. We recommend staying at one of the campgrounds with free shuttle service to one of the ferry services. Spend all day at Mackinac Island, which has been called the

The Long and Short of Going Home

If you have time for a scenic side trip before ending your trip, turn east on MI 72 at Grayling and drive through Huron National Forest. Bird-watchers come from all over the world to look for the rare Kirtland's warbler, a yellow-breasted beauty with a lovely song. It nests on the ground in stands of trees. Huron National Forest is one of Michigan's most popular vacationlands for outdoors-loving families. Fish, hike, paddle, and pedal for as long as your schedule allows.

MI 72 takes you east to the Lake Huron shore. Stay with US 23 and follow the beautiful Lake Huron coast south with stops at campgrounds and overlooks. At Standish, you can hop on Interstate 75 for a quick entry into Detroit. Or, drive MI 61 west to US 27 where you'll find hiking and fishing at Wilson State Park (800-447-2757). The park lies just north of the MI 61 exit.

If you have even more time, don't head west just yet. Continue down the Huron coast on US 23 around Saginaw Bay to Bay City with its 1,700-acre Tobico Marsh Wildlife Refuge. Climb observation towers for a look at the wetland, which teems with waterfowl and marsh denizens, including hundreds of bird and mammal species. Stop in Saginaw to admire the rose gardens, play in the children's zoo and water park, and see the museums. The art museum has a formal garden, and the Castle Museum is housed in a replica of a French chateau. From just south of Saginaw, MI 46 goes west to rejoin US 27 north of Lansing, and you're back on course.

Bermuda of the Midwest. It was originally French; then it was won by the English, who turned it over to the Americans, who lost it back to Britain briefly during the War of 1812.

Start your visit to Mackinac Island with a horse-drawn carriage tour, which points out the historic and natural high points. Then set off on foot or rent a bicycle. No cars are allowed on the island. Visit Fort Mackinac, the Governor's Residence, Victorian mansions, historic churches and homes, and the fantastic lilacs—one of the first and best summer bloomers—in Marquette Park. Stuart House Mansion has been furnished just as it was in 1810, when John Jacob Astor had a fur trading post here. The island's crown jewel is the Grand Hotel, one of the most opulent hotels in the state. To keep curious crowds at bay, the hotel charges $8 for a tour of the grounds and Victorian gardens. You can also have lunch or tea here.

The island has enough shopping, sightseeing, and dining to fill your day, but everything is pricey. If you're on a budget, bring a picnic to enjoy along the island's paved, 18-mile (28.8 km) shoreline trail. At the northern point, you'll come to British Landing, where the Redcoats came ashore in 1812 and overpowered the Yanks. You can pick up an island map almost anywhere downtown, and you'll be surprised at how much there is to discover once you get away from the tourist-packed areas near the dock.

From Mackinaw City, continue north on Interstate 75 and turn west into the Upper Peninsula, affectionately known as the U.P. Or cross Sault Ste. Marie into Ontario for more summer ramblings. If your vacation is nearing its end, however, it's a straight shot south on Interstate 75 to US 27 to Lansing and then to Interstate 69 back to Indiana.

CHAPTER 10

New Hampshire Splendor
A White Mountain Meander

MILEAGE
Approximately 300 miles
(480 km)

RESOURCES
- Franconia Notch Chamber of Commerce, P.O. Box 780, Franconia NH 03580, 800-237-9007 or 603-823-5661, *http://www. franconianotch.org.*
- New Hampshire Office of Tourism, 172 Pembroke Rd., P.O. Box 1856, Concord NH 03301, 800-FUN-IN-NH (800-386-4664) or 603-271-2665, *http://www.visitnh.com.*
- White Mountain National Forest, Supervisor, 719 Main St., Laconia NH 03246, 603-528-8721, *http://www.fs.fed. us/r9/white.*
- White Mountains Attractions, 200 Kancamagus Hwy., P.O. Box 10, North Woodstock NH 03262, 800-346-3687 or 603-745-8720, *http://www. visitwhitemountains.com.*

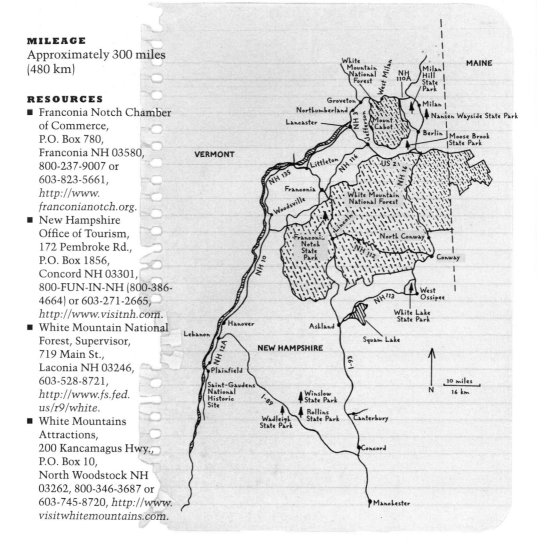

Lift Thine Eyes to the Hills

Our trip begins and ends in Manchester, a mill town like many others that sprang up as the United States entered the industrial age. Today the "mile of mills" and the mill houses that were home to the workers are relics of a bygone age. Learn about this era, as well as about local history going back to

Indian times, at the Manchester Historical Association, 129 Amherst Street, which is open Tuesday through Saturday. Admission is free.

See the Zimmerman House, which was designed by Frank Lloyd Wright, the Currier Gallery of Art (192 Orange St.; tours of the Zimmerman House begin here) with its superb collections of American and European works (Matisse, Sargent, Remington, and others), and the Lawrence L. Lee Scouting Museum. The Scouting Museum houses a library of Boy Scout books plus uniforms, memorabilia, and a stamp collection of scout commemoratives. The museum is open every day in July and August. Manchester also is home to the Science Enrichment Encounters Museum, 324 Commercial Street, with hands-on experiments for the kids.

Interstate 89 leads to Concord, where history goes back to 1727. The town is as modern as the space age, with a planetarium named for *Challenger* astronaut Christa McAuliffe; it is the official state memorial to America's first teacher in space. Learn about the area's past at the New Hampshire Historical Society, which is open daily except holidays. View displays depicting local Indian and pioneer history and a superb collection of Early American furniture. The Wells Fargo stagecoach you remember from the movies was actually a Concord Coach; you'll see a restored one here.

Rent a canoe to paddle the Merrimack River, go fishing, and reserve at least half a day for Silk Farm Wildlife Sanctuary. The

> ### New Hampshire's Seacoast
>
> *New Hampshire doesn't have a long seacoast, but what there is of it is easily accessed off the Blue Star Turnpike, a toll road connecting the Massachusetts and Maine stretches of Interstate 95. The New Hampshire shore is one long string of state parks, all of them just a few miles east of the highway. Go deep-sea fishing, sea kayaking, swimming, and whale watching. Have a clam bake. Attend concerts throughout the summer at the Sea Shell band shell at Hampton State Beach. See the roses at Fuller Gardens in North Hampton Beach at 10 Willow Avenue, 3 miles (4.8 km) south of Hampton Beach on NH 1A.*

home of the state Audubon Society, the sanctuary is threaded with trails through wetlands that sparkle with birds and small mammals. From the bird blind, you can see it all without disturbing the critters.

North of town just off Interstate 93 at Canterbury (stop now or on the way back), Shaker Village was once home to three hundred religious converts whose way of life led to the invention of a spare, practical, furnishing style. Tours lasting about an hour and a half, leave every hour. Return to

RICHARD COOK, CURRIER GALLERY OF ART

Zimmerman House, the only Frank Lloyd Wright–designed residence in New England.

Interstate 89 and follow it northwest through verdant mountain scenery.

Rollins, Winslow, and Wadleigh State Parks are along this route, so take time for hiking, fishing, and evenings around the campfire. The downhill drive into Lebanon is especially awe inspiring. The spellbinding scenery continues as you turn south from Lebanon on NH 12A to the Saint-Gaudens National Historic Site just south of Plainfield. Sculptor Augustus Saint-Gaudens is probably best known for designing the $10 and $20 gold pieces that are valuable collector items today. Some of his most famous sculptures are on display here, and his works can also be seen in Paris and Rome. Tour the sculptor's home, which was built as a tavern around 1800, his studio, and the gardens. Walk a 2.5-mile (4 km) trail, fish in Blow-Me-Down Pond and, if you're here on summer Sunday afternoons, take in a concert.

Just south of the historic site, the longest covered bridge in the United States crosses the Connecticut River into Vermont. Our compass, however, steers us back to Lebanon and north on green, leafy NH 10, which takes us through Hanover and the picturesque campus of Dartmouth

> ### About Bugs
>
> *Biting insects, especially voracious biting flies, aren't just a New Hampshire problem. You'll find them pretty much everywhere, at their worst in May and June. It always seems to us that the farther north we go, the hungrier and more desperate biting bugs get. Wear long trousers and long sleeves as well as plenty of strong insect repellent. In extreme cases in the most remote outback, anglers wear hats with veils that tuck in securely around the collar. Unlike mosquitoes, which are bad enough, the flies take a generous swatch of your hide and leave a real wound behind.*
>
> *The Northeast is also Lyme Disease country, so wear tick repellent—not just mosquito sprays. In each area, we ask locals for advice about what repellents work and what places should be avoided and when.*

College to Oxford. Continue north following this winding, lovely road along the Connecticut River to Woodsville and on to Littleton. At Littleton, pick up NH 135, which follows the river to Lancaster. You can drive all the way around Mount Cabot through stunning scenery.

Tip:
According to Barbara Radcliffe Rogers, author of **New Hampshire Off the Beaten Path**, the best weather in New Hampshire is from August through October. Reservations are suggested for July and August as well as during October's peak color.

Leave Lancaster on NH 3 through Northumberland to Groveton, head east on NH 110 through West Milan, and then follow NH 110A to NH 16 and south to Milan. Milan Hill State Park has campsites, and nearby Nansen Wayside State Park is in the shadow of the Mahoosuc Range. Both are clearly marked off NH 16.

Continue south on NH 16 to Berlin (rhymes with *Merlin*), a paper-mill town that is a good place to stock up on provisions before you continue south on NH 16

Currier Gallery of Art.

CURRIER GALLERY OF ART

Hampton Beach.

through scenery that just doesn't quit. West of the intersection of NH 16 with US 2, Moose Brook State Park also has camping. Continue west on US 2 to Jefferson, home of Santa's Village theme park. From Jefferson, take NH 116 to Littleton and Interstate 93, which takes you south to Franconia Notch State Park.

Franconia Notch State Park

One of the best state parks in the East, Franconia Notch State Park is watched over by the Old Man of the Mountain, a group of rock ledges forming the profile of a man from chin to forehead. At the Flume Visitor Center, see a film about the notch and its natural history.

In other mountain groups, a low place that presents a natural route might be called a *gap* or a *pass*, but in New Hampshire's White Mountains these low places are called *notches*. You'll see notches galore (and plenty of state parks) on this trip, but Franconia Notch is one of the most beautiful. That means, of course, that the state park can also be one of the most crowded, so be sure to make campground reserva-

New Hampshire offers plenty of shaded campsites.

Robert Frost Place

Just south of the community of Franconia off Interstate 93, follow NH 116 to Robert Frost Place. It's open daily in summer but from 1 P.M. to 3 P.M. only, so plan your trip for a leg-stretcher stop here. A brief audiovisual program tells the story of the poet, who made his home on this land. Some of Frost's original manuscripts are on display here, and the nature trail has places to pause and read lines from Frost poems.

tions well in advance and, whenever possible, stay off the roads on weekends. Weekenders fill the highways spring through fall, and in Franconia, where Interstate 93 narrows to two lanes to preserve the natural beauty of the area, speed limits are reduced.

Explore this state park by bicycle on the paved, 9-mile (14.4 km) bicycle trail. Take the aerial tram to the top of Cannon Mountain for a panoramic view of three states. Walk miles of trails in hopes of seeing deer, peregrine falcons, moose, or beavers busily damming a stream. The gorge, a glacial valley that is 8 miles (12.8 km) long and bracketed by peaks rising as high as 5,000 feet (1,524 m), is a little under a mile from the visitor center. The cafeteria serves meals and snacks, and a bus runs part of the way to the gorge. On the way, you'll cross one of

Profile ("Great Stone Face"), Franconia Notch State Park.

GAIL KIMBALL

the oldest covered bridges in New Hampshire. You could spend weeks here fishing, nature watching, hiking, and climbing.

When you do leave, briefly get back on Interstate 93 south to Lincoln, where the Kancamagus Highway (NH 112) leads you on a merry mountain chase. The highest mountain highway in the northeast, it cuts

White Mountain National Forest

White Mountain National Forest spreads from the Maine border across the northern third of New Hampshire almost to the Vermont border. Its ranges include eight peaks more than a mile high and twenty-two peaks higher than 4,000 feet (1,219.2 m). The highest, Mount Washington, is 6,288 feet (1,916.6 m). More than 100 miles (160 km) of roads thread through the forest, which has hundreds of campsites (not all of them RV accessible) and about 1,200 miles (1,920 km) of footpaths. Many more campsites are available in state and private campgrounds.

across the entire White Mountain National Forest, so you may want to come back and drive it all in autumn when it's in technicolor. For now, we go east to Conway, where you'll find a small Indian museum as you enter the town and Eastman Lord House right on NH 16, a twelve-room mansion built in 1818 and furnished in a dozen different periods from colonial times to the 1940s.

Take NH 16 south from Conway for another scenic roller-coaster ride with a view of Mount Chocorua, which is called the Matterhorn of America. If you're a heroic hiker and want a challenge, get a good map and give it a go. From the top you'll have awesome views of the mountains and lakes.

At West Ossipee, follow NH 113 west, with a stop at White Lake State Park if you like, and continue west to pick up Interstate 93 at Ashland. On the way, NH 113 runs north of the fun-packed Lake Win-

Take a Train Trip

If you have time, head up NH 16 to North Conway to ride the Conway Scenic Railway (800-232-5251 or 603-356-5251) or rent a canoe or kayak to paddle the Saco River. The area is crowded on weekends, however, throughout summer and fall and also during the winter ski season.

GAIL KIMBALL

Lupines blooming in the New Hampshire mountains.

nepesaukee vacationland but it passes directly by the Science Center of New Hampshire on Squam Lake, a 200-acre preserve where you can see nature displays, a maple sugar house, a steam-powered mill, and nature programs that involve the whole family. Don't miss the nocturnal exhibit, where you can have a Peeping-Tom's view of what forest creatures do at night while you're asleep. From here, Interstate 93 leads back to our starting point at Manchester.

Events:
- The New Hampshire Music Festival plays in Gilford, near Laconia, in July and August. Some of New England's top artists are featured in the Lakes Region Fine Arts and Crafts Festival at Meredith in August.
- In late June, the High Hopes Hot Air Balloon Festival flies at Milford.

Nashua

If your trip continues south to Nashua (take the toll F. E. Everett Turnpike for a quick ride down the west side of the Merrimack River or choose NH 3A for a slow meander along the east side of the river), more sightseeing treats await. Write ahead to the Nashua Conservation Commission (City Hall, 229 Main St., Nashua NH 03061) for a map of the Mine Falls Park Heritage Trail. This is a loop that follows a canal, with good views of the river. Parking is on Riverside Street. You can also launch a canoe on Mill Pond to reach the canal; write ahead for canoe trail information.

Massive mills were operated in Nashua by the river waters, which were channeled through a canal to create the 36-foot (11 m) drops needed to turn the mill. The story is told at the Nashua Historical Society, where you'll see artifacts from throughout New Hampshire's history including a full-size schoolroom. Also tour the stately Abbott-Spalding House, with its collection of Sandwich glass, next door to the historical society.

Autumn Trips

Work your way south with the winds, following the best of autumn color or a flurry of apple festivals from Canada to the Carolinas. After Labor Day, crowds are thinner, but more campgrounds and attractions are closed. You must plan more carefully, make reservations, and keep an eye on temperatures so you're not caught by a surprise freeze that cracks your RV's water hose.

Many RVers camp all year in all temperatures—the RV makes a snug and affordable ski lodge or ice fishing shack—but many others lay up their rigs in late fall. The latter involves lots of chores, but this is also a good time to make a wish list of RV accessories you want Santa Claus to bring. Enlist the family in using the down time to plan next year's RV trips to be bigger and better.

Scarlet Oak
(Quercus coccinea)

*Sugar Maple
(Acer saccharum)*

CHAPTER 11

Beautiful Ohio
Song of Shining Water

MILEAGE
Approximately
350 miles (560 km)

RESOURCES
- Athens Area
  Chamber of Commerce,
  5 No. Court St.,
  Athens OH 45701,
  740-594-2251,
  *http://www.
  athenschamber.com.*
- Athens County Conven-
  tion & Visitors Bureau,
  667 E. State St.,
  Athens OH 45701,
  800-878-9767 or
  740-592-1819,
  *http://www.athensohio.
  com.*
- Greater Cincinnati Con-
  vention & Visitors Bureau,
  300 W. 6th St.,
  Cincinnati OH 45202,
  800-246-2987,
  *http://www.cincyusa.
  com.*
- Hocking Hills County
  Regional Welcome Center,

13178 State Rd. 664 S.,
Logan OH 43138,
800-HOCKING (800-462-
5464) or 740-385-9706,
*http://www.hockinghills.
com.*
- Ohio Division of
  Travel & Tourism,
  City Center Mall,
  P.O. Box 1001,
  Columbus OH 43216,
  800-BUCKEYE
  (800-282-5393),
  *http://www.ohiotourism.
  com.*

- Ohio State Park Resorts,
  P.O. Box 550,
  Cambridge OH 43725,
  800-ATAPARK (800-282-
  7275),
  *http://www.dnr.state.
  oh.us/odnrparks/.*
- Ohio Valley Visitor Center,
  45 State St.,
  Gallipolis OH 45631,
  800-765-6482 or
  740-446-6882,
  *http://www.eurekanet.
  com/~ovvc.*

Cincinnati on the Rhine

Our trip really begins in Cincinnati, but if you have to travel through Dayton to get there, be sure to stop. See Dayton Aviation National Historical Park, which actually covers four different areas. Write ahead to the park (P.O. Box 9280, Wright Brothers Station, Dayton OH 45409) for maps and information, and allot at least two days to see it all.

Visit the Wright Cycle Shop, which housed Orville and Wilbur's bicycle shop, and Hoover Block, where the brothers had a printing business. The Paul Laurence Dunbar House was purchased by the writer, who was a friend of the Wrights, for his mother. Known for his short stories, poetry, and novels, Dunbar died here in 1906. The third unit of the Dayton Aviation National Historical Park is Wright Hall in Carillon Historical Park, which houses a restored 1905 Wright Flyer III. Stay on to see the entire park, which is filled with historic buildings. Also part of the national park is Huffman Prairie Flying Field at Wright-Patterson Air Force Base, where the Wrights established the world's first permanent flying school. While you're on the base, also see the Air Force Museum.

Now let's start that trip up the Ohio River. Legend has it that early German settlers felt at home as they approached Cincinnati, which spreads from hilltop to hilltop and peers out over the beautiful Ohio Valley. The settlers brought with them a love of culture, which blesses the city with fine music and arts, and a love of good wines made from grapes that grow on steep slopes found in this valley. Although World War I brought a big change in the city's attitude to things German (before the war, the city had German-language schools and newspapers), the German influence remains alongside the influence of other waves of settlers, including Irish, Italian, Greek, and Asian immigrants.

Tip:
Ohio wines, seldom sold outside the state, are among the finest in the nation. Ohio River Valley Region wineries include Meier's in Cincinnati, Moyer's in Manchester, and Valley Vineyards in Morrow. For information on Ohio wineries, call 800-227-6972 or 440-466-4417.

Cincinnati is surrounded by campgrounds galore, including one (Woodland Trailer Park, 513-931-8845) in the city itself

Dayton's Oregon District.

Event:
On Labor Day Weekend in Cincinnati, everyone gathers along the waterfront for concerts, skydiving, and fireworks. In mid-November a three-day International Folk Festival features ethnic foods, crafts, music, and dancing.

and several in nearby Hamilton. Reservations are always recommended, but they are especially important during leaf-peeping season and any time the Cincinnati Reds or Cincinnati Bengals have a home game. Loyal fans come from miles around, and many of them have RVs solely for the purpose of following their beloved teams.

Cincinnati isn't a city to sightsee in a big RV, but Metro buses are reliable and inexpensive. Take one of the river tours and a twenty-minute carriage tour of downtown. Note the fountain that appears in the opening footage of the old TV series *WKRP*. This impressive sculpture and its surrounding park are a favorite hangout for downtown workers and visitors; concerts often play during the lunch hour. On the tour, you'll also see the Roebling Bridge. Designed by the engineer who also designed the Brooklyn Bridge, it's on the National Register of Historic Places.

One of our favorite city stops is Union Terminal (1301 Western Ave.), which is loaded with nostalgic appeal for rail buffs and for anyone interested in the history of the homefront during World War II. Once a major terminus, the terminal thundered day and night with trains carrying troops. Its movie theater played newsreels, and its restaurant was tiled with now-priceless Rookwood ceramics. The terminal itself is an architectural triumph of arches, murals, marble, a domed rotunda, and art deco fixtures; it now houses world-class history and natural history museums. Special exhibits and a changing program of large-format movies are always playing, so one visit here isn't enough.

The Roebling Bridge is a Cincinnati landmark.

Other noteworthy museums are the Taft Museum (Pike and 4th Sts.), a mansion built in 1820 and furnished with period pieces, art works including a Rembrandt and a Whistler, and memorabilia connected with Ohio's powerful Taft family. Don't miss the gardens that surround the house, especially if you're here before the first frost. Also see the William Howard Taft National Historic Site (2038 Auburn Ave.), an 1853 Greek Revival mansion where the twenty-seventh president grew up.

North of downtown just off Interstate 275, Sharon Woods Village is a park containing nineteenth-century buildings that were moved here to save them from the wrecker's ball. The buildings include two log houses, a doctor's office, a Carpenter Gothic house, and a brick Federal-style home. Hours are limited in late fall, so call ahead (513-563-9484).

Rookwood Pottery on Mt. Adams east of downtown is worth visiting on two counts. The pottery made here is internationally famous, and the restaurant is great fun because some of the tables are actually inside giant kilns that once baked the pottery. Cincinnati has a green tiara of parks, more than most cities this size, but we'll save our nature watching for later in the trip.

Like many of the cities along the Ohio, Cincinnati gives you a double bang for the buck because it spills over into Kentucky, just a bridge away. Consider Covington and Newport, Kentucky, to be part of the package. Newport Aquarium, situated on the Kentucky riverfront across from Yeatman's Cove in Cincinnati, is part of Newport on the Levee, a dining and theater complex. See tanks filled with fish, amphibians, and other creatures from rivers around the world, and marvel at an aquarium full of bizarre sea life such as pufferfish and sea dragons. You'll also see a display of dangerous and deadly species that include piranha, and an aquarium filled with local species from the Ohio River.

Get your fill of zesty Cincinnati-Newport city life, great dining, and sightseeing, and then hit the road. Just as the Ohio Valley formed a vast supermarket for early hunter-gatherer tribes, it is a happy hunting ground today for RV campers who love to drive through nonstop scenery. We aren't taking the easy road; instead, we'll follow the slow, scenic route along the river.

Event:
In October, almost every hamlet in this heavily German area has a boffo Oktoberfest. Cincinnati's—which is actually held in September—is especially lively. So is Covington's, across the river at Mainstrasse Village.

Into the Valley

Take OH 32 east from Cincinnati to East Fork State Park, which has fishing and nature trails, and then head south on OH 133 to US 52, which follows the Ohio River. Pass bluffs awash with autumn color and timeless villages that are little more than a crossroads, a church, and a small gas station or convenience store. Almost every village has an Underground Railroad locale or legend. Once across the Ohio River, escaped slaves were in Union territory, with many friends who helped them find their way to safe havens in the North.

The entire community of Ripley is a historic district. See Rankin House (Rankin Rd.), where more than two thousand blacks were helped by the Reverend John Rankin, founder of the Ohio Anti-Slavery Society. It's open only on weekends in autumn. Come see it for its history and its hilltop view of the river. The Ohio Tobacco Museum on US 52 is also worth a quick stop. Although it has been discredited, tobacco played a big role in U.S. history and in Indian culture. The displays here help put this role into perspective.

Event:
On the third weekend of October, droves of people go to Shawnee State Park and Forest for hiking, scenic drives, and hoedowns amid the autumn splendor.

Continue along US 52 through the lovely autumn scenery with a stop at Shawnee State Park off OH 125 west of Portsmouth. The park is in the 60,000-acre Shawnee State Forest, where you can drive a panoramic loop tour to see miles of unbroken forest color from overlooks. Shawnee Indians had a settlement here where the Scioto River flows into the Ohio, and it's easy to imagine that it looks the same today as it did then.

Roy Rogers's hometown of Portsmouth is the nearest thing to a big city we'll see for a while, so it's a good place to stock up on provisions. Park wherever you can find a place and take a walking tour of the Boney-

You'll find plenty of campground choices along the Ohio River and its tributaries.

Event:
On Labor Day Weekend,
Portsmouth holds its River Days
Festival downtown.

fiddle historic district downtown. The old brewery is now the Brewery Arcade, a shopping and dining complex. Tour the 1810 House with its period furnishings as well as the Southern Ohio Museum and Culture Center. The massive flood wall is covered with murals, so walk along it to see a gallery 2,000 feet (609.6 m) in length.

Now continue your eastward river ramble from Portsmouth on US 52. To the north lies a great chunk of Wayne National Forest, which covers much of southern Ohio in several different parcels. Stop in for the camping, fishing, and hiking, or take the bridge over to Huntington, West Virginia, for some city sightseeing and shopping. Throughout your Ohio River ramble, you're only a bridge away from either Kentucky or West Virginia, and this is one case where city life can be found on the other side.

Gallipolis

We'll stay with the Ohio River on US 52 to OH 7, which takes us north into Gallipolis (rhymes with *valley police*). The first thing we love about this historic hamlet is that it has preserved a huge greenspace right downtown for its city park. Like most settlements along the river, this one dates to the late 1700s, when the wilderness was still impenetrable but the river formed a slick, quick interstate route to the sea. One of the nineteenth-century riverboats, floating helplessly after it broke a shaft, landed in Gallipolis and brought yellow fever ashore. Dozens died. In the park you'll see a monument to the broken shaft that caused it all.

Gallipolis still has a French aura remaining from its original settlers—aristocrats fleeing the French Revolution. They turned their hands to hard labor and wrested homes out of a forested wilderness. Learn their story at Our House State Museum (434 1st St.). The town also has an art colony and is the home of the Victorian-era Ariel Theater (426 2nd Ave.), where you might catch a play or a performance of the Ohio Valley Symphony.

Just up US 35 from Gallipolis at Rio Grande (pronounced *rye-oh grand*), you can see the original Bob Evans Farm. The Evans family is best known for its sausage and its chain of country restaurants. The farm and farmhouse are surrounded by old log cabins and other historic buildings. Nearby, the modern Jewel Evans Grist Mill is a superb example of Amish carpentry. Using original burrstones that came to Ohio by boat, the mill turns out grains and mixes that you can buy to cook in your RV galley.

Back to the River

The Beautiful Ohio calls us back to its bluffs and banks, so we return to OH 7 and a trip that leads to Forked Run State Park, where the lake is stocked with rainbow, golden, and brown trout, and saugeye and big catfish that can be caught below the dam. At Chester, leave OH 7 and follow signs to the park. The park provides boat ramps on the Ohio River and has two hiking trails, one 2.5 miles (4 km) and the other half a mile (0.8 km) long, both through a painted forest that is at its peak in mid- to late October. With luck, you might see a bald eagle, wild turkey, or

Chillicothe

If you have time for a side trip and don't mind some backtracking, the trip up OH 104 to join US 23 at Waverly and on to Chillicothe is a beautiful drive along the Scioto River. Chillicothe, the first capital of the Northwest Territory, is a history lover's mecca. See the museums and historic homes. Leave Chillicothe on OH 772, which winds and twists south through more gorgeous scenery. At Rarden, join OH 73, which takes you back to Portsmouth.

white-tail deer. Hunting is allowed in season at Shade River State Forest, which adjoins the park. Leaving the park, take OH 124 to Little Hocking and rejoin OH 7.

You'll have to cross the toll bridge to Parkersburg, West Virginia, to get an excursion boat to Blennerhassett Island, but we recommend making the trip rather than just looking at the island from afar on the Ohio shores. The story is a juicy one. It started when a wealthy Irish nobleman, Harman Blennerhassett, married his niece. The scandal drove them out of Ireland, and they settled on this island in the Ohio River, building a palatial mansion. They entertained in high style and attracted the rich and famous, including Aaron Burr. Burr, the former vice president who was then in disgrace after killing Alexander Hamilton in a duel, hoped Blennerhassett would bankroll his scheme to seize some Spanish territory and set up a separate country.

The plot was discovered and Burr arrested for treason. Burr was never convicted, but Blennerhassett was ruined and—to complete the tragedy—his mansion burned to the ground in 1811. The mansion has been faithfully replicated on the original site. Visit the welcome center and museum at Point Park in Parkersburg first. From here, a sternwheeler makes excursions to the island. For information, call 800-CALL-WVA (800-225-5982).

Back across the river, OH 7 takes you into Marietta, where the Muskingham River brought New Englanders south to the Ohio after the American Revolution. This is one of the Ohio's most comely river ports. Park and take a walking tour up one street and down the next to see grand old mansions from the flatboat era through the opulent steamboat years and on into the Sears Roebuck era (when townspeople could get a kit house by mail order). A trolley tour operates on weekends through October, and we recommend it for seeing the city's highlights.

Visit the original home built by General Rufus Putnam when he brought his flotilla here. See Campus Martius Fort (2nd and Washington Sts.), which the settlers

Event:
Marietta holds its Ohio River Sternwheel Festival on Labor Day weekend and its Indian Summer Days Arts and Crafts Festival in late September.

built to defend themselves in 1788. The museum here traces the settlement of Ohio. At Mound Cemetery (5th and Scammel Sts.) you'll see a 30-foot (9.1 m), cone-shaped mound built by ancient Indians and a cemetery where two dozen Revolutionary soldiers are buried. Take a tour aboard a riverboat for more history and stop into the historic Lafayette Hotel (101 Front St.) to eat in the elegant Gun Room and to shop the gift shop. Dining is also superb at the Levee House Cafe (127 Ohio St.), the only original structure left standing in Marietta after years of floods, fires, and demolition.

If you have time, continue up OH 7. For miles you'll have the fall forest fireworks of Wayne National Forest on your left and bold river scenery on your right. OH 7 takes you to Interstate 70, a main east-west interstate. Our plan, however, takes you west from Marietta on OH 550 through the beautiful fall colors of another portion of Wayne National Forest. The route takes you past Strouds Run State Park (south on OH 690 between Sharpsburg and Athens), which has hiking trails, good fishing, and a timeless spring that has made it a landmark since Indian times. Today you can still see the old springhouse.

Our route to the Hocking Hills, where an Ohio autumn is something to behold, takes us through Athens on US 50. Take OH 550 west to Sharpsburg, then drive southwest on OH 377 into Athens, and turn left onto US 50. A sizeable town where you can replenish your provisions, Athens is the home of Ohio University, founded in 1804 as the first university in the Northwest Territory. If the campus interests you, pick up a brochure at the visitor center on Richland Avenue and take a self-guided

Hocking Hills State Park is threaded with hiking trails.

tour. Otherwise, leave town on OH 56, which takes you northwest to the Hocking Hills. An alternate route is to take US 33 into Logan, especially if you haven't gathered information on the region in advance; it's the best place to pick up current information about events in the Hills.

The Hocking Hills

In the Hocking Hills, you'll find caves and cliffs, country lanes that twist themselves into pretzels, hiking paths through majestic scenery, private campgrounds galore, and a half-dozen state parks, some with camping. Everybody knows this is the place to be when the fall color is best, so it's going to be crowded. If possible, do your road touring during the week. We like to lose ourselves in the remote roads of the region (with the help of DeLorme's *Ohio Gazetteer*), stopping anywhere someone has hung out a shingle offering handicrafts. On weekends, stay off the roads and in a

campground where you can hike or fish.

At Hocking Hills State Park, which is 12 miles (19.2 km) southwest of Lancaster via OH 374 and OH 664, see the natural wonders of Ash Cave, Conkles Hollow, the Cantwell Cliffs, Rock House, Cedar Falls, and Old Man's Cave. The park has a swimming pool with water slides, a dining lodge, park rangers, a staff naturalist, and a 17-acre, spring-fed lake reached by a hiking trail.

A flash flood caused massive damage at Old Man's Cave State Park (in Hocking Hills State Park on OH 374/664) in 1998, wiping out stone bridges dating back to the 1930s, but reconstruction is now under way (for an update, visit the website at <*http://www.oldmanscave.com/trails*>). All the area's parks are as popular in winter as they are during the rest of the year because the cross-country skiing is good and the natural sculptures created on the rock formations by ice and snow are a photographer's dream.

At Nelsonville (midway between Athens and Logan on US 33), ride the Hocking Valley Scenic Railway, which runs daily in summer and puts on extra trains during the fall foliage season. Labor Day through mid-November, trains run on weekends only. Call 614-470-1300 or 800-967-7834 for details. The railway and the old depot are on the National Register of Historic Places.

After your stay in the Hocking Hills, US 23 from Circleville or US 33 from Lancaster takes you to Columbus and to interstates headed in every direction.

Event:
In mid-September, the Hocking Hills Indian Run offers 5K, 10K, 20K, and 60K runs through Hocking Hills State Park and Hocking State Forest. Write the Hocking Hills County Tourism Association (see resources section earlier in this chapter) for registration forms.

CHAPTER 12

A Coast through Maine
The Wonders Down East

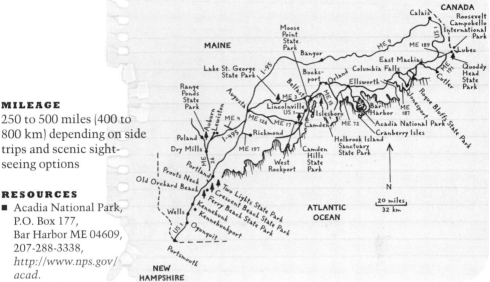

MILEAGE

250 to 500 miles (400 to 800 km) depending on side trips and scenic sight-seeing options

RESOURCES

- Acadia National Park, P.O. Box 177, Bar Harbor ME 04609, 207-288-3338, http://www.nps.gov/acad.
- Camden-Rockport-Lincolnville Chamber of Commerce, On the Public Landing, P.O. Box 919, Camden ME 04843, 800-223-5459 or 207-236-4404, http://www.visitcamden.com.
- Kennebunk-Kennebunkport Chamber of Commerce, 17 Western Ave., P.O. Box 740, Kennebunk ME 04043, 800-982-4421 or 207-967-0857, http://www.kkcc.maine.org.
- Machias Bay Area Chamber of Commerce, P.O. Box 606, Machias ME 04654, 207-255-4402, http://www.nemaine.com/mbacc.
- Maine Campground Owners Association, 655 Main St.,

Lewiston ME 04240, 207-782-5874, http://www.campmaine.com.
- Maine Office of Tourism, 325B Water St., P.O. Box 2300, Hallowell ME 04347, 800-533-9595 or 207-623-0363, http://www.visitmaine.com.
- Old Orchard Beach Chamber of Commerce, 1st St., P.O. Box 600, Old Orchard Beach ME 04064, 207-934-2500, http://www.oldorchardbeachmaine.com.
- Roosevelt Campobello International Park, P.O. Box 129, Lubec ME 04652, 506-752-2922, http://www.fdr.net.

Kennebunkport Beckons

Our trip begins at Portsmouth, New Hampshire, where we enter Maine via Interstate 95 or on US 1, which parallels the interstate and provides a more leisurely ramble to our first stop, Ogunquit. This is one of the picturesque villages that people love about Maine, an artist colony where you can stroll past galleries and studios and shop for just the right miniature to hang in the RV. Take a walking tour of Marginal Way, a footpath that hugs the bold shoreline and ends in pretty Perkins Cove. In fall you won't have a problem with crowds, but keep an eye on the tides be-

Down East

In the days when ships relied on wind power, prevailing winds from the southwest were favorable for the brisk trade that ships brought "down" to Maine on a following sea, thus the term "down East."

cause the crashing surf and occasional rogue wave can snatch at unwary walkers or straying kids. Leave town on US 1 for the short ride to the Wells area.

Wells National Estuarine Research Reserve is a 1,600-acre marsh where saltwater farming has been practiced for more than a hundred years. In fact, locals still call the place Laudholm Farm. Hike 7 miles (11.2 km) of trails through the wetlands, which include Rachel Carson Wildlife Refuge. The nature show goes on all year, but it's especially captivating on a ripe, sunny, dry day in autumn.

US 1 now leads to the communities known as the Kennebunks. Kennebunk is a year-round community. Kennebunkport is more touristy, but it is a joy after Labor Day, when the crowds have thinned. Until Columbus Day, most attractions are open at least part of the time, and after September 15 you no longer have to buy a $5 parking pass for the beach. At Union Street and Ocean Avenue, Kennebunk's welcome center (207-967-8600) is open every day spring through late fall. Kennebunkport has a welcome center at Dock Square.

See museums and historic homes at Kennebunk, which has been settled since the seventeenth century. In Kennebunkport, start at Dock Square for a stroll to Parsons Bay. It's a seaside walk along the boulder-strewn coast to see Spouting Rock and Blowing Cave, which are best viewed at half tide.

Emmons Preserve, a 148-acre woodland on Gravelly Brook, is the place to bask in autumn color and sightings of southbound flocks of migrating birds. From Dock Square in Kennebunkport, take North Street to Beachwood Avenue, turn right on Gravelly Brook Road and then left. Look for the trailhead on your left in about 2 miles

Ogunquit Harbor is littered with boats through mid-autumn.

MAINE OFFICE OF TOURISM

(3.2 km). Follow pink blazes for one trail, yellow blazes for the other; both are easy-going, so try both.

Picnic Rock on Butler Preserve is on the Kennebunk River a little more than a mile from the ocean. To get there from Kennebunk, take ME 35 West, then turn right onto Old Port Road. You'll see the Nature Conservancy sign on your right. Bring a lunch and linger to enjoy the view.

Take ME 9A North from Kennebunk, then turn right onto ME 99 for about 2 miles (3.2 km) to reach Kennebunk Plains Preserve, an 1,100-acre wilderness where you may luck into the last few blueberries of summer.

Back in Kennebunk, watch for the ME 9 turnoff to Old Orchard Beach.

Old Orchard Beach

Known locally as OOB, Old Orchard Beach is the 7-mile (11.2 km) stretch of satin sands between the Saco and Scarborough Rivers and the postcard views of Prouts Neck, Hills Beach, and the Woods Island Lighthouse. All the fun is still here as you remember it from your childhood: cotton candy, the highest Ferris wheel in Maine, fried dough, caramel popcorn, a pier extending 500 feet (152.4 m) into the ocean, and tireless tides.

Headquarter in the OOB area while you tour New England's largest salt marsh (off ME 9 in Scarborough), Winslow Homer's studio in nearby Prout's Neck, and Ferry Beach State Park (Bay View Rd. off ME 9 in Saco) with its beaches and bicycling. Settlers first came to OOB, the "Garden by the Sea," in 1657. In time, an apple orchard was planted on high land above the beach and, by 1837, summer boarders were paying $1.50 a week to stay at the farmer's house. When the railroad came in from Montreal in 1853, Canadian visitors flocked here for the fine beaches; even today, you'll have ample opportunity to practice your French here. Canadian coins begin showing up in your pocket change, and even though they are worth less than U.S. currency, they'll be more widely accepted as you get closer to the border.

Event:
In mid-September, Old Orchard Beach holds its Tow Truck Meet and Parade, which is followed a week later by an annual Classic Car Show with fun for the whole family.

The summer crowds are gone now, and many of the amusements are quiet ones, which is all the better for the RV family who prefers combing deserted beaches, watching birds, riding horses in a world of bright red and yellow hardwoods, bicycling park paths, playing golf, and finding easy parking for the RV. Striped bass and bluefish are still biting after Labor Day, and the original soda fountain in the heart of Ocean Park still serves homemade ice cream. A concert or workshop might be playing at the historic Ocean Park Temple, which was built in 1881. Ocean Park at the southwest end of OOB is a state game preserve where you can walk trails through the majestic pines.

Thanks to its popularity, this area abounds with great campgrounds—some of them complete resorts with Jacuzzis and swimming pools, lobster bakes, miniature golf, tennis, and planned activities. Most stay open until mid-October, but check ahead and get reservations.

Heading Inland

US 1 is the scenic route along the coast, but to make tracks now to the uplands where fall color is most glorious, hop on Interstate 495 at Portland and head north toward the twin cities of Lewiston and Auburn. On the way, get off the interstate at the Gray exit, watching for signs to Dry Mills on ME 26, and continue to Poland Spring, whose famous waters are now bottled by Perrier.

Fall is the perfect time to walk the nature trails of Range Ponds State Park, which is just south of Poland off ME 26. Insects, a plague in summer, are banished by the first

MAINE OFFICE OF TOURISM

Maine State Capitol Building, built about 1910.

frost. If you have a canoe, you can launch it here. Retrace your steps to Interstate 495 for the fastest way to get into the twin cities.

Tip:
Maine's state gem is tourmaline. You'll find it in custom-made pieces in specialty boutiques and jewelry shops.

Lewiston and Auburn are divided by the Androscoggin River, which provided the rush of waters that drove the area's giant mills in the eighteenth century. Auburn, on the west bank of the river, is the Androscoggin county seat. In downtown Lewiston, see Bates Mill, a massive brick complex that once produced miles of textiles and employed hundreds of people. Today it houses restaurants, offices, and the Creative Photographic Art Center, which is open all year. If you're a photo buff, tour the galleries. Peek into Saints Peter and Paul Cathedral (Bartlett and Ash Sts., Lewiston), a Gothic Revival masterpiece.

Hike 3 miles (4.8 km) of trails at Thorncrag Bird Sanctuary, which covers 228 acres on the east side of Lewiston. In the fall, hardwoods change color to contrast with the evergreens. Bring a picnic lunch and your binoculars, and spend the day looking for unusual birds among the residential and migrating species.

The best bicycling in this area is at Lost Valley, where you can mountain bike all day for about $5. Bicycle-racing events go on here through September; skiing usually begins in late November or early December. Lost Valley is on ME 4 just north of Lewiston.

Interstates 495 and 95 take you to Augusta. It may be the state capital, but it's still a small, friendly town where you can tour the state house any time. (When the legislature is in session, however, parking is hard to find.) See the Maine State Museum with historic displays on Maine shipbuilding, fishing, and farming, and visit regal Blaine House, which was built in 1833; both are in the State House Complex at

State and Capitol Streets. Blaine House is open Tuesday to Thursday all year. Old Fort Western (City Center Plaza, 16 Cony St.) downtown is a living history museum, open only on weekends in the fall, that was built during the French and Indian War in the 1750s. In 1775, it sheltered Benedict Arnold and his men during their grueling march to attack the British stronghold at Québec City.

Hike the 3.5-mile (5.6 km) trail through Pine Tree State Arboretum, a 224-acre refuge at 153 Hospital Street in Auburn, where you can identify trees and birds. In fall, apple trees will be bearing modern as well as rare antique varieties. If an early snow falls during your visit, the trails will be open for cross-country skiing.

Swan Island, which is reached by boat out of Richmond (take Interstate 95 or US 201 south to the ME 197 exit), is open only through the third week in September. You

At Fort Western, guides dress as the inhabitants did in 1754.

MAINE OFFICE OF TOURISM

must get reservations because access to this island in the Kennebec River is strictly limited to sixty people a day (call 207-547-4167 several weeks in advance for details and a reservation form; a reservation fee and admission are charged). Once home to nearly a hundred farmers, the island is now populated by deer, wild turkeys, and bald eagles. Bring a picnic lunch to enjoy along the hiking trails or at the primitive campground, which has fireplaces. (Don't confuse this freshwater island with Swans Island, which is in the Gulf of Maine off Bar Harbor.)

Midcoast and Down East Maine

If you come to Maine in summer, Augusta may be the point from which you'll take off northward into the wilderness, but as autumn deepens we stay nearer the coastline. Heading east from Augusta on ME 3, explore Lake St. George State Park, with its hiking trails and fishing lake. Or, leave Augusta on ME 17E, and then follow ME 90E from West Rockport and US 1N through Camden. If you have time, take a sea-kayaking lesson in Camden Harbor. Leaving the village again, continuing on US 1 N, stop at Camden Hills State Park, with its outstanding mountain hiking paths and views of Penobscot Bay and Megunticook Lake from Mt. Battie and Mt. Megunticook. The park campground is open through September but closes in October; for schedules, call the park directly (207-236-3109) or the Maine State Park Reservation line (800-332-1501 within Maine or 207-287-3824 from outside the state). Then continue north on US 1 to Lincolnville Beach.

From there, take the ferry to Islesboro for a day outdoors. Take your bicycles or tow car but not a big rig. Roads are narrow and winding. Penobscot Bay is dotted with state parks, and it's easy to be seduced by the many country roads that ramble off toward the shoreline. Spend a day birdwatching here, another day fishing there, and yet another day hiking. Pay a visit to Moose Point State Park (207-548-2882), which is off US 1 just east of Belfast.

DAN KIRCHOFF

Midcoast Maine is popular with sea kayakers because of the lovely harbors, coves, and inlets.

Take a self-guided walking tour of historic Belfast, which has three separate National Historic Districts. Then relax at Belfast City Park on Northport Avenue, where you'll find tennis courts, a terrific playground for the kids, good views of the bay, and picnic tables. Ride the Belfast and Moosehead Lake Railroad to see autumn color. Locally called the Bull Moose Railroad, the B&ML (207-948-5500 or 800-392-5500) runs train excursions through the peak of the fall-color season. The train schedule is complicated, so plan well ahead. You can also see the autumn glory of the Camden Hills on a scenic flight out of Belfast Municipal Airport (207-338-2970 or 800-338-2970). Reservations are essential.

Continue up US 1 through Bucksport. Historical museums are found in both Bucksport and Orland, and you can also park along the Narranmissic River here and photograph the scenery. Fort Knox, which overlooks Bucksport Harbor, is open through October. Explore its dank and scary tunnels.

Just past Orland, watch for ME 15 and turn right to Brooksville. Between West Brooksville and South Brooksville, ME 15 takes you to ME 176; from ME 176 travel west on Cape Rosier Road to Holbrook Island Sanctuary State Park. The route is well marked. There's an easy trail that takes about half an hour, or a steep trail up Backwoods Mountain for a magnificent view. Bring the dog on a leash. There's no camping here, no bicycles are allowed on the trails, and the park is closed after October 15.

Leaving Holbrook Island on ME 15 toward Blue Hill, take ME 172 into Ellsworth. Steamers brought Bostonians to this area as

Event:
The third weekend in September, the Maine Organic Farmers and Gardeners Association holds its Common Ground Country Fair in Unity with food booths, folk dancing, crafts, and a celebration of organic and made-in-Maine foods. And Belfast has its Church Street Festival—with arts and crafts, a parade, children's activities, and food booths—on the first Saturday in October.

early as the 1840s. Ever since, it has been a tourism mecca for what locals call *summercators*. Stop at the L.L. Bean Factory Store (207-667-7753) in Ellsworth for bargains on overstocks and other outlet merchandise. Unlike the retail store in Freeport, which is open around the clock, this one is open 9 A.M. to 9 P.M. Monday through Saturday and 9 A.M. to 6 P.M. on Sunday.

As you leave Ellsworth on Bar Harbor Road (ME 3), look for Birdsacre, a 130-acre bird sanctuary that is open every day during daylight hours. Admission is free; a small fee is charged for the museum in the old Stanwood Homestead. Injured birds are brought to Birdsacre for rehabilitation, so donations are much appreciated.

Bar Harbor

Bar Harbor is a tourism powerhouse, so appealing that the fun stretches on long after Labor Day. This means that campgrounds stay open longer (a few are open all year),

Golfing is big in Maine, particularly along the coast. Here, a course in Bar Harbor.

MAINE OFFICE OF TOURISM

but it also means that things can be as crowded during September's warm days, especially on weekends, as they are in July and August. Visit St. Saviour's Episcopal Church with its wealth of Tiffany windows. It's open daily, dawn to dusk. The Bar Harbor Oceanarium is entertaining for kids and adults alike, and the Natural History Museum has a hands-on section for children. The small, private Abbe Museum (207-288-3519), a showcase of Indian artifacts, is south of town at Sieur de Monts Spring. Next door are the Wild Gardens of Acadia, where you can see plants native to the area.

Take a guided walking tour of Bar Harbor (until mid-September) and one of the bus tours (through mid-October). Reservations are advised even after Labor Day because the tours are so popular at leaf-peeping time. Call Acadia National Park Tours at 207-288-3327. Later you can explore on your own, but the insights you'll gain on the guided tours are invaluable. Thanks to the extended season, you can also sail aboard the schooner *Margaret Todd* and book a whale-watching excursion well into October. Through September, guided sea kayaking tours are also offered. When it's time to move on, head west out of Bar Harbor on ME 233 to the headquarters of Acadia National Park.

Acadia National Park

Acadia National Park encompasses three distinct areas totaling 39,000 acres. Mount Desert (rhymes with *alert*) Island is the main section of the park, and it includes the town of Bar Harbor. On the Schoodic Peninsula, the second section, you can drive or bicycle scenic loops day after day, stopping for picnics and hikes. The third section of the park—Isle au Haut can be reached only by boat. During high tourist season, propane-powered buses now run free of charge on six routes through the park. Passengers can bring their bicycles aboard, as well.

If you have been in Maine for more than a few days, you probably already carry a tide clock in your head. Knowing the times

JEFF GREENBERG, COURTESY MAINE OFFICE OF TOURISM

Acadia National Park offers miles of scenic driving, hiking, bicycling, and climbing.

of high and low tides is an important ingredient in planning trips for the best scenery, safest hiking, and peak surf. High tide at Schoodic Point, when big combers break into crystal shards against the pink cliffs, is unforgettable. Start your park visit at the welcome center, where you can get maps, guidance, and schedules of park events as well as see a 15-minute orientation video.

Drive the park's 20-mile (32 km) scenic loop and go up Cadillac Mountain Summit, the highest point on the East Coast. You can make it in a motor home, but this kind of sightseeing is no fun with a big travel trailer under tow. Settle into a campground, unhitch, and enjoy the park in your tow car.

Get a Maine fishing license and fish the park's lakes for brookies, pickerel, perch, and bass. No license is required for saltwater fishing, which is a way of life here. Bring bicycles and pedal the 57 miles (91.2 km) of carriage road trails (originally built for horse-drawn carriages) that thread through the park. One of the two campgrounds in the park, Blackwoods, is open all year. If you stay long enough for snow, the park is a favorite for ice skating, iceboating, ice fishing, and cross-country skiing. Forty-three miles (68.8 km) of trails have been designated for snow vehicles. Take the ferry to Little Cranberry Island to see the museum and nature center.

Way Down East

When it's time to tear yourself away from Acadia, continue east on US 1 and Alternate US 1 through stunning scenery and timeless villages. Columbia Falls is the site of the Ruggles House. Built in 1818, it's open through mid-October. While at the house, ask for a free walking tour map of the village and stretch your legs. Detour on ME 187 out to the Jonesport Peninsula, where you can ask about the legend of Tall Barney and eat at the restaurant named for this real-life giant. At the tip of the peninsula, the 1,500-acre preserve at Great Wass Island is owned by the Nature Conservancy. Dress for soggy going, and hike the two trails. Bring snacks and water with you. There are no facilities, and campfires aren't allowed.

Continue east on US 1 to Roque Bluffs State Park, which has no camping and will be quiet at this time of year—the perfect place to hike, add to your bird-watching list, and picnic. The beach is always open during daylight hours, but the park itself closes by mid-September.

Some of the best hiking along this coast is on the Bold Coast Trail. At East Machias, look for ME 191 to Cutler. Go about 4.5 miles (7.2 km) from the center of Cutler to the parking area for the trail, which is in Cutler Coast Preserve. Follow blue blazes along the cliffs for 5 miles (8 km) of hiking that is ranked moderately difficult for healthy hikers but dangerous for children and older folks. A trail extension leads on another 2.2 miles; you'll need four to six hours to make the entire loop and all day if you stop to bird-watch and take pictures. For more information, call the Maine Bureau of Parks and Lands at 207-287-3821.

If the weather holds, there are plenty of places along the coast to launch your own or a rented sea kayak. Most of the outfitters rent through October. Contact the Machias Bay Area Chamber of Commerce (see resources section earlier in this chapter) for more information.

ME 191 and ME 189 bring us to Lubec, the gateway not just to Roosevelt Campobello International Park but also to miles of meandering coastline dotted with picturesque fishing villages. Every Sunday, all year, a group called the Pathfinders go on walks in the area; nonmembers are welcome to tag along at no charge. Call 207-733-2129 for walk schedules.

Beach-comb, picnic, and photograph the distinctive lighthouse at Quoddy Head State Park. The park doesn't have campsites, but there is a challenging hiking trail

along the cliffs and an easier 1-mile (1.6 km) hike along a boardwalk. You can also take a flight-seeing trip—an excellent way to see the autumn splendor—out of Lubec Municipal Airport. Reservations (207-733-2124) are essential. Just across the bridge from Lubec lies Campobello Island in Passamaquoddy Bay.

Roosevelt Campobello International Park

Acreage and a home on this island were bought in 1883 by the father of Franklin D. Roosevelt. The complex grew, even though FDR's visits were infrequent after he was crippled by polio in 1921. Nevertheless, this island was his summer home, and it is now maintained as a tribute to his memory by a joint United States–Canadian commission. Although it is reached by bridge from Lubec, the island is actually in New Brunswick, Canada, and the nearest camping is in Herring Cove Provincial Park (506-752-2396), just across the Canadian border from Lubec. The campground will accept U.S. dollars at whatever exchange rate applies during your visit.

In the park, start at the visitor center in the thirty-four-room Roosevelt Cottage. The park is open at no charge until Canadian Thanksgiving in October. Pick up maps and take as many of the driving tours as you can. Picnic next to the lighthouse or at Friar's Head, where grills and picnic tables are available. If you're a hardy hiker, dare the 2-mile (3.2 km) trail between Liberty Point and Raccoon Beach. Otherwise, find easier going on the beach and breathtaking views from observation platforms along the drives.

We've now traveled as far "down east" as the road can take us. US 1 leads to Calais, where you can join ME 9 and return to Bangor through beautiful mountain scenery dressed in its gaudiest fall colors. Time your trip to pull off at the picnic area at Peaked Mountain (between Wesley and Beddington) for lunch. At Bangor, pick up Interstate 95, which will take you back to your starting point at Portsmouth, New Hampshire.

Pennsylvania, Ohio, and Indiana
In the Path of the Plain People

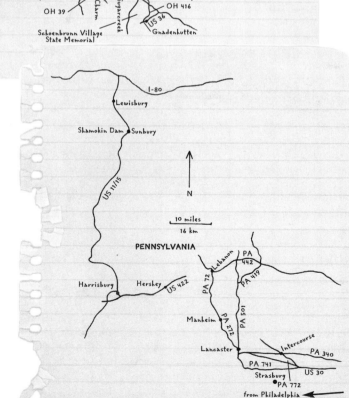

MILEAGE
Approximately 1,000 miles (1,600 km)

RESOURCES
- Elkhart County (Indiana) Convention & Visitors Bureau, 219 Caravan Dr., Elkhart IN 46514, 800-517-9739, *http://www. amishcountry.org.*
- Holmes County (Ohio) Tourism Bureau, 35 N. Monroe St., Millersburg OH 44654, 330-674-3975, *http://www. visitamishcountry.com.*
- Indiana Division of Tourism, Department of Commerce, 1 N. Capitol St.,

Indianapolis IN 46204, 800-289-6646 (or 800-291-8844) or 317-232-4685, *http://www.state. in.us/tourism.*
- Ohio's Amish Country Visitors Bureau, P.O. Box 117, Berlin OH 44610, 330-893-3467.
- Pennsylvania Center for Travel, Tourism, & Film, 404 Forum Bldg., Harrisburg PA 17129, 800-VISIT-PA (800-847-4872), *http://www.visit. state.pa.us/.*
- Pennsylvania Dutch Convention & Visitors Bureau, 501 Greenfield Rd., Lancaster PA 17601, 800-PA-DUTCH (800-723-8824)

or 717-299-8901, *http://www. 800padutch.com.*
- Philadelphia Convention & Visitors Bureau, 1515 Market St., Philadelphia PA 19102, 800-321-9563, *http://www.pcvb.org.*
- Steuben County Tourism Bureau, 207 S. Wayne St., Angola IN 46703, 800-LAKE-101 (800-525-3101) or 219-665-5386, *http://www.lakes101.org.*
- Susquehanna Valley Visitors Bureau, RR 3, 219D Hafer Rd., Lewisburg PA 17837, 800-525-7320 or 570-524-7234, *http://www.svvb.com.*

W e're on our way to Indiana, where Elkhart is the center of the RV industry. Our route follows the trail of the Amish, Mennonites, and other sects descended from the Anabaptist movement that preceded the Protestant Reformation. It leads us through some of the most beautiful, bountiful farmlands in the country's breadbasket region.

The logical place to begin is in the East, in the heart of Pennsylvania Dutch country at Lancaster, Pennsylvania, but we spend a few days in Philadelphia first. Originally a Quaker settlement, the "City of Brotherly Love" is a sightseeing bonanza that deserves attention in its own right. Some of the most popular spots include Independence National Historical Park (Visitor Center at 3rd and Chestnut Sts.), where the Liberty Bell is; Society Hill (2 blocks south of the historical park) and Penn's Landing (between Market and Lombard Sts. along the Delaware River); and the trails in Fairmount Park along the Schuylkill River.

From Philadelphia, US 30 takes you west to Lancaster, the heart of Pennsylvania Dutch country. You'll find the visitor

information center on the highway just past the gas station west of where you cross PA 340, the Old Philadelphia Pike. Pick up a ninety-minute audiotape that provides a self-guided tour. Through narration, music, and sound effects, the tape makes the area come alive. Settle into a campsite in the Lancaster area and take the route at your own pace, preferably over several days. Tourist information centers are also found in downtown Lancaster, on PA 896 in Strasburg, and at the Reamstown (US 222) exit off the Pennsylvania Turnpike.

Abhorring such modern conveniences

Pennsylvania Dutch

Pennsylvania Dutch *refers to the people of central Pennsylvania whose ancestors emigrated primarily from Germany (*deutsch, *thus* Dutch*). Although the "Plain People" of Pennsylvania are all also Pennsylvania Dutch, not all Pennsylvania Dutch are "Plain," which refers to the Amish, Mennonite, Brethren, and people of similar religious sects.*

Historic Strasburg lies in the heart of Amish country in Lancaster County, Pennsylvania.

KEITH BAUM, PENNSYLVANIA DUTCH CONVENTION & VISITORS BUREAU

as electricity and automobiles, the Amish use horse-drawn carts and carriages, which calls for careful driving on your part. Buggies have the same highway right-of-way as other vehicles, but the driver's vision is more restricted and the horsepower is more unpredictable. Buggies are not required to take to the shoulder to get out of your way, so pass only when space allows. Don't blow your horn; it could spook the horses.

As a reward for taking the slow lane, you'll spend most of this trip on pastoral country roads out of another era. You can shop for homemade cheeses, apple butter, heavenly baked goods, jams, and relishes. Take home an heirloom quilt. Stop at restaurants where homestyle meals are served in generous portions at modest prices.

Lancaster is the home of the oldest continuously operating central market in the nation. Buy fresh produce, cheeses, sausages, and handmade goods of all kinds. At the Mennonite Information Center

Understanding the Amish

Educate yourself and your family so your trip into Amish country isn't uninformed. Before you leave, dip into the pages of Pennsylvania Dutch: The Amish and the Mennonites, *or* German and Swiss Settlements of Colonial Pennsylvania. *Once you're in Amish country, you're likely to find* The Puzzles of Amish Life, 20 Most Asked Questions about the Amish and Mennonites, *or* Our People *in local bookstores (see appendix).*

While wending your way through the countryside and through markets, bear in mind that this way of life isn't a sideshow staged for our cameras. The people of most sects object to being photographed at all, so limit your photographs to the scenery and respectfully leave local folk out of your shots.

Event:
Kerosene lamp tours are held at the Amish Farm and House in Lancaster through the end of October. In downtown Lancaster, a street fair with strolling musicians, street entertainers, and food booths is held the first Friday in October.

(2209 Millstream Rd.), pick up brochures and information, see a free video and exhibits depicting the Anabaptist faiths, and browse the gift shop. It's open 8 A.M. to 5 P.M. every day except Sunday. Lancaster Newspapers Newseum shows the history of newspaper publishing; the city also has a wax museum and several museums devoted to local and regional history.

The area east of Lancaster and west of Intercourse is a good place to cruise up and down country roads. You may see a country school with shoes neatly lined up on the front porch, an Amish clothesline filled with black work trousers and white aprons, dozens of buggies, and acres of farm fields abuzz with horse-drawn harvesters. Red geraniums and bright mums bloom in courtyards; woodlands are bright with reds and golds.

Intercourse, east of Lancaster where PA 340 meets PA 772, is the home of Kitchen Kettle Village. This is a popular stop for tour buses, so there is plenty of parking space for big RVs. A bluegrass group is usually twanging away in the courtyard. Shop the thirty-two shops, take a ride in a horse-drawn wagon, or just sit in the shade and hum along. Just west of Intercourse on PA 340, the Amish Country Homestead is a nine-room house where you can see how people live without electricity. On US 30 east of Lancaster, tour the Amish Farm and House and sample Pennsylvania Dutch treats in the food pavilion.

The best place to get a buggy ride is at Bird-in-Hand, which is just west of Intercourse on PA 340. It's also the home of the Americana Museum. Weavertown Amish Schoolhouse, open through October, gives you a peek into an authentic Amish classroom. It's 1 mile (1.6 km) east of Bird-in-Hand on PA 340.

Southeast of Lancaster on PA 741 at Strasburg, Historic Mill Bridge Village has three National Historic Landmarks: a double-span covered bridge, an 1812 Amish-style home, and a 1738 grist mill. Ride the Strasburg Railroad (717-687-7522) a Victorian parlor car pulled by a steam locomotive. Lunch and dinner are served in the dining car. The National Toy Train Museum and

First-Prize Pineapple Rhubarb Pie

This recipe won a blue ribbon in an annual contest during the Kitchen Kettle Village Rhubarb Festival in Intercourse.

Crust
- 3 cups flour
- ¾ teaspoon salt
- ¼ teaspoon ginger
- ¼ cup confectioners sugar
- 1 cup butter
- 2 egg yolks, beaten
- ¼ cup pineapple juice

Filling
- 1 26-ounce can crushed pineapple, drained
- 4 cups fresh rhubarb, cut into 1-inch pieces
- 1¾ cups granulated sugar
- ⅓ cup Clear Gel, mixed with the sugar
- 1 tablespoon orange juice
- 1 tablespoon cold unsalted butter, cut into small pieces

Glaze
- 1 egg beaten with 2 tablespoons heavy cream

To make the pastry, combine the first four ingredients in a mixing bowl and cut in the butter to resemble corn meal. Blend in the egg yolks, alternating with the juice. Don't overmix. Handling the dough as little as possible, divide it into two round balls and roll out one of the balls in a floured circle to fit the pie pan with a half inch overlapping the edge. Fold this edge under and flute to make a standing rim. Roll out the other ball and cut into strips to make a lattice top.

To make the filling, combine the rhubarb and pineapple in a large bowl. Sprinkle with sugar, Clear Gel (available in food stores in Amish country), and orange juice. Toss and mix. Spoon the mixture into the piecrust and dot with butter. Top with the lattice crust and brush with the glaze. Bake at 375°F for 40 minutes or until the crust is brown.

Choo Choo Barn are at Traintown USA (east of Lancaster via US 30 and PA 896 on Paradise Lane, Strasburg), a model train buff's dream come true. See seventeen operating trains and shop for anything needed for your own train layout. The Amish Village (2 miles/3.2 km north of Strasburg on PA 896) is yet another chance to glimpse the Amish way of life; it is open all year. For salt-glazed stoneware, shop Eldreth Pottery (246 N. Decature St., Strasburg).

Back at Lancaster, travel north on PA 72 through the picturesque "Dutch" community of Manheim, where Zion Lutheran Church was established in 1772. Continue north on PA 72 to Lebanon, home of delicious Lebanon Bologna. If you have time, head east on US 442 and then south on PA 419 to Newmanstown, home to one of Pennsylvania's oldest forts. Fort Zeller was originally built from logs and was rebuilt with stone in 1745. Two miles (3.2 km) north of Lebanon on PA 72, you'll find Coleman Memorial Park, a 100-acre preserve that is the perfect place to picnic on a warm autumn day or warm up with a game of tennis if the day is chilly.

US 422 now takes us west from Lebanon to Hershey. The whole town smells deliciously of chocolate. Take the free tour of Hershey's Chocolate World on PA 30 and visit the 23-acre Hershey Gardens (Hotel Rd.), where fall flowers keep a sunny face until the first hard frost.

Cross the Susquehanna River at Harrisburg and head north on US 11/15, following the river until you reach Interstate 80. Along the way, spend pleasant hours roving the riverside, through small towns, and past Shamokin Dam. Across the river in Sunbury, Fort Augusta dates to 1757. Cross the bridge for a look. Or, continue north to Lewisburg to visit Packwood House Museum (15 N. Water St.), a twenty-seven-room, three-story log and frame structure filled with period furnishings and Americana. It's closed Mondays and holidays. Slifer House Museum, a mile north of

town on the grounds of Lewisburg United Methodist Homes, is a restored, twenty-room Victorian mansion. It's open daily except Monday until December.

Interstate 80 offers a straight shot west across the beautiful, sparsely populated mountains, with the Allegheny National Forest to the north and south. The road runs uphill until just past Clearfield, where you climb the highest point on Interstate 80 east of the Mississippi River. Continue on the interstate to the Ohio border.

Ohio's Amish Country

Enter Ohio on Interstate 80 at Youngstown, where Mill Creek Park is a good place to stop for a day of walking green paths, smelling the roses, or touring a woolen mill that was built along the creek in 1821. There's no camping in the park, but you'll find private, state, and local campgrounds here and in the Akron area. From Akron take OH 93 South 8 miles (12.8 km) to Portage Lakes State Park where you can go boating and fishing for saugeye and walleye on the Nimisila Reservoir (no gasoline or diesel motors are permitted). The park's lakes, gouged out by the glacier that shaped the north half of Ohio, were part of the path that Indians paddled on their way from Lake Erie to the Ohio River. The only portage required on the route was a short stretch here between the waters.

Mesopotamia

If you want to make a side trip from Youngstown to a tiny pocket of Amish life, go north on OH 11 to OH 87 and then travel west to Mesopotamia. The village's End of the Commons General Store has been in business since 1840. Some of the store's old-fashioned goods are for sale; some are just for display. Stroll the village commons and around the community to see many homes built before the Civil War.

From Youngstown, take OH 11 south to Boardman and then follow US 224 west to Canfield. From Canfield, head southwest on US 62 to Canton and then south on In-

If you're lucky, you'll come across an Amish barn raising.

OHIO DIVISION OF TRAVEL & TOURISM

terstate 77 to New Philadelphia. Jump back out of the twenty-first century here at Zoar State Memorial, the site of a village founded in 1817 by a German group known as Separatists fleeing religious persecution in their homeland. Their commune here, owned by the Society of Separatists, lasted eighty years. Tour the restored buildings and the garden.

Tip:

To see Ohio's widespread Amish country with a guide who was raised in the Anabaptist culture, call Joanne Hershberger at Shrock's Amish Farm and Home (330-893-3232).

Take OH 416 south from New Philadelphia and pick up US 36 East to the quaint German settlement at Gnadenhutten (pronounced *ja-NAY-den-hutton*). Just south of the hamlet is a monument to ninety Christian Indians who were massacred here in 1782, ten years after a community was established. See the Indian burial mound, reconstructed church, cooper's cabin, and museum. The oldest tombstone in Ohio is also part of this site. Return north on OH 416 toward US 250. Just after Goshen, turn right from OH 416 onto OH 259 to Schoenbrunn Village State Memorial, where Moravian missionaries led Christian Indians in the building of a village in 1772. Continue

Event:

In mid-October, Gnadenhutten holds Apple Butter Days, a festival at which apples are boiled in a copper kettle over an open fire to produce apple butter.

up US 250 to Interstate 77 and then travel north one exit to Dover.

At Dover, the Warther Museum (half a mile east of Interstate 77) houses wooden miniatures created by the late master carver Ernest Warther. The complex is a delightful mishmash of elaborate carvings, buttons, Indian arrowheads, and railroad memorabilia.

By this time you have already seen some Amish buggies and bonnets. Now head west from Dover on OH 39 through Sugarcreek, where you'll find the Alpine Hills Historical Museum and several good restaurants with traditional fare. Next pass through Walnut Creek, where an enormous indoor flea market is open April through November. In town, the German Culture Museum next to the post office is devoted to local German and Swiss settlers. North of the community, Yoder's Amish Home features a modern, ten-room Old Order Mennonite home, a 116-acre working farm, and an 1866 Amish-Mennonite home. Take a ride in a buggy or a hay wagon. When you leave, stay on OH 39.

Tip:

Throughout Amish country, October is filled with the kinds of special events that make country travel so rewarding. Stop to read posters on storefronts and power poles, in coin laundries, and along roadsides for news of church suppers, craft shows, and festivals.

The heart of Ohio's Amish country is Berlin (Holmes County is home to even more Amish people than Pennsylvania Dutch country is). Berlin offers more chances to sample hearty Amish cooking, shop for foods, and immerse yourself in Amish culture. The Mennonite Information Center here known as Behalt has a cyclorama about the Anabaptist movement and how these people arrived here. The center is on OH 77 off US 62 near Berlin. In addition to the impressive cyclorama, it has clean rest rooms, maps, brochures, and friendly people who will direct you to nearby spots where you can pursue your own special interests in crafts, quilting, fishing, or shopping.

US 62 leads from Berlin to Millersburg. Here, don't miss the stunning, twenty-eight-room Victorian mansion that houses the Holmes County Historical Society. Shop for blankets and sweaters at Rastetter Woolen Mill. For more shopping, head south on OH 557 (from US 62 between Millersburg and Berlin) to Charm, where Miller's Dry Goods sells items used by the Amish, including the dark fabrics that are unique to each sect.

Back in Millersburg, head northeast on OH 241 to Kidron Road, turn left on US 250, and then right on Emerson Road to reach Kidron and Lehman's hardware store, which handles mail orders from all over the world. This store is the nation's best-known supplier of gas refrigerators, horse-drawn plows and mowers, treadle sewing machines, wood cookstoves, hand-cranked laundry wringers, and other items that go with the electricity-free way of life. These items sell like mad to tourists, locals, survivalists, and people anywhere in the world who don't have electricity. The store is worth a special trip from anywhere in this part of Ohio. When you're finished shopping, leave Kidron by traveling west on Emerson Road, which brings you to US 250 and into Wooster.

The home of the stately College of Wooster, known since 1866 for its liberal arts programs and excellent music school, Wooster is worth a day or two of sightseeing. It also offers modern shopping malls and supermarkets if you are due for some restocking after your sojourn on the back roads. Wander the grounds of the Ohio Agricultural Research and Development Center to see orchards, rose gardens, research gardens, and the Secrest Arboretum

Event:

The Wayne County Fair is held in Wooster, Ohio, the first weekend after Labor Day. In October, the city has a living history encampment called the Colonial Williamsburg Festival.

OHIO DIVISION OF TRAVEL & TOURISM

Make way for carriages. Horses can be more unpredictable than engines.

(1 mile/1.6 km south of Wooster on Madison Ave.), where trees will be wearing their brilliant autumn robes. In the Wayne County Historical Society Museum (546 E. Bowman St.), view Native American collections, a country schoolhouse, a log cabin, and Ohio pioneer memorabilia. Have lunch at the charming Wooster Inn (801 E. Wayne Ave.).

From Wooster, take OH 83 north and turn west on OH 162. At Huntington, turn north on OH 58 to Findley State Park for fishing or primitive camping. Hike the state park as well as the surrounding 200-acre Wellington State Wildlife Area. They're both heavily forested in hardwoods that turn brilliant colors in autumn. Continue north on OH 58 through pretty farm country to Wellington and pick up OH 18, which leads west to Norwalk. From Norwalk, travel west on US 20. US 20 parallels the Ohio Turnpike (Interstate 88/90), so if you're ready for travel by interstate, get on the turnpike and head west. You can, however,

take US 20 all the way to Elkhart, Indiana, where we pick up the Amish thread again.

On to Indiana

It's easy to follow the Heritage Trail through northern Indiana's Amish country with audiotapes guiding your way. Although some backtracking is involved, we recommend headquartering in the Elkhart area so you can make day trips from here to Amish country, using an audiotape as a guide. Stop at the Elkhart County Visitor Center off Interstate 80/90 and borrow a tape for a small deposit. The visitor center downtown is always open. When the counter is not staffed, brochures and telephone information are available.

Elkhart is the home of the American RV industry, the perfect place to order your next RV right at the factory. Factory tours are offered free at forty-two local RV manufacturers! Well in advance, get a list from the Convention & Visitors Bureau shown in the resources section earlier in this chapter and plan your time; some tours are by appointment only and others are offered only on certain days or at certain hours.

Before you leave town, see some of the country's first trailers at the RV/MH Heritage Foundation on IN 19 downtown. It's open weekdays free; donations are accepted. About forty old cars are on view at the S. Ray Miller Antique Auto Museum (2130 Middlebury St.), where admission is $4 for adults and $3 for seniors over age sixty-two and children ages seven to seventeen. While in Elkhart, also visit the New York Central Railroad Museum and the Midwest Museum of American Art (429 S. Main St.). Cruise the St. Joseph River aboard the *River Queen* on Sunday afternoons through October (219-522-1795).

Following the audiotape or an Amish tour map you pick up at the visitor center, make a loop tour out of Elkhart. In Middlebury (take IN 13 north from US 20), shop for quilts and crafts, have a meal, and buy a kuchen for tomorrow's breakfast. Walk the grounds of Krider Garden, which was built as a horticultural exhibit for the Chicago World's Fair in 1934. It's an outstanding display that covers 4 acres. At Bonneyville Mill Park, buy flour at Indiana's oldest operating gristmill and hike 233 acres of woods and meadows that are dressed in autumn finery.

Elkhart County is a grid of east–west and north–south roads that we like to drive randomly, admiring farm scenes, stopping at shops and restaurants, and photographing American heartland scenes. From Middlebury, drive east on US 20 to IN 5, which leads to Shipshewana. Attend the Shipshewana Flea Market and Auction. Stock up on fresh produce and have an Amish meal here. Within the complex are seven carry-out locations, so pick up roasted chicken

and hot potato salad for dinner tonight in the campground. Yoder's Shopping Center in Shipshewana offers ten thousand hard-to-find items such as linen toweling, ladies' cotton stockings, and shoes and jeans in unusual sizes. Shipshewana is also home to the Menno–Hof Mennonite–Amish Visitors Center, where a house and barn, museum, and multimedia program tell the story of the sects.

From Shipshewana, travel back west on US 20 to IN 13, which takes you to IN 4 and into Goshen, the Maple City. The city

> **Event:**
> The Michiana Mennonite Relief Sale held in late September in Goshen, Indiana, is one of the nation's best folk events. A fortune in handmade quilts and antiques is auctioned, and home-baked foods that taste great in the RV are sold. Also this month, the Nappanee Apple Festival offers a weekend of family fun.

is threaded with bicycle and hiking trails that are beautiful in their autumn dress. See the county courthouse (a Greek Revival masterpiece) and the "police booth," a fort built at Main and Lincoln in the 1930s to protect the town from bank robbers. Stop by the Old Bag Factory—built as a buttermilk soap company in 1895—to shop for hand-carved gifts, hand-thrown pottery, candles, stained glass, sculpture, jewelry, and hearty breads. Go south from Goshen on IN 15; then head west on US 6 to Nappanee.

At Nappanee, the Amish Acres Historic Farm (1 mile/1.6 km west on US 6) houses a restaurant, theater, and shops as well as a typical Amish house and barn. It's open daily through December. The local Apple Festival is held in the old Plaza Depot (Main and Lincoln Sts.), which is worth a look any time of year if you're a rail buff.

> **Event:**
> The Amish Harvest Festival is held in Middlebury, Indiana, in early October.

Wayne County

If you have time to dip deep into southern Indiana, you can explore two more areas where the "plain people" are found. Richmond, due east of Indianapolis on the Ohio border at Interstate 70, is the newest Amish settlement. Thirty families came here to Wayne County in recent years from Lancaster County, Pennsylvania. Stop at the welcome center in Richmond for a self-guided driving-tour map and information on Amish shops and restaurants.

In the local country market in Borkholder Dutch Village (US 6 West from Nappanee, then north on County Road 101), more than 400 booths offer foods, crafts, and quilts.

Now let's head back to Elkhart on IN 19.

Another group of Anabaptists settled in southwestern Indiana's Daviess County in the Washington area just east of Vincennes.

The famished traveler should have no trouble finding a family-style meal in Amish farm country.

Interstates don't serve the area, which makes it a pleasant destination for "shun-pikers" with plenty of time to enjoy the scenery. Old-order Amish first settled here in the mid-1800s, bringing with them their talented crafters, German language, and old ways that don't allow the use of electricity or automobiles. The area has eight one-room schools where Amish children study until they are twelve or thirteen years old. The children then learn a trade and live out their lives in the same way their parents and grandparents did.

Write ahead (see resources section earlier in this chapter) for a map and a list of Amish businesses before making the rounds. At Amish Kountry Korner, stock up on bulk foods, candies, homemade cheese, and crafts. The Gasthof Amish Village serves family-style meals. Enos Graber makes furniture and sells bulk foods. Knepp's Country Kitchen makes candies. You can also buy new buggy wheels or have old ones repaired, order a horse collar, shop for quilts and baskets, or attend the lively Friday-night auction in Washington. It starts at 6 P.M. with miscellaneous items. Small animals and poultry are sold next, followed by homegrown produce. By 7:30, the auction of antiques and furniture begins, followed by the livestock auction at 8 P.M.

For recreation, go fishing in the Glendale Fish and Wildlife Area 10 miles (16 km) south of Washington, or stay close to town and fish in the city's West Boggs Park. Just east of Daviess County spreads the Hoosier National Forest with colorful hiking trails, lakes for canoeing and fishing, and plenty of campsites.

St. Jacobs

If you want to explore Amish culture further, add a side trip to your journey around Lake Erie (chapter 15). Just north of Waterloo, Ontario, in the Mennonite community at St. Jacobs, see a multimedia presentation at the Meeting Place, shop for quilts and crafts, and visit the St. Jacobs Market to buy fresh produce from local farms.

KEITH BAUM, PENNSYLVANIA DUTCH CONVENTION & VISITORS BUREAU

CHAPTER 14

New York and Vermont
Autumn in a Neon Forest

MILEAGE
600 to 800 miles (960 to
1,280 km)

RESOURCES

- Addison County
  Chamber of Commerce,
  2 Court St.,
  Middlebury VT 05753,
  800-733-8376.
- Albany County Conven-
  tion & Visitors Bureau,
  25 Quackenbush Sq.,
  Albany NY 12207,
  800-258-3582,
  http://www.albany.org.
- Columbia County
  Tourism, 401 State St.,
  Hudson NY 12534,
  800-724-1846 or
  518-828-3375.
- Dutchess County Tourism,
  3 Neptune Rd. Suite M-17,
  Poughkeepsie NY 12601,
  800-445-3131,
  *http://www.
  dutchesstourism.com.*
- New York Convention
  & Visitors Bureau,
  810 Seventh Ave.,
  New York NY 10019,
  800-NYC-VISIT
  (800-692-8474),
  http://www.nycvisit.com.
- New York State Division of
  Tourism, Empire State
  Plaza Rm. 110,
  P.O. Box 2603,
  Albany NY 12220,
  800-225-5697, *http://
  www.iloveny.state.ny.us.*
- Vermont Department of
  Forests, Parks & Recreation,
  103 S. Main St.,
  Waterbury VT 05671,
  802-241-3650.
- Vermont Dept. of Tourism,
  134 State St.,
  Montpelier VT 05602,
  800-837-6668, *http://
  www.travel-vermont.com.*

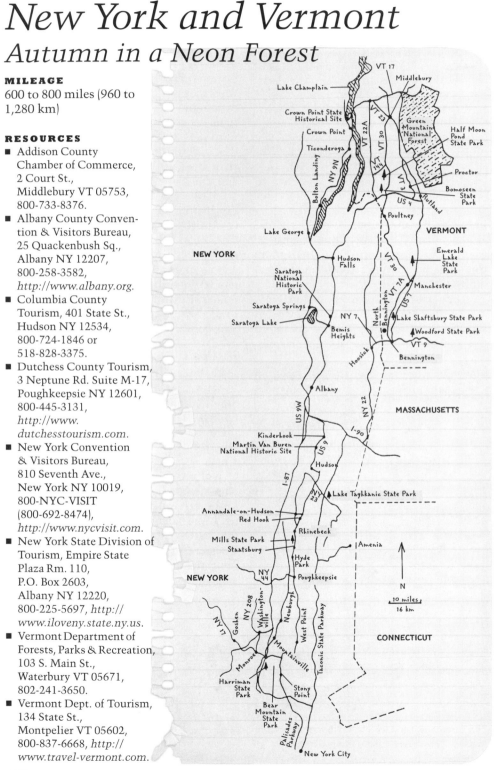

New York City

Our trip begins and ends in the last place on earth where you would want to drive an RV. New York City has long been a staple in our travels, however, because we can camp just outside the city, catch a bus, and be in Manhattan in just a few minutes. This is one way to take great, greedy bites of the Big Apple without having to pay $200 a night for a hotel room the size of a broom closet. We have seen RVs in the city, where they are a staple for film crews and fashion shoots, but we can't recommend taking your camper—or even your car—into Manhattan.

Look under both New York and New Jersey in campground guides. Some campgrounds are close to public transportation into the city; others, such as the KOA at Newburgh, New York (800-KOA-7220/800-562-7220), run daily bus tours into Manhattan. The closest KOA to Manhattan, the Newburgh campground is also a good place to headquarter while exploring such Hudson Valley gems as West Point, Hyde Park, and the wineries as well as historic sites in Newburgh itself.

Tip:

For current information on Vermont road conditions, call 802-828-2648 Monday through Friday, 7:00 A.M. to 3:30 P.M.

Once you get into Manhattan, take one of the bus tours, such as Gray Line (212-397-2600). The New York guidebooks in our travel library ignore guided tours, but the truth is that you get a lot of rubbernecking for the money, reams of fascinating trivia and historical background, and orientation that will come in handy for future explorations on your own.

We have also taken guided walking tours, which are more specialized than bus tours and focus on many topics from cemeteries to architecture. Among the best tours are those of Harlem or historic Lower Manhattan. Circle Line sightseeing cruises (212-563-3200) offers cruises and excursions with breathtaking views of the Statue of Liberty, the city skyline, and Ellis Island. A skinflint way to see the harbor is to ride the Staten Island Ferry. After a tour or two of the city, you'll be oriented and will find New York easy to navigate. For a list of tours and guides, call 800-NYC-VISIT (800-692-8478).

Leaving the City

Now let's get out into the countryside where hardwood forests are aflame with reds and yellows and every little village is holding an apple pie supper or a cider pressing. From the city, drive up the Palisades Parkway on the west side of the Hudson River on steeply wooded shores. Only 25 miles (40 km) north of Yonkers, Bear Mountain State Park is a bonanza of hiking trails and fall color. So is Harriman State Park, located nearby in the heart of what will be ski country in a few months. To reach either park, go west on NY 17A from the Stony Point exit.

Just west of Interstate 87 on NY 17 at Monroe, the living history Museum Village stays open until early December. Its "residents" busily blacksmith, dip candles, weave, make brooms, and print with primitive, movable type. Continue west on NY 17 to Goshen, home of the Trotting Horse Museum and the oldest trotter track in the country. It's in the heart of onion-growing country. Farm stands may still have some onions for sale during your visit. Shop too for apples by the peck and a pumpkin just the right size for carving.

From Goshen, retrace your path east on US 17 past NY 94 and then travel northeast to Washingtonville on NY 208. Here, the Brotherhood Winery has been making wine since 1839. Autumn is grape-stomping

Event:

From Labor Day to Halloween, the I Love New York Fall Festival is held along the Hudson River. Every riverside town has displays and special events.

time, so stop in for a tasting and a look at the winemaking process.

You're in the shadow of Storm King, a famous mountain, where the 400-acre Storm King Art Center (Old Pleasant Hill Rd.; watch for signs off NY 32 in Mountainville) displays works of some of the world's best-known sculptors against a background of awesome mountain scenery. To reach the art center, head northeast from Washingtonville on NY 94 to NY 32 and then south to Mountainville.

Throughout this route you're on lands that figured crucially in the Revolutionary War. Continue north on NY 32 into Newburgh (home of the KOA already mentioned), where George Washington waited for word that the war had officially ended. Tour the Jonathan Hasbrouck House, which was Washington's headquarters, and the New Windsor Cantonment, where reenactors portray the military camp commanded by Washington.

Travel north out of Newburgh on NY 9W to NY 44, which crosses the Hudson River via a toll bridge to Poughkeepsie. See Locust Grove (2 miles/3.2 km south of Mid-Hudson Bridge on US 9), once the home of telegraph inventor Samuel F. B. Morse and now a 150-acre park and wildlife sanctuary.

The house and exhibits are open limited hours in September and October, but the nature show on the grounds is at its most glorious. Stop at James Baird State Park for some mountain hiking if you like. To reach the park, take NY 55 east from Poughkeepsie 9 miles (14.4 km) and then go north 1 mile (1.6 km) on the Taconic Parkway.

Leaving Poughkeepsie on US 9, continue north through color-drenched foothills to Hyde Park and the Franklin D. Roosevelt National Historic Site. Tour the mansion called Springwood, which is furnished exactly as it was when FDR lived here. It's open daily through October and Thursday to Monday during the winter. FDR himself planted many of the trees on the estate, creating an experimental forestry station that wears its autumn colors for your visit.

The beaux-arts mansion built for Frederick Vanderbilt is also open through the fall (on US 9 in Staatsburg). Walk the grounds to get breathtaking views of the Hudson and the distant Catskill Mountains. Mills State Park in Staatsburg, on US 9, 3 miles (4.8 km) north of Hyde Park, has stunning overlooks of the river. Stop in for a tour of the historic Mills Mansion. It's open Wednesday to Sunday spring through October.

Hyde Park, the home of Franklin D. Roosevelt.

NEW YORK STATE ECONOMIC DEVELOPMENT

Stop frequently in your trip along the Hudson River to enjoy the views.

Continue up US 9 to Rhinebeck, where air shows at the Old Rhinebeck Aerodrome continue through October. Take a barnstormer ride in a vintage aircraft, and tour the museum's superb collection of pre–World War II airplanes. Go north on US 9 to NY 9G to Annandale-on-Hudson to visit Montgomery Place, a mansion that dates to 1805. Tour the house to see antiques and treasures, and walk the grounds for a grand view of cataracts falling to the river. The mansion is open daily except Tuesday through October and on weekends in November and December. Picnicking is permitted anywhere on the estate, and you can stock your RV larder with luscious apples from its pick-your-own orchards.

A mile south of Annandale-on-Hudson on NY 9G, pick up NY 199 East to Red Hook.

Autumn's fireworks continue as you take this road through Red Hook to the Taconic State Parkway; turn north on the parkway and take the West Taconic exit (NY 82). Travel southeast, following signs to Lake Taghkanic State Park. This park is busy in summer and winter but is likely to

be blissfully uncrowded now— when the hardwoods are at their brightest.

Return to NY 82 and head northwest to join NY 23 into Hudson. Visit the American Museum of Fire Fighting here. Hours are limited after October 1, so write ahead to Columbia County Tourism (see resources section in this chapter). Continue north on NY 9 toward Kinderhook, watching for signs to the Martin Van Buren National Historic Site. America's eighth president retired here on a 20-acre estate. Tours of the thirty-six-room mansion continue through October. In Kinderhook, stop to see the historic James Vanderpoel House, which was built in 1820. Hours are limited after Labor Day, but with luck you'll get a shot of the home wreathed in fall color. From Kinderhook, take US 9 north into Albany.

The Capital District

Albany is a busy state capital and a transportation hub since the earliest days of Dutch exploration, when Henry Hudson made his way up the river from New York,

NEW YORK DEPARTMENT OF ECONOMIC DEVELOPMENT

Take a fall-color cruise on Lake George.

and even before, when it was a crossroads of Indian trails. Robert Fulton's steamboat *Clermont* arrived in 1807. When the Erie Canal opened in 1825, the city boomed with water traffic.

If you have time to explore the city, take a free tour of the State Capitol and go to the Empire State Plaza, which houses state offices and the New York State Museum. View exhibits depicting natural and cultural history; then take the free ride to the observation deck in the Tower Building. Seek out the Shaker Heritage Society, where Shaker patroness Mother Ann Lee is buried. It's the site of the first Shaker settlement in the nation. Stop to see Historic Cherry Hill and the Schuyler Mansion, both historic mansions steeped in early New York history.

Take Interstate 87 north to Saratoga Springs. The village has been a spa visited by people coming to "take the waters" for centuries. It is also a cherished art colony and home to the Saratoga Performing Arts Center. The performance season will be over by fall, and so will the famous Sara-

toga horse races, but the National Museum of Racing and Hall of Fame is open all year. Bring containers to the spring for a taste of the stinky, fizzy, sulphury mineral water. We find it tangy and refreshing, but it isn't to everyone's taste.

Leave Saratoga Springs heading southeast along Saratoga Lake on NY 423 to Bemis Heights. Turn north on US 4 to Saratoga National Historic Park. Visitors can take a self-guided driving tour through 9 miles (14.4 km) of battlefields, earthworks, and exhibits that explain the American victory over the British here at the Battle of Saratoga in 1777. This victory brought the French into the fray on the American side and is considered to be the turning point of the Revolution.

Begin at the visitor center by seeing the film and exhibits, and take it from there depending on the weather and how much time you have. The park is open daily except major holidays. Activities and reenactors are fewer in the fall, but the sweet, cold air, blue skies, and florid autumn color make up for the lack.

Continue driving deeper into the Adirondacks, the high peaks well to the north and west of this route, as you skirt the Tongue Mountain Range. From Saratoga National Historical Park, travel north on US 4 toward Lake George. At Hudson Falls, go west on NY 254 for 2 miles (3.2 km) to US 9 and the community of Lake George, then continue north along scenic NY 9N to Bolton Landing. This is a summer community that won't revive again until ski season. Take a boat to the Lake George Islands for a picnic or hike. Almost anywhere here you're likely to see deer, especially at dawn and dusk. Be alert when driving. When you're in hunting territory, take special care not to be mistaken for venison.

Lake George has a long boating history dating back to early racing, especially during Prohibition when speedy boats had a particular value because they brought Canadian whiskey to thirsty Americans. You'll probably see shiny wood Hackers on the lake, taking their last outings before winter. For a special treat, have a gourmet lunch or dinner at the historic Sagamore at Bolton Landing. It's one of the Empire State's most splendid resorts, the last of dozens of enormous, wooden hotels where wealthy New Yorkers and Philadelphians came to escape city summer heat in the 1890s. Continue north on NY 9N to Ticonderoga.

Fort Ticonderoga has been a lookout point since before European settlement when this area was a portage for Indians going from Lake Champlain to Lake George. The fort was built in 1755 by French troops from Québec and was fortified against the British, who captured it in 1759. The British were in turn ousted by Ethan Allen's Green Mountain Boys in 1775, an early and badly needed victory for American revolutionaries. Climb the stone ramparts for sensational views of the surrounding waters and forests, and see the superb collections in the museum. The fort is open until mid-October.

When you see the scenery, you'll understand why this area has so many state parks, attractions, and private campgrounds. In spring and summer it's a god-send of green. In autumn, it's a kaleidoscope of reds and yellows; in winter, a crystal palace popular with downhill and cross-country skiers. You can continue north until the weather closes in if you like, but our inner compass is already calling for us to turn back south. Cross Lake Champlain into Vermont on NY 17 (which becomes VT 17) just north of Crown Point. Stop at Crown Point State Historical Site to see the

Event:

In late September, many Vermont villages hold apple festivals and apple pie suppers. Watch for local posters and join in the homespun fun.

ruins of a stone fort that was built by the French in 1734, and then enter Vermont at Addison, approaching Green Mountain National Forest.

The Green Mountain State

Of all the autumn scenery we have seen in our years of travel, none compares with Vermont's. Depending on your pulling power, take back roads anywhere in Green Mountain National Forest, which covers a large patch of the western part of the state from Middlebury south to Rutland. Another portion of the forest covers almost the entire southeastern third of the state. Most Vermont state park campgrounds officially close after Labor Day, but some camps stay open when the weather is warm. Most private campgrounds stay open until mid-October or later, and some stay open through hunting season and into ski season. Here more than anywhere, it's important to have reservations.

After entering the state on VT 17, continue through Addison and take VT 23 southeast to Middlebury. This is a picturesque village that seems little changed from its appearance in the late 1700s. Visit the Sheldon Museum (1 Park St.), housed in

VERMONT DEPARTMENT OF TOURISM AND MARKETING

Not all covered bridges can accommodate RVs: read clearance signs before attempting to cross.

a nineteenth-century home, and the John Strong Mansion (west of town on VT 125), where you'll see secret rooms big enough to hold three dozen people. These rooms serve as a reminder of how hostile the frontier could be in the 1790s when this house was built. Tour the Congregational Church on the Common, which dates to 1806. Through the fall, the Vermont State Craft Center—housed in an old mill overlooking Otter Creek Falls—features more than 250 crafters who demonstrate, create, and sell.

The most scenic routes south from Middlebury are VT 30 (the Seth Warner Memorial Highway) or US 7, which leads directly to our next stop at Rutland. Along VT 30, pass Bomoseen and Half Moon Pond State Parks. North of Rutland on US 7 in Pittsford, stop at the New England Maple Museum to sample Vermont foods and see collections of sugaring antiques.

Watch a sculptor at work at the Vermont Marble Exhibit, which is north of Rutland on VT 3 at Proctor. Open daily except Sunday in autumn, the site has exhibits that show how marble is formed, a

movie, a marble market, and a gift shop. Wilson Castle on West Proctor Road is a thirty-two-room mansion on a 115-acre estate. Truly a castle and filled with antiques and stained glass, it's open through mid-October. The crown jewel of this area's sightseeing is the Norman Rockwell Museum, which has more than two thousand of Rockwell's pictures on display. East of Rutland on US 4, it's open all year except major holidays.

Event:
The Vermont State Fair is at Rutland in early September.

From Rutland, travel west 7 miles (11.2 km) on US 4 to see Hubbarton Battlefield and Museum. The Green Mountain Boys fought the only battle staged on Vermont soil here when they beat back the British. Walk the trails, have a picnic, and tour the museum, which is open until Columbus Day. Continue west to VT 30 and turn south to continue the scenic drive to Poultney and Lake St. Catherine State Park, where a jewel-like lake sparkles in a green forest setting. Stay with VT 30, which angles east to join US 7, to reach Emerald Lake State Park nestled in the shadow of Mount Tabor, which is more than 3,000 feet (914.4 m) high.

Continuing south on US 7 (Ethan Allen Parkway) reach two of the Green Mountain State's most popular summer playgrounds: Manchester and Manchester Center. At Lye Brook Wilderness Area (east of Manchester

Bennington Monument honors Revolutionary War heroes and provides a panoramic view of the surrounding hills.

1.5 miles/2.4 km on VT 11/30 to East Manchester Rd., then south to Glen Rd.), hike a 2-mile (3.2 km) trail to the waterfalls. At the Southern Vermont Art Center (off West Rd.), hike botanical trails and shop for artwork. Tour Hildene (south of Manchester on VT 6A), a twenty-four-room mansion overlooking the Battenkill Valley. Until 1926, this was the summer home of Robert Todd Lincoln; many of his personal effects are still on display here. Stay on US 7 southbound, or take VT 7A for spectacular scenery along the Equinox Sky Line Drive toll road if you have a small, powerful, maneuverable rig. VT 7A is a steep, mountain road that can be dicey—even for cars—in heavy fog or freezing rain.

Stop next at Bennington on US 7, the home of the Green Mountain Boys. See the Bennington Battle Monument, a 306-foot (93.3-m) monolith that dominates the scene for miles around. From its top, you'll have a million-dollar view of Vermont's autumn splendor, so bring your camera. In Old Bennington explore this colonial village, including the Old First Church, built in 1805, and the Old Burying Ground, where Revolutionary soldiers and the poet Robert Frost are buried.

In North Bennington (on NY 7A west of US 7), tour the Park-McCullough House, which was built in 1865. Open daily through October, this thirty-five-room mansion is filled with Victoriana. The Long Trail, a hiking path over the Green Mountains to the Canadian border, begins east of Bennington. If you have time for local exploring near Bennington, visit Woodford State Park, the highest park in the state at 2,400 feet (731.5 m), and Lake Shaftsbury State Park, which lies in 101 acres of wetlands and woods.

Take VT 9 west from Bennington back into New York, where the road becomes NY 7. Immediately turn south at Hoosick on NY 22 and wind through country villages that time forgot. The route follows the Little Hoosic River, paralleling the Taconic State Parkway. Stay with NY 22 until Amenia, where US 44 takes you back to the Taconic and your return to the Big Apple.

CHAPTER 15

Lake Erie
All the Way Around

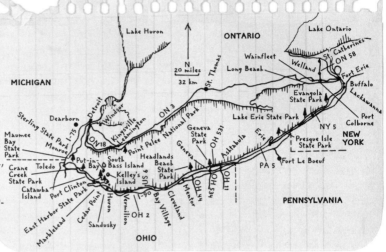

MILEAGE

Approximately 640 miles (1,024 km)

RESOURCES

- Convention & Visitors Bureau of Windsor, Essex County, & Pelee Island, 333 Riverside Dr. W., Windsor ON N9A 5K4, Canada, 800-265-3633 or 519-255-6530, *http:// www .city. windsor.on.ca/cvb*.
- Detroit Metro Convention & Visitors Bureau, 211 W. Fort St. Suite 1000, Detroit MI 48226, 800-DETROIT (800-338-7648), *http://www.visitdetroit. com*.
- New York State Division of Tourism, Empire State Plaza Rm. 110, P.O. Box 2603, Albany NY 12220, 800-225-5697, *http://www.iloveny.state. ny.us*.
- Ohio Division of Natural Areas & Preserves, Bldg. F, 1889 Fountain Sq., Columbus OH 43224, 614-265-6453, *http://www.dnr.state.oh. us/odnr/dnap/dnap.html*.
- Ohio Division of Travel & Tourism, P.O. Box 1001, Columbus OH 43216, 800-BUCKEYE (800-282-5393), *http://www.ohiotourism. com*.

- Ohio Fall Color Hotline, 800-BUCKEYE (800-282-5393) or 614-265-7000.
- Tourism Ontario, 1 Concorde Gate 9th Fl., Toronto ON M3C 3N6, Canada, 800-ONTARIO (800-668-2746), *http://www.travelinx. com*. Reservations at Ontario provincial parks can be made at 888-ONT-PARKS (888-668-7275 from Canada or the U.S.) or *http://www. OntarioParks.com*. A $9 nonrefundable fee is charged.
- Niagara Falls Tourism, 5515 Stanley Ave., Niagara Falls ON L2G 3X4, Canada, 905-356-6061, *http://www. niagarafallstourism.com*.

Erie, Pennsylvania, and the Wonders of Presque Isle

Fall color creeps to a crescendo along the shores of beautiful Lake Erie, and few places are lovelier than the Presque Isle peninsula, which crooks a finger out into the lake to form a sheltered bay. The name Presque Isle means "almost island,"—good news for RV travelers because the island is accessible by car. The speed limit, by the way, is 25 miles per hour. Believe it.

Get started right after Labor Day. If it's still warm enough, swim in the surf. If not, enjoy the bird watching, which is spectacular anytime but especially during migration seasons. The 3,200-acre Presque Isle State Park is a bonanza for the

Presque Isle State Park juts 7 miles (11.2 km) into Lake Erie.

outdoors-loving family. Bicycle or hike the trails, fish, canoe marshes that are alight with wildlife, picnic, tour the educational displays at the visitor center, or rent a boat from the marina. The park doesn't offer camping, but commercial parks can be found in the Erie area.

Tour the US Brig *Niagara* (150 E. Front St. at the Erie Maritime Museum), a replica of the flagship that carried Oliver Hazard Perry to victory over the British in the Battle of Lake Erie in 1813. On deck are guns like those used in the battle and down below are crew living quarters and hammocks like those where crew slept. The northeast corner of Presque Isle Bay, called Misery Bay, is where the fleet spent a bitter winter. Tour the monument to Perry found here (you'll see another monument to Perry when you get to Put-in-Bay in Ohio). At the foot of Dunn Boulevard, visit the first lighthouse on the Great Lakes, which was built in 1813.

To see another layer of lake history, drive south of the city on US 19 about 16 miles (25.6 km) to Fort Le Boeuf. It was one of a chain of forts that stretched from Presque Isle inland in the French and Indian War. When they left the fort, the French torched it, but it was rebuilt by the British in 1760, burned again in 1763, and refortified by the Americans in the 1790s. In the museum, see a model of an Iroquois village and artifacts that have been unearthed in the area. A statue of George Washington commemorates his diplomatic service here as a British officer. The statue shows him delivering a demand from the British to the French to abandon their Ohio holdings.

Heading east, take Interstate 90 for speed, US 20 for city stops, or PA 5 for scenery. You won't see a lot of the lake, but the grand homes and lawns along the way make for good sightseeing and you'll pass many parks where you can picnic or launch a boat. From here to the New York border along PA 5, you're in vineyard country. Almost two dozen red and white varieties of grapes are grown here by the Mazza family and made into sweet, dry, and sparkling wines. Stop at any of the vineyards or cellars that offer wine tastings, and stock up. Production is so small, you won't find these wines outside the state.

Into New York

Once across the state border, stay with NY 5 or Interstate 90 and stop at Dunkirk to photograph the lighthouse, which was built in 1875. Guided tours are available of the tower and the lighthouse keeper's quarters, which are furnished in Victorian style. In summer the lighthouse is open daily, but after Labor Day it's open only Monday, Tuesday, and Thursday to Saturday. Lake Erie State Park and Evangola State Park,

COURTESY OF PRESQUE ISLE

both off NY 5, have nature trails. Fall color and bird watching are superb now and, if you're caught by an early snowfall, you can cross-country ski miles of trails here.

The "shunpiker" instinctively tries to get through busy Buffalo as quickly as possible, but this major port and rail terminus has history and class. If you want to see the sights, write ahead to the Greater Buffalo Convention & Visitors Bureau (107 Delaware St., Buffalo NY 14202) for maps and information. Attractions include a superb botanical garden with 150 acres of florals indoors and out, a zoo, a science museum, and a twenty-sixth-floor observation tower with a great view of Lake Erie.

Across the Frontier

At Lackawanna, NY 5 joins Interstate 190 and soon crosses the toll Peace Bridge into Ontario. We've never had problems entering Canada in our RV, but do remember that this is another country and U.S. citizens are visitors there. Handguns are prohibited, but you can bring a rifle or shotgun if you're going hunting. Declare fruits and vegetables if asked, and be prepared to produce the paperwork for your vehicle, proof of citizenship (a driver's license won't do), and proof of rabies vaccination plus a veterinarian's certificate of health for any pets that travel with you. Customs officers have never hassled us about personal items we have on board, but we don't advise bringing large stocks of groceries that can just as well be bought along the way as needed. (All of this assumes that this is a pleasure trip, not a commercial venture.)

Our first stop in Canada, Fort Erie, was built by the French as a trading post and then wrested away by the British, who fortified it against the upstart Americans. Today it guards the border between the United States and Canada. If you've never seen Niagara Falls, this is the place to peel off in that direction. Take Queen Elizabeth Way (QEW) north to see the Canadian side of the falls. Then go west on ON 420/20 and stop at the viewing complex near St. Catherines to watch ships from all over the world navigate the Welland Canal. There's also a museum here depicting the history of the canal, an engineering wonder.

Take ON 58 south through Welland to Port Colborne and join ON 3, which follows the Lake Erie shore. Head west along ON 3. After Wainfleet and Long Beach, ON 3 is no longer the closest road to the shore. Hop on almost any road south toward the lake, and you'll find a provincial park at the end of almost every road. All of the parks are worth a special stop if you have time. Most have campsites.

This is still farm country, a green and giving land filled with tidy farms, grazing dairy cows, and tobacco farms inland and picturesque fishing villages lakeside. The largest community midway through the route is St. Thomas, where you can stop for provisions and see historic homes dating to the early 1800s. Leave St. Thomas on ON 3, which again clings to the shoreline. At Leamington, stop at Point Pelee National Park. Here, you'll see rare plants and mammals found almost no place else in Canada. Bird watching is unequaled as migrating geese, swans, ducks, and monarch butterflies swoop past on their journey south. At Kingsville, which is a few miles west of the park on ON 18, visit Jack Miner's Bird Sanctuary, a resting place for migrating birds. Jack Miner pioneered the practice of bird banding. The sanctuary is open daily except Sunday at no charge (call 877-289-8328 or send an e-mail to <info@jackminer.com>). Continue on ON 18 to Windsor.

Windsor is a sophisticated city with an eye-popping riverfront park and fountain, a casino, a living history village, museums, and historic mansions. To see fall color at its best, visit Willistead Manor, a 1906 mansion surrounded by woodlands, or take a sightseeing cruise aboard the *Pride of Windsor* (800-706-2607 or 519-971-7797). When it's time to go, take the bridge (ON 3) or tun-

Event:
Harness races run at Windsor (Ontario) Raceway starting in mid-October.

Event:
On Labor Day weekend, the Fort Montreaux Jazz Festival in downtown Detroit features more than eighty concerts. The Michigan State Fair starts in Detroit in late August and runs through early September.

nel (ON 3B) to Detroit. Rely on signage because at this writing Detroit is thoroughly torn up with new construction. If you want to continue around the lake and get out of the city as quickly as possible, follow signs to Interstate 75 South and keep going.

Back to the United States

Entering Detroit, you're back in the United States in a vibrant city that offers so many attractions, you may be tempted to stay on and on. More than a dozen campgrounds are within 45 miles (72 km) of downtown, where you'll find all the things expected in a great city: museums, galleries, shopping, mansions, fine restaurants, the second-largest theater district outside Manhattan, churches and memorials and, of course, major league sports. For the best view of the surrounding city, take the elevator for a small charge to the observation deck in the Renaissance Center, which locals call the RenCen. The view is especially spectacular after dark; you feel afloat in a sea of twinkling lights.

Two of the Detroit area's most important attractions are the Henry Ford Museum and Greenfield Village in Dearborn. From the bridge or tunnel, head north on Interstate 96 to Interstate 94 and then take the Oakwood Boulevard exit. Follow signs to the Henry Ford Museum and Greenfield Village complex. If you take our Land of Lincoln route (see chapter 2), you'll visit a replica of the courthouse where Abraham Lincoln practiced law. At the Henry Ford Museum, you'll see the real thing. The courthouse was purchased by Henry Ford,

dismantled, and brought here for reassembly. More than eighty other authentic buildings representing some of the most important moments in American history are found here: mills, factories, laboratories, homes, schools, and workshops connected with Thomas Edison, the Wright brothers, George Washington Carver, Luther Burbank, Harvey Firestone, and many more. And you're welcome to tour the grounds with your (leashed) dog!

There is always something going on here. You could spend days watching people crafting, doing their chores, and otherwise portraying life in the eighteenth and nineteenth centuries. The 12-acre Henry Ford Museum has collections representing industry and arts. It's one of the most important collections of American historical artifacts in the country.

Both the village and the museum are open all year. If you're here in late fall when it snows, you can take a tour of the village on a sleigh. Suwanee Park, an amusement park that can be included in admission to the complex, has limited hours in fall.

Event:
Greenfield Village in Dearborn hosts an Old Car Festival in mid-September and Fall Harvest Days in early October.

While you're here, tour Henry Ford's estate Fair Lane. When he built it in 1915, it cost more than $2 million. The grandeur includes the mansion plus 72 acres of property decked in its autumn best, a boathouse, and a children's playhouse.

The quickest way down the Lake Erie shore is via Interstate 75. Where the route crosses the Raisin River, which flows into Lake Erie, stop at Sterling State Park (take the Monroe exit). The park is open all year, so stop to swim if it's warm, or to fish, explore, launch a boat, and let the kids enjoy the playground. The Monroe County His-

PHOTO COURTESY OF HENRY FORD ESTATE, UNIVERSITY OF MICHIGAN—DEARBORN

Fair Lane, the Henry Ford Estate.

torical Museum in Monroe has exhibits honoring General George Custer, a country store, and displays depicting area battles, Indians, and early pioneers. It's open every day in summer, but after Labor Day it's closed Monday and Tuesday.

On to Ohio

So far we have passed through states that have only a small claim on Lake Erie, but now we enter Ohio, where the lake spans the almost entire northern rim of the state like a sparkling tiara. Even in the grittiest industrial towns, the lakefront spreads its beauty. In the marshes, villages, and islands, the lake is a constant presence—sometimes lashing and sometimes calm, but always a force. In autumn when the trees turn and roadside stands are piled high with ruby-red apples and pumpkins the size of potbelly pigs, Ohioans take to the highways just to drink in the beauty of it all.

Toledo, known for its glass manufacturing, is blessed with shores on both Lake Erie and the Maumee River. The Toledo Museum of Art (2445 Monroe St.) is one of the finest in the nation, showcasing paintings, sculpture, textiles, and glass from all

over the ancient and modern worlds. The museum is open at no charge daily except Monday. Something is in bloom all year at Toledo Botanical Garden, which is just off the West Central exit from Interstate 475. See the floral displays, arts, and pioneer homestead. Free to the public, the garden is open daily. The Toledo Zoo (3 miles/4.8 km south of downtown on US 25) has the only place that we know of to observe hippos underwater. For information on other local attractions, contact the Greater Toledo Convention & Visitors Bureau, 401 Jefferson Street, Toledo OH 43604 (800-243-4667 or 419-321-6404).

If your travels focus on wildlife, you'll find great bird watching at Maumee Bay and Crane Creek State Parks plus fishing (including ice fishing in winter), hiking, and picnic tables. Just east of Maumee Bay State Park, Cedar Point National Wildlife Refuge (not to be confused with the Cedar Point at Sandusky) juts into the lake. Waterfowl are so abundant here, wealthy sportsmen bought up most of these lands at the turn of the century and turned them into private hunting preserves. This action saved the lands from being drained and covered with factories. Continuing east on OH 2, stop at the lake overlook just west of Port Clinton. It's a good spot for a picnic.

Port Clinton is a delightful harbor in its own right as well as the jumping-off point for exploring the Lake Erie islands. For travel to the islands, Miller Boat Lines (800-500-2421) can accommodate motor homes and travel trailers at prices that range from $10 round trip for a car to $30 round trip for a 26-foot (7.9 m) motor home or trailer. RV camping is found on Middle Bass Island and at Put-in-Bay, but don't miss the other islands. See them on day trips.

In Port Clinton, visit the Ottawa County Historical Museum with its exhibits on Indians and the Battle of Lake Erie. Fish for

Event:
In Toledo, horse racing at Toledo Raceway Park goes on through early December.

Event:

In Early October, Port Clinton's Harvest Festival features wine tastings, contests, and other entertainment.

perch, bluegill, bass, and crappie at Catawba Island and East Harbor State Parks. Both parks have launch ramps. To reach Catawba, take OH 163 East from Port Clinton, then OH 53 North and west on West Catawba Road; it's another 5 miles (8 km) to Moores Dock Road. Again from Port Clinton, drive 7 miles (11.2 km) west on OH 163, then turn north on OH 269, to get to East Harbor.

To reach Kelleys Island, take Neauman's Ferry (800-876-1907 or 419-626-5557) or Kelley's Island Ferry (888-225-4325 or 419-798-9763). You can also get there by air with Griffing Flying Service (800-368-3743 or 419-626-5161). The island is famous for its romantic remoteness and its dramatic glacial grooves, which were caused by the slow passage of glaciers over the bedrock millennia ago. Hike 5 miles (8 km) of trails through the state park here, or go bicycling to hunt for fossils, photograph wildflowers, fish, and watch the September flyby of migrating birds and monarch butterflies. Bikes and golf carts are available for rent near the ferry dock.

Tip:
Transportation is usually priced one way when making day trips to the Lake Erie islands. For no added cost, you can take the ferry over and fly back for two different travel experiences.

At Inscription Rock, see Indian petroglyphs. Through September, see the old toys and watch the video at Lake Erie Toy Museum. Or, just hang out "downtown" at a sidewalk café and watch the world go by.

Marblehead, at the end of a long peninsula east of Port Clinton (take OH 163

East), is one of the most photographed spots on the shore. Its lighthouse, built in 1821, is the scene of the Autumn Lighthouse Festival in October. Off the tip of the peninsula, Johnson's Island has a Confederate cemetery at a site where prisoners of war were kept during the Civil War. The causeway charges a small toll.

The village of Put-in-Bay on South Bass Island has a colony of year-rounders, but early fall is a sweet, uncrowded time between the summer-fishing and ice-fishing seasons. To get there from Catawba you can take Miller Boat Line (800-500-2421 or 419-285-2421). Perry's Victory and International Peace Monument is a dazzling, 352-foot (107.3 m) granite Greek Doric column that dominates the scene for miles around. When you reach the observation deck (there's a small fee for the elevator ride), you'll be 317 feet (96.7 m) above the lake, with a seagull's view of blue waters, white sails, creamy wakes, and puffy clouds. The monument honors Oliver Hazard Perry's victory over the British in the War of 1812.

Event:

Historic Weekend is held at Put-in-Bay in mid-September with a parade, a concert, arts, crafts, and an 1812 military encampment.

From Port Clinton, take OH 2 east to Sandusky and the toll road to Cedar Point. The Sandusky area has been one of Lake Erie's favorite playgrounds since the days when Knute Rockne was a lifeguard at Cedar Point and Enrico Caruso came here to sing at the famous Hotel Breakers (for more information on local attractions, contact the Sandusky Area Convention & Visitors Bureau, 231 W. Washington Row, Sandusky OH 44870, 800-255-ERIE/800-255-3743).

Drive out the long finger of land that leads to the point, and camp at what seems like the edge of the world. The amusement park here has some of the world's oldest,

Event:
In late September, a Wood Carving Festival featuring nationally known wood-carvers is held at the Merry-Go-Round Museum in Sandusky.

newest, highest, fastest, and steepest roller coasters. The area offers a total vacation experience with beaches, a marina, fishing, rides, dining, and activities. After Labor Day, Cedar Point is open on weekends into October.

Returning to the mainland, travel east on US 6 to Huron and two of the best wildlife refuges on the lake. More than three hundred bird species have been spotted at Sheldon Marsh State Nature Preserve. Old Woman's Creek National Estuarine Research Reserve and State Nature Preserve provides an observation deck over a unique estuarine habitat. So rich in bird sightings is the Lake Erie flyway that the Lake Erie Wing Watch has been formed to promote bird watching here. Call 800-255-ERIE (800-255-3743) for more information. To continue, travel east on US 6 to Vermilion.

Vermilion, where the Vermilion River empties into Lake Erie, has retained the look of a quaint harbor town. Its Inland Seas Maritime Museum has a wealth of collections describing Great Lakes maritime history, lore, commerce, and disasters. The old settlement dates back to just after the Revolution when settlers whose homes were lost during the war were given land grants here on what was then the western frontier.

Interstate 90 can whisk you through crowded Cleveland, but if you stray off the interstate you'll be rewarded with surprises and sightseeing. Take US 6 at least as far east as Bay Village. The nearest campgrounds to Cleveland are in the suburbs. Leave your travel trailer or motor home and travel around in your tow car or by public transportation, which is excellent. We recommend Trolley Tours of Cleveland (800-848-0173 or 216-771-4484) for a one- or two-hour tour of downtown Cleveland. The riding is

easy, and the narration is filled with information to help you decide what you want to see on your own. An excellent source of general information is the Greater Cleveland Convention & Visitors Bureau, 3100 Terminal Tower, 50 Public Square, Cleveland OH 44113 (800-321-1001 or 216-621-4110).

The Rock and Roll Hall of Fame and Museum is a must. Also visit the steamship *William G. Mather*, an ore freighter built in 1925, and the USS *Cod*, which is permanently moored at the lakefront. The *Cod* is the only World War II submarine that is still in the water in its original condition. Tour the Flats, an old industrial area that has been converted to smart restaurants, nightclubs, and apartments.

Cleveland has major league sports, theater, dining, symphony, dance, and shopping as well as a massive greenbelt that girdles the city. No matter where you are in the city, you're never far from a park. Between Cleveland and Akron, the Cuyahoga Valley National Recreation Area is the home of the esteemed Blossom Music Festival plus endless trails for hiking and skiing, meadows covered with wildflowers, forests, and a sightseeing train. It's worth leaving the lake to dip south and spend time here, especially in fall when the woods are a riot of reds and golds.

Heading east from Greater Cleveland, take Interstate 90 to Mentor to see Lawnfield, the mansion where President James A. Garfield lived before leaving for the White House. Holden Arboretum (south of Mentor on OH 306) has 3,100 acres with lakes, hiking trails, and a forest that at this time of year wears coats of many colors. Continuing east on Interstate 90, stop at Headlands Beach State Park on the lake. (Take the OH 44 exit from the interstate.) This park is the northern terminus for the Buckeye Trail and, while it is packed in summer, it's al-

Event:
Held in October, the Woolly Bear Festival in Vermilion is a small-town festival with games, food, and fun for children.

A historic railroad runs all year through the Cuyahoga Valley.

most deserted on some autumn weekdays. Fish from the dock or the bridge and hike miles of trails here and in the adjoining Mentor Marsh State Nature Preserve.

Geneva State Park is also on the lakeshore (north on OH 534 from Interstate 90). Exposed to all the wild fury, heat, cold, calm, and pounding surf that Lake Erie can dish out, this place is an exciting place to be when lake storms growl. Swim, picnic, watch sunsets and cloud formations, fish from the breakwall, and look for unusual plants found in marshes and shores here.

We've saved Ashtabula (north on OH 11 from Interstate 90) for last in hopes

Covered Bridge Clearances

Four of Ashtabula County's covered bridges can be seen from bypass roads. For the drive-across bridges, clearances range from 8 feet to 16 feet, 2 inches (2.4 to 4.9 m).

Signs that show the way through a self-guided driving tour of the bridges are up all year, not just in October during the Covered Bridge Festival. Take the trip at any time. For a map that also describes each bridge and its history, contact Ashtabula Covered Bridge Festival, 25 W. Jefferson St., Jefferson OH 44047, 440-576-3769.

you'll arrive by the second full weekend of October in time for the Covered Bridge Festival. Thirteen bridges have been beefed up and modernized here. You can drive them all if you have a small rig or a tow car. Restrictions for the bridges differ, so call the Ashtabula County Convention & Visitors Bureau (800-3DROP-IN/800-337-6746) for descriptions and limits for individual bridges. A memorable trip at any time of year, a visit here is especially delightful now when the fall colors are at their zenith and the whole county turns out to offer hot cider, crafts, and special events.

In Ashtabula, an important ore and coal port, visit the Hubbard Homestead, which was a refuge on the Underground Railroad, and the Great Lakes Marine and U.S. Coast Guard Memorial Museum, which is housed in a lighthouse keeper's home built in 1898.

Heading east again, follow OH 531 along the shore or take the Conneaut exit from Interstate 90. Stop at the Conneaut Historical Railroad Museum. It's closed after Labor Day, but you'll still see the old depot and the engine and caboose outside. Leave Conneaut traveling east on Interstate 90, which leads back to the trip's starting point. You have circumnavigated one of the greatest Great Lakes—and then some.

Winter Trips

Our winter RV travels take us to Florida, Alabama, Georgia, and Louisiana. Nippy days aren't alien to southern climes: we've shivered even in Key West during the one or two cold fronts that dip that far south in most winters. You'll be camping now with an older, quieter crowd, but the campground camaraderie is even closer in winter. Cold days are perfect for the most vigorous hiking, tennis, and jogging. Rates may be higher in snowbird centers, particularly Florida, but pleasant surprises await in the northern South, where crowds are thin and rates are often discounted.

If you have an all-weather rig, you can follow almost any route in this book, winter or not, with careful planning to ensure the highways are passable and campgrounds open. Plan shorter driving days so you can reach camp in plenty of time to set up before darkness falls. And allow for frequent wash jobs to remove salt or road chemicals from your RV.

LOUISIANA TRICENTENNIAL COMMISSION

*American Holly
(ilex opaca)*

LOUISIANA TRICENTENNIAL COMMISSION

Showy Orchid
(orchis spectabilis)

CHAPTER 16

A Georgian Idyll
Colonial Coastings
and Swamp Crossings

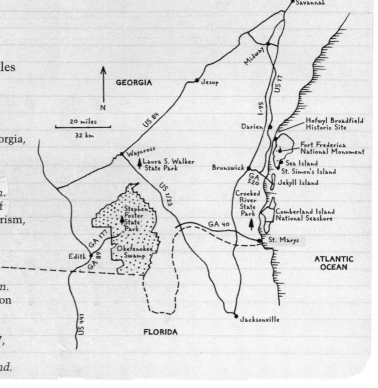

MILEAGE
Approximately 280 miles
(448 km)

RESOURCES
- Brunswick &
  the Golden Isles of Georgia,
  4 Glynn Ave.,
  Brunswick GA 31520,
  912-265-0620,
  http://www.bgivb.com.
- Georgia Department of
  Industry, Trade, & Tourism,
  P.O. Box 1776,
  Atlanta GA 30301,
  800-VISIT-GA
  (800-847-4842),
  http://www.gomm.com.
- Jekyll Island Convention
  & Visitors Bureau,
  45 S. Beachview Dr.,
  Jekyll Island GA 31527,
  800-841-6586,
  *http://www.jekyllisland.
  com.*
- Okefenokee National
  Wildlife Refuge,
  Rte. 2, Box 3330,
  Folkston GA 31537,
  912-496-7836.
- Savannah Area Convention
  & Visitors Bureau,
  301 Martin Luther King Jr.
  Blvd, P.O. Box 1628,
  Savannah GA 31402,
  877-728-2662,
  http://www.savcvb.com.

T his short loop begins in
Jacksonville, Florida,
and it ends not far from
there at Okefenokee National
Wildlife Refuge. Our
goal is to go up the coast
through lands that saw the
very earliest dawn of American
history and into the
cotton era, with stops at
every island we can reach.
Along the way we'll have
some of the best wildlife
watching in the east, beaches
that we'll have almost ex-
clusively to ourselves in
winter, hunting, fishing,
and shirtsleeve tempera-
tures that last through most
of the season. In exchange
for the occasional cold
spell, you'll find off-season
rates and few tourists.

Tip:
Call 404-656-5267
anytime for information
on Georgia highway
conditions.

Cumberland Island National Seashore

The St. Marys River forms the border between Florida and Georgia, but it is known mainly as a navy base. To travelers, however, it is the gateway to Cumberland Island National Seashore. Take exit 1 or 2 off Interstate 95 and travel east on GA 40. Camping is available at Crooked River State Park (912-882-5256), located north of GA 40, or at private campgrounds in the area.

You can't take the RV to Cumberland Island; you can overnight on the island itself only by staying in the fairly pricey bed and breakfast inn or by taking backpack equipment for primitive camping at Sea Camp Beach. A visit to the island is best taken as a day trip on the ferries that leave from St. Marys at 9 A.M. and 11:45 A.M. (call 912-882-4335 for reservations). Returns are at 10:15 A.M. and 4:45 P.M., which means you can stay just an hour on the island or explore all day if you wish. The ferry trip should be reserved in advance, although bookings aren't as heavy in winter as in spring and summer.

The entire refuge of Cumberland Island covers 36,545 acres of seashore, freshwater lakes, and marshes. The forty-five-minute

Sunrise along the Colonial Coast.

ferry ride is part of the fun as you cross Cumberland Sound. Keep an eye out for U.S. Navy ships from King's Bay Naval Base nearby. The base is home to one of the East Coast's major fleets.

A small visitor center is located at the Cumberland Island dock, and another small center can be found at Sea Camp Beach, a short walk across the island to the Atlantic side. Rest rooms and drinking water are available on the island. Bring everything else with you, and take any trash back to the mainland. Bring tackle and fish the surf for red bass, bluefish, and spotted trout. In the sound, fish for croaker, red bass, and drum.

When we stepped ashore on Cumberland Island, we were greeted by a living zoo of deer, raccoons, squirrels, leggy shorebirds, alligators, sea otters, swooping pelicans, and peregrine falcons in a natural setting of wind-sculpted live oaks draped with Spanish moss. We even saw some wild horses, but we didn't see any wild boar, which also inhabit this incredible island.

Many bird species nest here and, in addition to the year-round residents, winter brings a population of seasonal residents, accidental visitors, and migrating species that stop here for a rest on their journeys north and south. The marshes create a fertile broth for the nurturing of fish and shellfish, which in turn provide dinner for the many birds you'll see on this side of the island. In summer, the air is insufferably steamy and buggy except on the beach. Winter is the best time for exploring the island's interior, which has the most interesting wildlife, romantic ruins, and a deer population said to number in the thousands.

The British fortified Cumberland Island in the early 1700s, but after the Revolution attention turned to planting the rich soil. Dungeness Plantation grew oranges, olives, and Sea Island cotton. Nathaneal Greene, a general in the Revolutionary War, began building the first Dungeness mansion but died in 1786 before it could be finished. The four-story mansion was completed in 1814. Its guests included Eli Whitney and General "Lighthouse Harry" Lee, father of Robert E. Lee, who was taken ill in 1818

GEORGIA DIVISION OF TRADE, INDUSTRY, & TOURISM

The dunes at Cumberland Island, off Georgia's southeast corner.

while sailing along the Georgia coast. He came ashore here and was nursed by the Greene family, but he died a few weeks later. Members of the Greene family are buried here. Lee's grave was here until 1913, when his remains were removed to Virginia.

Thomas Carnegie, Andrew Carnegie's brother, bought the island in 1880 and built a mansion for himself and one for each of his children. The Carnegie family began deeding the land to the National Park Service in the 1960s, so it is gradually returning to the wild. When you're ready to leave, return to Interstate 95 for the trip north to Brunswick. Or, take historic US 17, an equally scenic but slower route.

Brunswick Beckons

As the gateway to the Golden Isles, Brunswick always seemed to us just a place to stop at the welcome center on our way to the good stuff. Then we learned we were missing a good bet. Historic Downtown Brunswick, which is east of Interstate 95 (take the GA 520 exit), is one of forty designated Main Street cities in Georgia. The Old Town National Historic District, built

in a grid pattern designed by General James Oglethorpe, is a good place for a walking tour. Head up one street and down the next.

For a good view of the marshes and the seas of grass that turn to bronze in low sun—giving the Golden Isles their name—stop at Overlook Park on US 17. Then continue up US 17 briefly to Gloucester Street and turn left. Note the Lanier Oak here. You'll hear a lot about poet Sidney Lanier in Georgia. It was under this tree that he is said to have been inspired to write "The Marshes of Glynn," his most famous poem.

Continue on Gloucester Street and then turn right on Union Street to see the historic courthouse, which is surrounded by trees from different nations including a pistachio from China. Returning to Gloucester on Union Street, find yourself in the center of the most interesting walking. Between Gloucester Street and Prince Street (on Albany, Ellis, Union, Reynolds, and Bay Streets), you'll see historic homes in a variety of architectural styles.

End your visit at Mary Ross Waterfront Park, which has a lively farmers market, a replica of the Liberty Ships that were built here during World War II, and a good view of the picturesque shrimp fleet that makes its home port here. Tuesdays through Sundays, a casino ship sails from here on gambling cruises lasting about six hours, so it's best to avoid the port when crowds of passengers are entering and leaving.

Brunswick Stew: The Official Recipe

This is a practical recipe to throw together in the biggest pot you have in your RV galley. Invite a crowd, serve this one-dish feast in sturdy, disposable bowls, and pass the hot sauce for those who want extra zing. Many recipes exist for Brunswick stew, some of which call for squirrel or other game. What all of the recipes have in common is the inclusion of more than one kind of meat as well as of corn to contribute a sweet, creamy sauce. We cheat by using canned chicken to avoid the mess of cooking and boning chicken, but here is the official version.

1 3-pound whole chicken
1 pound lean pork
1 pound lean beef
3 medium onions, chopped

Place the meat in a large, heavy pot. Season with salt and pepper. Add onions, and cover with water. Cook several hours or until the meat falls from the bones. Cool; then shred the meat. To the meat and stock add

4 1-pound cans tomatoes
5 tablespoons Worcestershire sauce
1 tablespoon Tabasco sauce
2 bay leaves
1 teaspoon dry mustard
½ stick butter

Cook one hour, stirring occasionally to prevent sticking. Then add

3 tablespoons vinegar
2 1-pound cans cream-style corn
1 15-ounce can English peas
3 small Irish potatoes, diced
1 box frozen okra (optional)

Cook slowly until the stew is thick and the potatoes are tender. Ladle into soup bowls.

Jekyll Island

From US 17 just south of downtown Brunswick, a causeway leads to Jekyll Island on GA 520. In the 1890s, Jekyll Island was the Newport of the sun belt. Roosevelts, Cranes, Goulds, Pulitzers, and J.P. Morgan were among the millionaires who established an exclusive hunting club here. They brought in their own chef to create gourmet feasts at the palatial Jekyll Island Club, which is now a grand resort. Stop in for a meal and a snoop around. In time, they needed more room for their families and guests and began building "cottages," each more extravagant than its neighbor.

Today this cluster of mansions makes up the Jekyll Island Historic District. The entire island is managed by the state, which also provides a campground (912-635-3021). In season, there's a fourteen-day limit, but in winter you can get a monthly rate. Cold fronts can be icy, but we love this island in winter when the crowds are gone. The campground allows pets and has a laundry, camp store, and full hookups including cable TV.

On your visit to the historic district, take one of the guided tram tours for the excellent narration and easy riding. Then

Fishing the Golden Islands

Think of this region as one of the world's greatest seafood supermarkets. Fish the freshwater lake at Blythe Island Regional Park near Brunswick. Drop a line from any of the bridges where fishing is permitted and parking is available. Surf cast from the beaches of St. Simons or Jekyll Island, or from the piers that both islands provide. (These piers are also good for crabbing.) From the marinas on the mainland or islands, charter a fishing boat to angle offshore for cobia, Spanish mackerel, king mackerel, grouper, snapper, and amberjack.

The best fishing is May through September, but a professional guide will be able to tell you what is biting when. Inshore river fishing for trout, flounder, sheepshead, and whiting goes on through the winter. A license is required for all fishing and netting by anyone over age sixteen.

make future visits on your own, allowing more time to see each site. Self-guided walking tours are welcome and—with 20 miles (32 km) of bike paths—the island is also ideal for bicycling. Thirty-three of the original buildings remain, including mansions and Faith Chapel, which has Tiffany windows. The village had everything that could possibly be needed by the millionaires, from a generator house to their own infirmary, indoor tennis courts, a golf course, and a marina for their fabulous yachts. Many of the service buildings now house smart gift shops or restaurants.

Take the time to enjoy the island's natural charms as well. Kayak the creeks. Ride horseback on the beach and through a maritime forest, and charter a boat to go dolphin watching or deep-sea fishing. Drive all the way around the island, stopping at radiant beaches, picnic tables under skyscraper-size live oaks, and historic ruins. See the remains of the Horton Brewery, which supplied beer to the troops at nearby Fort Frederica, and visit the Horton House, which was built in 1742. Nearby are the graves of early settlers, the duBignon family.

Shrimping is a major industry in the Golden Isles.

The island has an eighteen-hole championship golf course, a nine-hole oceanside course built by the original millionaires, an advanced tennis center with clay courts, and markets that sell basic supplies. Do your major provisioning on the mainland.

St. Simons Island

Return to US 17 and head north, where another vacation kingdom awaits on St. Simons Island. Reach the island from the mainland on a causeway that charges a very small toll. There is no campground here, so make your visit a day trip from your base at Jekyll Island or Brunswick.

Start your driving tour by turning right on Kings Way, which takes you to Retreat Avenue, site of Retreat Plantation. Drive down this avenue of oaks to the coast, checking out the plantation ruins. There's a fishing pier at the south end of the island, and a fine little museum in the 104-foot (31.7 m) lighthouse. Continue back north on the ocean road to the site of the Battle of Bloody Marsh. Here in 1742, the English turned back the Spanish before they could attack Fort Frederica, decisively saving Georgia for the British crown.

Drive up Frederica Road to Fort Frederica National Monument, where you can spend several hours roaming among the ruins of an impressive fort that was built in 1736, three years after Savannah was founded. Start at the visitor center by viewing the film, which is shown every half hour. Then take a ranger-led tour or wander around on your own. Christ Church was built in 1883, but a congregation met here as early as 1736, when John and Charles Wesley preached under the oaks. The fort is open daily except Christmas.

The communities of Sea Island and St. Simon's Island are playgrounds for the rich and famous. We once stayed at the Cloister here, one of Georgia's most exclusive resorts, but this isn't an area to wander in your RV. Besides, the estates are so thoroughly surrounded by high hedges, you can't see anything. Naturalists present daily interpretive programs on the beaches of Little St. Simons Island, but don't blunder into side roads where you're not welcome.

After visiting the islands, leave the Brunswick area northbound on US 17. Stop at Hofwyl Broadfield Historic Site, and walk the trail through a canopy of live oaks from the museum to the homestead. A trail leads to the remains of a rice dike, which was built long ago by slaves. Fortunes were made in the Low Country by planters who grew rice, indigo, and Sea Island cotton.

Also walk the remains of an old rice-dike system at Champney Wildlife Interpretive Trail in Darien. Darien, the next town north on US 17, is also the home of Magnolia Bluff Factory Stores, the largest group of factory outlets along the Colonial Coast. Explore the old city, the second oldest along the coast, as well as the ruins of a warehouse and slave cabin built from tabby, a building material made from oyster shells. The many tabby ruins you'll see along the coast testify to its staying power. Continue north on US 17.

The string of barrier islands, which can be seen across the golden marshes as you drive north, continues up the Colonial Coast. Most of the islands are wildlife refuges with limited public access—especially in winter—but all of them are drenched in history, ghost stories, and romance. Early settlers homesteaded on most of these barrier islands, and many of them are occupied today by wealthy home owners, research facilities, or both.

Before European settlement, Indians lived on the barrier islands for centuries, harvesting the rich abundance of the sea and estuaries. More than six hundred archaeological sites—some of them going back to 2000 B.C.—have been identified on St. Catherines Island alone. As you pass by, ask whether boat tours are available to any of the islands while you're here.

On to Savannah

In our view, Savannah is the fairy-tale princess in the royal family of Georgia tourism. It isn't an easy city to drive, but plenty of parking for RVs is available at the visitor's center on the north side of town, just south of where US 17 crosses the river to South Carolina. Take Interstate 95 to Interstate 16 and stay with it until it ends in the heart of the city. The visitor's center is housed in the old Central of Georgia Railroad Station, which dates to about 1860.

Savannah was planned as a walking city in the days before motorcars. Like London, the historic district is a series of twenty-two regal squares surrounded by elegant townhouses. Restoration is tightly controlled, so most of what you see is authentic to the city's eighteenth-century origins designed by James Oglethorpe. Forming the largest registered urban historic landmark district in the United States, the area covers 2.2 square miles (5.7 sq. km) and contains more than 1,200 restored structures.

Start at the Savannah History Museum next to the visitor center by seeing the eighteen-minute audiovisual presentation. The Central of Georgia Railway Roundhouse here is the oldest and most complete American locomotive repair shop in the nation. If you want to see it turn, simply ask. Next take a guided tour that leaves from the visitor center by trolley or bus. Then set off on foot or take a harbor cruise to complete your orientation. A good place to spend half a day shopping, observing activity on the Savannah River, and dining is Historic River Street, where old cotton warehouses have been transformed into a smart plaza. High on the bluff above the street, cotton merchants once conducted their business on Factors Walk. Cobblestone ramps lead to the river from here.

Your second day in the city might start at the City Market and City Market Arts Center, where more than thirty artists are at work. By now you'll know which of the many historic homes and museums you want to explore more thoroughly.

Downtown, view two bronze cannons on Bay Street between Drayton and Bull Streets. They were seized at the Battle of Yorktown and presented to Savannah's Chatham Artillery in 1791 by George Washington. Street vignettes such as this intrigue us the most about Savannah. Every square seems to have a statue or fountain or garden and, even though this is winter, camellias will be in bloom against a backdrop of evergreens.

Have fun studying every square. Johnson

> **Event:**
> In March, Savannah's St. Patrick's Day Parade and celebration is one of the largest in the east. Local Irish founded the Hibernian Society here in 1813.

Square has a monument to General Nathaneal Greene, whose story you encountered at Cumberland Island. Greene Square was named for him. In 1825, the Marquis de Lafayette spoke to a crowd gathered under the balcony of the Owens-Thomas House on what is now called Lafayette Square. Chippewa Square commemorates the 1814 Battle of Chippewa in Canada. Wright Square contains the grave of Yamacraw chief Tomo-chi-chi, who welcomed Oglethorpe and the area's original colonists.

The Pirate's House Restaurant (20 E. Broad St.) has been here forever, and it's still an important stop on the visitor's itinerary. The food is classic Low Country, children get their own combination souvenir menu and pirate mask, and the restaurant's legend is a lollapalooza. It's said that in the early days, sailors were shanghaied through a secret tunnel that led from the inn to the river.

At the end of US 80, visit Tybee Island, which is also the home of Fort Screven. This fort was built in 1875 and saw service in the Spanish-American War and World War I. The museum, located in one of the bastioned vaults, displays relics from colonial and pre-colonial times. If the day is warm, scout the island's beaches for seashells. The Marine Science Center here also has educational fun for the whole family. Tybee Lighthouse, built in 1736 and restored in 1887, is still open to the public.

At the junction of Interstate 95 and US 80, stop to see the Mighty Eighth Air Force Heritage Center, which has aircraft on display, a museum, a gift shop, and memorabilia.

North of Savannah on US 17, the Savannah National Wildlife Refuge covers 26,000 acres in South Carolina. In winter,

GEORGIA DIV. OF TRADE, INDUSTRY, & TOURISM

Carriage ride, Savannah Historic District.

hunting for feral hogs and waterfowl is permitted. The wildlife watching from the observation points is outstanding.

Okefenokee Swamp

Leaving Savannah, take Skidaway Road southbound, and stop at Skidaway Marine Science Complex and Aquarium. Operated by the University of Georgia Marine Extension Service, this is a good place to see marine life specific to Georgia waters.

The most direct route to our next stop, Okefenokee Swamp, is to travel south from Savannah on US 17 and then right on GA 196 to Midway and southwest on US 84, which has a pretty picnic pull off at Jesup. Continue on US 84 to Waycross. The closest camping to Okefenokee is at either Laura S. Walker State Park (912-287-4900) here at Waycross or Stephen Foster State Park (912-637-5274), which is in the heart of the swamp. Pick up camping information at any of the visitor centers along the way.

Once part of the ocean floor, the enormous saucer that holds Okefenokee Swamp is now more than 100 feet (30.5 m) below sea level. What appears to be solid ground are actually peat islands as much as 15 feet (4.6 m) deep, which are afloat on the bog. The name Okefenokee is as close as European translators could come to the Indians' name for this place, which means "trembling earth."

Covering more than 350,000 acres, the swamp is a national wilderness area and a national wildlife refuge. Connect with as many of the canoe trips, ranger-led excursions, and programs as you can manage. In summer it can be incredibly hot and buggy here, but winter is another world. Take vigorous hikes. Canoe for miles. Take a bicycle tour. Rent a boat and motor. Tramp through the wilderness looking for wildlife and birds.

By November sandhill cranes are stopping through here on their migration south, and you'll also see the occasional robin. Sweet gum, swamp maples, and sumac turn red in fall, and cypress trees blush a deep bronze. There's always a chance of spotting a bald eagle in winter, and more

Beyond Savannah

Traveling out of Savannah on Bay Street (which becomes Prospect Street), watch for a left turn to Fort Jackson. This fort was built to guard Five Fathom Hole, an important, deep-water haven for early merchant ships and gunboats. Built from 1809 to 1842, it's the oldest brick fort remaining in the city.

Twenty-five miles (40 km) southeast of town on GA 144, visit Fort McAllister, a Civil War earthworks fort that stood fast until the end of the war. Situated on the Ogeechee River, it fell to Union forces in 1864. Fort Pulaski, located 15 miles (24 km) east of Savannah at the end of US 80, is a national monument built between 1829 and 1847. It was Robert E. Lee's first post after his graduation from West Point.

otters come out of hiding because cold weather makes alligators less hungry. You'll see egrets, herons, and white ibis in the wetlands.

By January, the swamp has its full winter population of ducks, coots, greater sandhill cranes, and green-winged teal. Keep your binoculars on osprey nests in February, which is their nesting season here. As spring creeps closer, wild turkeys mate and sandhill cranes begin their conjugal ballet. Winter birds start heading north, but purple martins and eastern kingbirds arrive. Alligators come out to bask in warm sun. Bass spawn.

By early April, both the bass fishing and wildflowers are at their best. Look for carnivorous pitcher plants and the many varieties of wild orchids. Alligators begin their noisy mating ritual. In osprey nests high in the trees and in sandhill crane nests in the bullrushes, proud new parents feed their young. Nature's drama continues in May as new fawns appear, but this is a winter trip. It's time to move on south.

From Waycross, travel on US 1/23 back to Jacksonville. Or, from Stephen Foster State Park follow the Suwanee River south by taking GA 177 to Edith and GA 89, which becomes US 441 at the Florida border just north of Lake City.

CHAPTER 17

An Amble through Alabama: *Winter in the Heart of Dixie*

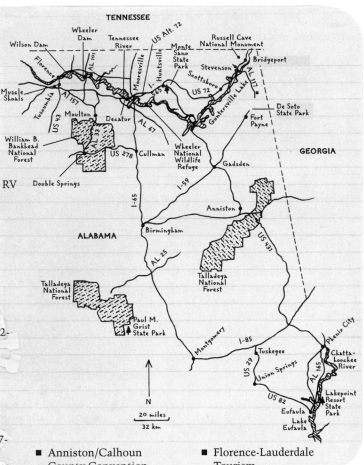

MILEAGE
Approximately
780 miles (1,248 km)

RESOURCES
- Alabama Association of RV Parks & Campgrounds, Executive Director, P.O. Box 70, Spring Hill TN 37174, 800-359-3218 or 334-774-3219.
- Alabama Bureau of Tourism & Travel, 401 Adams Ave., Montgomery AL 36103, 800-ALABAMA (800-252-2262), *http:// touralabama.com.*
- Alabama High Points Association, 1330 Quintard Ave., P.O. Box 1087, Anniston AL 36202, 800-489-1087 or 256-237-3536.
- Alabama Mountain Lakes Tourist Association, 25062 North St., Mooresville AL 35649, 800-648-5381 or 256-350-3500, *http://www. almtlakes.org.*
- Alabama State Parks Division, 64 N. Union St., Montgomery AL 36230, 800-ALA-PARK (800-252-7275), *http://www. dcnr.state.al.us.*

- Anniston/Calhoun County Convention & Visitors Bureau, 1330 Quintard Ave., P.O. Box 1087, Anniston AL 36202, 800-489-1087, *http://www. calhounchamber.org.*
- Decatur–Morgan County Convention & Visitors Bureau, P.O. Box 2349, Decatur AL 35602, 800-524-6181 or 256-350-2028, *http://decaturcvb.org.*

- Florence-Lauderdale Tourism, 1 Hightower Pl., Florence AL 35630, 888-FLO-TOUR (888-356-8687) or 256-740-4141, *http://www.flo-tour.org.*
- Gadsden-Etowah Tourist Board, 90 Walnut St., Gadsden AL 35901, 256-549-0351, *http://www. cybrtyme.com/tourism.*
- Greater Birmingham Convention & Visitors Bureau, 2200 Ninth Ave. N., Birmingham AL 35203,

800-458-8085 or
205-458-8000,
http://www.bcvb.org.

- Historic Chattahoochee
  Commission,
  211 N. Eufaula Ave.,
  Eufaula AL 36027,
  334-687-9755,
  http://www.
  hcc-al-ga.org.
- Huntsville Convention &
  Visitors Bureau,
  700 Monroe St.,
  Huntsville AL 35801,
  800-SPACE-4-U

(800-772-2348),
http://www.huntsville.
org.

- National Forests
  in Alabama,
  2946 Chestnut St.,
  Montgomery AL 36110,
  334-832-4470,
  http://www.r8web.
  com/alabama.
- Pickens County Tourism
  Association,
  P.O. Box 417,
  Carrollton AL 35447,
  205-367-2186.

- Scottsboro–Jackson County
  Chamber of Commerce,
  407 E. Willow St.,
  Scottsboro AL 35768,
  800-259-5508
  or 256-259-5500,
  http://www.
  sjcchamber.org.
- Union Springs–Bullock
  County Tourism Council,
  P.O. Box 5236,
  Union Springs AL 36089,
  334-738-TOUR (334-738-
  8687).

Alabama under the Stars

Our trip begins in Huntsville and takes us through thousands of years of natural history, Civil War sites, and some of the most beautiful drives in the South. Alabama has four national forests and twenty-six state parks. A wealth of natural wonders is also found just across the border in Florida, Georgia, Mississippi, and Tennessee. Fish freshwater or salt water. Explore mountains that were once home to Creek, Cherokee, and Chickasaw. Discover the Sipsey Wilderness, waterfalls, spelunking, and white-water rafting as well as America's southernmost ski slope at Mentone.

Alabama has fourteen covered bridges, the largest golf project anywhere in the

> **Event:**
> In late November through December, Christmas lights glow throughout the state. The Phenix City Amphitheater puts on a good light show and also holds special holiday programs.

world, ten major Indian powwows a year, and some of the brightest, whitest beaches in America. It's the primary setting for the movie *Forrest Gump*, the birthplace of Jesse Owens and Hank Aaron, and the home of the celebrated Alabama Shakespeare Festival. It is mountains, sandy seashores, farm fields, and forests all wrapped in a warm southern welcome.

An estimated two hundred thousand stars peppered Alabama when a rare meteor shower fell on the night of November 13, 1833. The song "Stars Fell on Alabama" is a Big Band classic, and legend today says that the starfish found on Alabama's Gulf of Mexico beaches are the stars that fell that night.

Robert Trent Jones Golf Trail

The largest golf project in the world, Alabama's Robert Trent Jones Golf Trail has a total of twenty-one courses offering 375 holes of championship golf in eight locales, none of them more than 15 miles (24 km) from an interstate. The state-owned courses are professionally operated to country club standards. They're found in Huntsville, Calhoun County (northeast Alabama), Birmingham, Auburn/Opelika, Greenville, Dothan, and Mobile. Some travelers make the golf trail the focus of their trip, traveling from course to course and playing the entire circuit. If this prospect appeals to you, call 800-FORE-ALA (800-367-3252) for more information.

Huntsville

Let's start with our eyes on the stars at the U.S. Space and Rocket Center at Huntsville (AL 20 exit off Interstate 565). The center

The U.S. Space and Rocket Center at Huntsville is a vital link in the American space program.

has its own year-round campground (256-830-4987) with full hookups. If you are a day visitor, you'll find plenty of parking for your rig. Plan to spend at least one day, and more if you want to take one of the space camp programs. The programs range from multiday children's programs for grades 4 and up to learn-to-fly programs for adults. Parent-child programs are also offered.

While Houston and Cape Canaveral grab the headlines during space launches, it was here in Huntsville that Dr. Werner von Braun and his team of scientists brought the United States into the space age. Huntsville is the heartbeat of the space program. Children love the hands-on displays, and nostalgia buffs enjoy memorabilia from the dawn of the space program in the 1930s

through the 1960s. See a dazzling large-format movie, picnic outdoors or eat in the cafeteria, ride the 4G Space Shot, and view outdoor displays that include dozens of rockets, a full-size space shuttle, and a rare titanium SR-71 Blackbird that can fly 2,200 miles per hour. The center is open every day but Christmas.

If you want to see the city of Huntsville, start at the visitor information center at the Von Braun Civic Center downtown at 700 Monroe Street. Take a trolley tour of the historic area to see Alabama's oldest operating hardware store, which dates to 1897, and historic neighborhoods with one of the highest concentrations of antebellum mansions in the South. Also see the 1860 rail depot. You can hop off and on the trolley, stopping at points of interest and catching the next trolley as it passes.

Huntsville–Madison County Botanical Garden on Bob Wallace Avenue is open all year. Winter is a quiet time to stroll among the evergreens and camellias. Walk the nature trail, visit the biosphere, watch black swans in the pond, and look for birds and small mammals that winter here. Downtown at Big Spring Park just west of Courthouse Square, see where Huntsville was founded along Indian Creek. Watch waterfowl, have a picnic, and walk the Friendship Bridge. If the day is sunny, stroll Maple Hill Cemetery among huge cedars and elaborate memorials. To reach the cemetery,

For More Information

Alabama Welcome Centers are found at Collinsville on Interstate 59 South, Elmont on Interstate 65 South, Robertsdale and Grand Bay at Interstate 10 West, Heflin at Interstate 20 West, Slocomb on US 231 North, Valley on Interstate 85 South, and Cuba on Interstate 59 North. Never pass up welcome centers. They're an excellent source of information, maps, discount coupons, and clean rest rooms. Parking is never a problem for an RV, and centers often offer dog-walking areas and sometimes a picnic table or other facilities.

travel east on Governors Drive past the hospitals, and then turn left on California.

At Monte Sano State Park (east on US 431), walk nature trails among native trees and interesting plants and flowers that were introduced from Japan. The park's Bavaria-like mountain setting prompted many of the German scientists at the space center to build homes here.

Alabama's Mountain Lakes

The Tennessee River creates a sapphire necklace of lakes across northern Alabama. Take Interstate 565 west from Huntsville and exit at little Mooresville, a village that could have served as a movie set for Tom Sawyer and Huckleberry Finn. The hamlet was established in 1818, and it is still a twelve-block time warp of structures that appear to be frozen in the early nineteenth century. This isn't a tourist town, so respect the residents' privacy while you stroll the old streets and stop at the post office where residents still get their mail in wooden pigeonholes used during the Civil War. Head west out of town on US Alternate 72.

In Decatur, stop by the city's visitor's center on US 31 in the center of town. Pick up maps, brochures, and a self-guided walking-tour map. Founded in 1823, Decatur opened its first bank, the Old State Bank, in 1833. This bank is the city's oldest structure and, if you know where to look, you can see scars made by bullets during the Civil War. Inside, view exhibits from the city's past. As a key rail junction, Decatur was a hot spot during the Civil War. When the smoke cleared after the war, the Old State Bank on Bank Street was one of only four buildings left standing. Construction soon resumed with a bang, filling the city with Victoriana.

Today you can walk old streets to see one of the most intact Victorian neighbor-

Mooresville, just outside Huntsville.

hoods in the state. The neighborhood covers more than 116 acres. Take a self-guided walking tour; then shop the galleries and boutiques in the historic shopping district.

You can also take a self-guided Civil War tour, which has ten interpretive markers explaining the city's role in the war. Visit Cook's Natural Science Museum (412 13th. St. SE) with its fine collections of wildlife, seashells, insects, and butterflies common to the Tennessee Valley. It's open daily except major holidays, and admission is free.

Point Mallard (on Point Mallard Dr. SE) in Decatur is the home of America's first wave pool. The wave pool closes in winter, but the rest of the attraction stays open all year. Play miniature golf or the eighteen-hole championship golf course, hike the 3-mile (4.8 km) riverside nature trail, go bicycling, or skate on the year-round ice rink.

East of town on AL 67, Givens Wildlife Interpretive Center, part of Wheeler National Wildlife Refuge, is one of the South's largest centers for the study of waterfowl and wildlife. The refuge is home to the state's largest concentration of wild geese, hundreds of deer, and three hundred species of birds. View the wildlife from the glass-enclosed observatory. They can't see you, so

Event:
The Southern Wildlife Festival in Decatur in late November features fine arts with a wildlife theme.

you'll have an unhurried view of the great spectrum of wildlife that thrives here in a variety of habitats. This time of year at the 34,500-acre refuge, wintering waterfowl will be starting their migration north. Year-round species will be nesting in spring.

Heading toward Florence on US 72, watch for signs to Wheeler Dam. Another part of the massive complex that controls the Tennessee River, this dam impounds a 74-mile (118.4 km) lake that is a favorite spot for anglers. Fish for channel catfish, crappie, spotted bass, smallmouth, largemouth, and drum. Jump back on US 72 and continue west to Wilson Dam. This is one of the great engineering marvels of the East, so take in the free show of massive barges and tows locking through hour after hour in a lift lock that raises them 100 feet (30.5 m).

US 72 continues west to Florence on the north side of the river and Alt. US 72 parallels it on the south side. If you take the northern route, turn north on Greenbrier Road 8 miles (12.8 km) east of Huntsville to find the original Greenbrier Restaurant, which was built in 1952. It's open every day for lunch and dinner, offering the very essence of southern country fare and drawing loyal regulars for miles around. Feast on catfish, ribs, ham, barbecued chicken, fried or boiled shrimp, and all the trimmings.

If you take the southern route, visit the Wheeler Home along the way. General Joe Wheeler commanded Confederate troops in 127 battles and had sixteen horses shot out from under him. Robert E. Lee called him one of the outstanding cavalrymen of the War Between the States. Wheeler's daughter, Annie, who was born after the Civil War, was a nurse in the Spanish-American War and earned the title "Angel of Santiago." In World War I she served in England and France. She lived in the home here until her death in 1955. On the plantation you'll see the 1872 home plus a double log cabin that dates to before 1818 and a two-story, Federal-style house.

The Shoals

Florence, Muscle Shoals, and Tuscumbia—collectively known as the Shoals—straddle

Decatur's Old State Bank survived the Civil War.

the Tennessee River in Alabama's northwest corner. We had to be dragged to the Alabama Music Hall of Fame in Tuscumbia, but we ended up loving it even though we're not country music fans. Lose yourself in music nostalgia, see the motor home used by the group Alabama on tour, and tape your own hit single in the recording booth. The museum honors not only country and western but also gospel, soul, rock, rhythm and blues, opera, and the velvet-voiced, Alabama-born Nat King Cole.

Tuscumbia (take US 43 south from Florence) is also the home of Ivy Green, the birthplace and childhood home of Helen Keller. Born healthy in 1880, she was nineteen months old when an illness left her blind and deaf. The moving story of how she learned to communicate is told in William Gibson's play (later a movie) *The Miracle Worker*. Now you can see the home where it all happened, and picture the crackling dramas that played out in these rooms, at this pump, on this furniture. In summer, scenes from the play are performed outdoors at Ivy Green; the home and grounds can be toured year-round.

Return to Florence on US 72. An unusual sight greets visitors at 601 Riverview

Drive in Florence, where a Frank Lloyd Wright house sits incongruously among traditional southern homes. Wright's assistant supervised the building of the house in the 1930s and 1940s. Here, Stanley and Mildred Rosenbaum raised four sons and lived out their lives. The house, now open to the public as a museum, was also furnished by Wright, whose designs were so impractical that Mrs. Rosenbaum gave the kitchen chairs to her maid because the little boys kept toppling over on them. Considered one of the best preserved of Wright's Usonian houses, it's the only Wright structure in Alabama and is open daily for tours. Call 256-764-5274 to make arrangements.

The great blues composer W. C. Handy was born in a log cabin in Florence. Today his birthplace is a museum and library that contains many of his handwritten compositions. See his trumpet, the family parlor, and the piano on which he composed "St. Louis Blues." Have lunch at Renaissance Tower on the north side of the river on AL 133. It's the tallest structure in the state, and it has the best view of the Tennessee Valley below. See Pope's Tavern, which dates to 1830 and was a stagecoach stop and Civil War hospital. Also on the north side of the river, the tavern faces Hermitage Drive; parking is behind it.

South from the Shoals

From Florence, take AL 157 southeast toward Moulton, and pick up AL 33 to enter William B. Bankhead National Forest. The forest is home to great stands of wildflowers, oak leaf hydrangea, and a rare club moss called ground cedar, but in winter you could find anything from snow to spring flowers. Come to camp, ride horseback, and hike the Sipsey Wilderness, which is the only remaining stand of old-growth trees in the state. With luck you'll see some exceedingly rare species, such as Alabama Streak Sourus fern, Alabama croton, club moss, and the flattened mush turtle.

While here, picnic and fish at Brushy Lake (electric motors only) and explore Pine Torch Church and Cemetery, which date to 1808. For reasons long forgotten,

graves in the old churchyard are covered with white sand. The practice continues to this day, and services are still held in the church. Campsites are available at Brushy Springs and Double Springs (205-489-5111).

US 278 runs east to Cullman, where tourism has a delightful German accent with a southern drawl. In the fine little museum, see mementos of the area's early German settlers who dreamed of building a self-sufficient community of German immigrants in the late 1800s. Lonely on the new frontier, they requested that priests be sent to start schools. St. Bernard's Abbey—a working monastery that today offers schooling, retreats, marriage encounters, and counseling—was established a century ago. Walk the shaded paths of Ave Maria Grotto, which is filled with miniature cathedrals and villages built over the years by one of the monks. The abbey is 3 miles (4.8 km) east of Interstate 65; follow the signs.

From here, you can take Interstate 65 straight south toward Montgomery or leave the interstate south of Birmingham and jog west on AL 25 to explore Talladega National Forest. Camp in the forest at Paul M. Grist State Park (334-872-5846). For additional information about the forest, call the ranger station at 256-362-2909. If it's a warm winter, the first warm rain will start the song of tree frogs. Chickadees, purple finches, and cedar waxwings love this forest. You'll sight opossums, saddleback caterpillars, and tent caterpillars that locals will tell you are good bream bait. Look for ginseng, bloodroot, purple coneflowers, and Queen Anne's lace, which old-timers here use in an exotic jelly recipe. Later in the season, big colonies of oak-leaf hydrangea burst into full bloom. Local folks call hydrangea "Seven Bark."

Tip:

Alabama's woodlands and waterways are full of game and fowl. Hunting seasons vary according to the type of hunting and the county, but something is in season from November through March. For more information, contact the Game and Fish Division, Alabama Department of Conservation, at 334-242-3465.

Montgomery

Montgomery, the state capital, is zesty and alive with history and arts. The city's visitor's center is a tourism showpiece in Union Station (300 water St.); pick up maps that describe self-guided walking or driving tours of the city's landmarks here. It's open daily except major holidays.

The Thompson Mansion at the corner of Madison and Hull Streets is another popular historic building. The mansion was built in about 1850 but was disassembled, taken elsewhere for restoration, and then reassembled on this site.

Everyone loves the zoo, which is open 10 A.M. to 4:30 P.M. in winter. Ride a miniature train to view more than eight hundred animals. To reach the zoo, take Fairground Road to Vandiver Boulevard. The entrance is well marked.

Visit the State Farmers Market, which is open daily and is a nonstop state fair of homegrown foods and homespun crafts. Ask what's playing at the Alabama Shakespeare Festival. All types of theater are offered, not just plays by the Bard. If you're an F. Scott Fitzgerald fan, see the home where he and Zelda lived from 1931 to 1932. It's now a museum with a short film about the couple, paintings by Zelda, and personal artifacts.

Tuskegee

Leaving Montgomery, take Interstate 85 east to Tuskegee, where Tuskegee Institute is now a national historic site. Booker T. Washington and George Washington Carver are the major heroes of this success story. Seeing a need for education for rural black children, Washington founded this school on a shoestring. Almost everything here was built by students, who were required to learn a trade in addition to their academic studies. Not only did they raise the buildings but they also made the bricks that built them.

The video is spellbinding, and the museum is a fascinating look at hardscrabble Alabama farming in the years after the Civil War and into the twentieth century. Of special interest are the works of George Washington Carver, who was not only a brilliant scientist but also a gifted artist. He died here in 1943.

Follow US 29 south from Tuskegee to Union Springs, where a southern country dinner at Zelda's costs less than $10 for all the ham, biscuits, greens, corn pudding, sweet tea, and other southern specialties you can handle. The town of Union Springs is tiny, but its streets are lined with 106 architecturally important old homes. Take a self-guided tour to see historic houses, churches, a Carnegie Library, and a gothic-style jail complete with a gallows on the third floor with a trapdoor that still works.

Along the Chattahoochee

Leave Union Springs eastbound on US 82, which takes you to Eufaula on the Chattahoochee River. If you haven't tired of historic homes, you'll find more of them here than in almost any other place in the state. We recommend taking a bus tour. The narrations are invaluable as you rubberneck your way past nearly six hundred historic homes built between 1834 and World War I. Most of them are privately owned by passionate restoration buffs. Tour the Shorter Mansion (340 N. Eufaula Ave.) as well as Sheppard Cottage (504 E. Barbour St.), which houses Eufaula's visitor center. Also seek out Hart House (211 N. Eufaula Ave.). Built about 1850, it is the headquarters of the Chattahoochee Trace of Alabama and Georgia.

The Chattahoochee Trace is a trip in itself, one that takes you up the Alabama side and down the Georgia side (or vice versa) of this historic river. Ask about it while you're here, and start planning your next trip for autumn when the bird life along the Chattahoochee Flyway will be at

Event:
The Sweet Potato Festival held at Tuskegee Institute the second Saturday in October honors George Washington Carver, who found more than a hundred uses for the sweet potato.

its most active. Lake Eufaula forms one of the state's best recreation resources, and Eufaula Wildlife Refuge is a feast for fishermen and wildlife watchers. Pick up a checklist at the visitor center and see how many of the 281 known species you can spot at the refuge: deer, marsh wrens, ruby-crowned kinglets, northern harriers, black-crowned night herons, scaups, snow geese, and Canada geese, which nest here. Lakepoint Resort State Park (334-687-6676) is more than a campground. It's a resort with restaurants, planned activities, and fishing that will knock your socks off.

For the scenic route along the Chattahoochee, take AL 165, or for a quick route north take US 431. Stop at Phenix City if you want to see the courthouse with its Roman Doric columns. Built in 1868, it's one of the oldest in the state. Or, skip the city and stay with US 431 through another part of Talladega National Forest and on to Anniston. This prim, old, southern city was founded in 1872, and its magnificent Church of St. Michael and All Angels (W. 18th St. and Cobb Ave.) was built in 1888. The church is open daily, so stop to see its marble altar, angel statues, and stained glass windows. See mummies and a dinosaur at the Anniston Museum of Natural History (800 Museum Dr.). Stop also at the Women's Army Corps Museum at Fort McClellan, at the north end of Anniston off AL 21.

Continue on US 431 to Gadsden, where the waterfall at Noccalula Falls Park should be a strong, silvery veil if there's been enough rain. It's beautiful even during dry spells, when there's only a wisp of a flow. A deep cave can be seen beneath the falls, and overlooking the drop is a statue of Noccalula, the Indian maiden who supposedly leapt to her death here because she couldn't marry the brave she loved.

Interstate 59 takes you to Fort Payne, the gateway to De Soto State Park with its canyons and waterfalls. Covering 5,067 acres, the park includes Lookout Mountain, Little River Canyon, De Soto Falls, and De Soto Lake. The campground (256-845-5075) is open all year. Take the scenic drive around the canyon, and hike miles of rugged trails. Visit the nature center, fish

the lake, swim in the swimming pool, and eat in the rustic park restaurant.

At Sequoyah Caverns (at the intersection of AL 117 and Interstate 59), fish for trout, walk through caverns that stay 60°F all year, and see limestone formations and a rainbow-colored underground waterfall. If it's a good snow year, ask about skiing in the area.

AL 117 leads across the Tennessee River to US 72, which takes you back to your starting point at Huntsville. You'll go through Scottsboro, which was founded in 1820 and is the home of the famous First Monday Trade Day. Since 1868—when the first Monday of the month meant the arrival of the circuit court—people came to town to sell produce, trade mules, go to church meeting, and talk politics. Today the first Monday of each month is a delightful country market. However, Scottsboro's shopping includes something even more exciting. At the Unclaimed Baggage Center you'll find bargains and surprises from bags that were unclaimed at airline carousels. The center is open daily except Sunday. Huntsville is only a short drive past Scottsboro.

Or, turn north from the Sequoyah Caverns area on US 72, and travel toward Bridgeport and Russell Cave National Monument. Evidence of human habitation going back as far as 7000 B.C. has been found here. Stop at the visitor center; then take a guided walk to the cave. Each year, a Native American Festival brings tribes together here for demonstrations and programs. Returning to US 72, stop in Stevenson, one of the South's most important rail junctions during the Civil War. Visit the Cowan Home (which was occupied by Union troops in 1863), the rail depot museum, and the ruins of the Little Brick, where Union officers headquartered. The old Stevenson Hotel, built in 1872, was a stopping point for train travelers. The log cabin you see in town was built in 1821 from native hardwoods.

A third possibility after leaving the Fort Payne area is to linger in the Guntersville Lake area (6 miles/9.6 km northeast of Guntersville off AL 227), which has campgrounds galore and one of the South's greatest fisheries.

CHAPTER 18

Tampa to Pensacola
Florida's "Long, Lonely Leg"

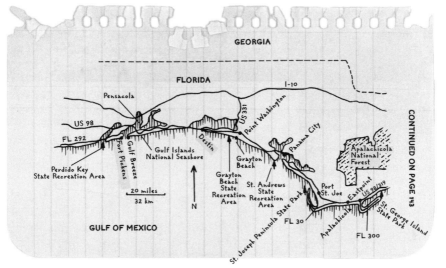

MILEAGE
Approximately 450 miles
(720 km)

RESOURCES
- Apalachicola Bay Chamber of Commerce,
  99 Market St. Suite 100,
  Apalachicola FL 32320,
  850-653-9419,
  http://www.homtown.com/apalachicola.
- Cedar Key Area Chamber of Commerce,
  480 2nd St., P.O. Box 610,
  Cedar Key FL 32625,
  352-543-5600,
  http://www.cedarkey.org.
- Emerald Coast Convention & Visitors Bureau,
  1540 Hwy. 98 E., P.O. Box 609, Fort Walton Beach FL 32549, 800-322-3319 or 850-651-7131,
  http://www.destin-fwb.com.
- Gulf Beaches of Tampa Bay,
  6990 Gulf Blvd.,
  St. Pete Beach FL 33706,
  800-944-1847 (U.S. only) or 727-360-6957,

http://www.gulfbeaches-tampabay.com.
- Panama City Beach Convention & Visitors Bureau,
  17001 Panama City Beach Pkwy.,
  Panama City Beach FL 32413, 800-553-1330,
  http://www.800pcbeach.org.
- Pensacola Convention & Visitor Center,
  1401 E. Gregory St.,
  Pensacola FL 32501,
  800-874-1234 (U.S. only) or 850-434-1234,
  http://www.visitpensacola.com.
- Seaside, County Rd. 30-A,
  P.O. Box 4730, Santa Rosa Beach FL 32459,
  800-277-TOWN (800-277-8696) or 888-SEASIDE (888-732-7433),
  http://www.seasidefl.com.
- South Walton Tourist Development Council,
  25777 U.S. Hwy. 331 S.,
  P.O. Box 1248,
  Santa Rosa Beach FL 32459,
  800-822-6877 or

850-267-1216
http://www.beachesofsouthwalton.com.
- St. Petersburg–Clearwater Convention & Visitors Bureau,
  14450 46th St. N.
  Suite 108,
  Clearwater FL 33762,
  800-345-6710 or 727-464-7200, *http://www.floridasbeach.com.*
- Tallahassee Area Convention & Visitors Bureau,
  106 E. Jefferson St.,
  Tallahassee FL 32301,
  850-413-9200,
  http://www.co.leon.fl.us/visitors/index.htm.
  A visitor information center (850-413-9200) is downtown in the Capitol on S. Duval St.
- Tampa-Hillsborough Convention & Visitors Association,
  400 N. Tampa St.
  Suite 1010,
  Tampa FL 33602,
  813-223-1111,
  http://www.gotampa.com.

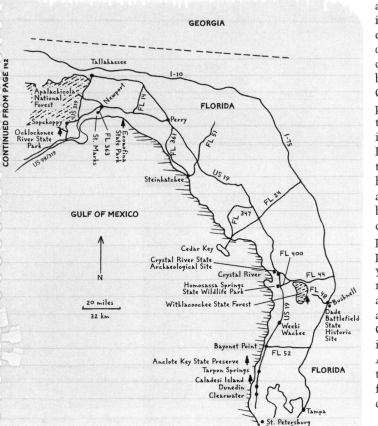

CONTINUED FROM PAGE 142

GEORGIA

Tallahassee

I-10

FLORIDA

Apalachicola
National
Forest

Sopchoppy

Ochlockonee
River State
Park

US 98/319

Newport

FL 14

Perry

St. Marks

FL 363

Econofina
State Park

FL 361

FL 57

I-75

Steinhatchee

US 19

GULF OF MEXICO

FL 24

N

FL 347

20 miles
32 km

Cedar Key

FL 400

Crystal River State
Archaeological Site

Crystal River

FL 44

Homosassa Springs
State Wildlife Park

FL 48

Withlacoochee State Forest

US 19

Bushnell

Dade
Battlefield
State
Historic
Site

Weeki
Wachee

Bayonet Point

FL 52

Anclote Key State Preserve
Tarpon Springs

FLORIDA

Caladesi Island

Dunedin

Clearwater

Tampa

St. Petersburg

Egmont Key State Park

and superb nature watching. We can't say it often enough. One trip to any of Florida's theme parks doesn't mean you have been there and done that. Competition among the parks is so fierce that they are all changing and improving constantly. In a visit of only one or two days, you probably hit only the high spots and miss many of the best scenes. Many Florida families buy annual passes and come to the parks often. The more you love nature, the more you'll find to enjoy about the flowers, birds, and animals at Busch Gardens here. The show is different every day. Across the street, Adventure Island is a water park filled with splashy fun to cool you off.

Ybor City is Tampa's Cuban core, a National Historic Landmark District. By night it's often a street party; by day it is a place to lose yourself in a sunbaked Latin landscape. Walking tours (813-248-3712) are available free on Thursday and Saturday at 10:30 A.M. Hear how Ybor City was settled in the 1880s by Vincente Martinez Ybor, whose cigar factory attracted hundreds of Cuban workers. Cuban liberator Jose Marti raised funds (and a little cane) here for his cause. Teddy Roosevelt rallied his Rough

Tampa and St. Petersburg

Our trip begins and ends in Tampa Bay, one of Florida's favorite vacationlands, and takes us up the coast that sailors call the "long, lonely leg" because Gulf-front communities are so few. The main road is miles inland, which means that you have to drive for miles through boggy wetlands—and some of the best wildlife watching in the state—to reach coastal settlements like Cedar Key and Steinhatchee.

Let's start, though, with some fun. Busch Gardens Tampa Bay is an excellent theme park with heart-in-mouth roller coasters, rides galore, dazzling shows, good restaurants, shopping, showplace gardens,

Event:
The Florida Strawberry Festival
is held in Plant City, near Tampa,
each February.

Riders here before they sailed off to the Spanish-American War.

Today the old cigar factory is the center of a revitalized area. Dine in smart restaurants. Shop boutiques and galleries. See cigar makers hand-roll stogies in the timeless way. Have lunch at Columbia Restaurant, which has been here since 1905 or, better still, come for dinner on an evening when there's a flamenco show. Other Columbia Restaurants are found on the Pier at St. Petersburg (which we recommend for its museum, aquarium, and shopping-dining complex), and at Clearwater Beach. They're family owned, so the quality is consistent and the Cuban cuisine is deliciously authentic.

Another history lesson not to be missed is the Henry B. Plant Museum (401 W. John F. Kennedy Blvd./US 60), now a part of the University of Tampa. Plant was a railroad magnate who brought trains down the Gulf Coast and established a palatial hotel to attract wealthy, fin de siècle sunseekers. Built in the flamboyant Moorish-Mediterranean extravagance of the times, the hotel and its rooftop minarets dominated the landscape. Some rooms are furnished as they originally were. Others are devoted to many layers of local history.

Visit the Florida Aquarium at the Port of Tampa (701 Channelside Dr.), the Museum of Science and Industry (4801 E. Fowler Ave.), and the children's museums in both Tampa (7550 North Blvd.) and St. Petersburg (Great Expectations, 1120 4th St. S.). To get from Tampa to St. Pete, you have a choice of three routes, listed north to south: the Courtney Campbell Causeway (FL 60), I-275, or the Gandy Bridge (US 92). During rush hours, they're all crowded, so try to avoid busy times.

Ask what's showing at Florida International Museum in St. Petersburg (100 2nd St. S.). The museum isn't always open, but its shows are blockbuster exhibits that may appear at only one or two other places in the United States. Its Treasures of the Czars show was the first time the priceless artifacts had been seen outside the Kremlin. The Salvador Dali Museum in St. Pete (1000 3rd St. S.) is one of the largest collec-

tions of Dali works in the world. Take one of the docent-led tours.

Campgrounds abound in this popular area, both on the mainland and along the Gulf beaches. Winter temperatures are mild, making it a good time for water sports, wildlife watching, and children's activities. Our recommendation is to stay a few nights on the mainland while you see the city attractions; then move to a Gulf-front campground for the breezes and beaches. Traffic is heavy, and commuting from the beaches to city sightseeing can be cumbersome.

If you have a boat, get out to Egmont Key State Park, which is at the mouth of Tampa Bay southwest of Fort De Soto Beach. Its strategic location has made it a landmark since the dawn of Florida history. Photograph the lighthouse, watch birds and wildlife, swim, and hunt seashells. Imagine this windblown key as a Union Navy base during the Civil War and, before that, when captured Indians were kept here during the Third Seminole War.

From St. Pete Beach, Dunedin, and other beach communities, US 19 takes you north. Ride the ferry to Caladesi Island State Park for a day at a picturesque beach. Crowds tend to cluster near the concession, so you'll probably have the hiking trails to

---

Anglers' Alert

Separate fishing licenses are required for saltwater and freshwater fishing in Florida. Call 888-FISH-FLO (888-347-4356), a 24-hour line where for $3.95 plus the cost of the license, you can get a fishing license by mail. A three-day permit is $6.50; seven-day, $16.50; and one year, $31.50. All prices are for nonresidents. Floridians pay $13.50 a year.

For freshwater fishing information, contact the Florida Game and Fresh Water Fish Commission, 620 South Meridian Street, Tallahassee FL 32399, 850-488-4676, <http://www.state.fl.us/gfc>. For saltwater fishing information, contact the Office of Fisheries Management and Assistance Services, 3900 Commonwealth Boulevard, Tallahassee FL 23299 (850-488-5757).

yourself. The nature show is a year-round pleasure. Look for shorebirds, raccoons, and turtle nests, which should be given a wide berth. It's illegal to disturb them. Honeymoon Island—which was once attached to Caladesi Island before a hurricane drove a channel between them—can be reached by road. Take FL 586, the Dunedin Causeway. Enjoy the beach and picnic area, hike nature trails through one of the area's last stands of virgin slash pines, and try your fishing luck.

Just as Ybor City took you back to old Cuba, Dunedin shows you a bit of old Scotland (especially in March during the High-

Event:

In March at New Port Richey, which is north of Tarpon Springs, the Chasco Festival celebrates the community's Indian heritage.

land Games), and Tarpon Springs takes you to Greece. Reach both communities via US 19. Early in the twentieth century, Greek divers (who had depleted the sponge beds of Key West) and newcomers from the Aegean settled in Tarpon Springs to dive for sponges in the Gulf at the mouth of the Anclote River. The invention of synthetic sponges and a blight that killed the natural ones dealt a one-two punch to the industry and, by World War II, its heyday was over. Still, the area's Greek heritage shines, especially during festivals. Today's fishing boats come back with shrimp, not sponges, but some sponging is still done here as a show for tourists.

Anclote Key State Preserve off Tarpon Springs can be reached only by boat, so make arrangements in town for a visit. See the 1887 lighthouse, bald eagles, stark pines with their osprey nests, and, on the beaches, a world of shorebirds. Bring everything with you, and carry any trash back to the mainland. The island has no facilities.

In Tarpon Springs, we like to stroll

Dodocanese Boulevard just to soak up the ambience. It's touristy, but the Greek shops and luscious Greek food set it apart from other Gulf-front tourist attractions. St. Nicholas Greek Orthodox Cathedral (36 N. Pinellas Ave.) is a Byzantine treasure. Stop in for a look. At the Universalist Church on Grand Boulevard, view a large collection of works by landscape artist George Inness Jr.

Into the Countryside

Take a respite now from overcrowded US 19. At Bayonet Point north of Tarpon Springs, follow FL 52 to Interstate 75 northbound. Drive through patches of the Withlacoochee State Forest. The forest lies on the Withlacoochee State Trail, a 41-mile (65.6 km) rails-to-trails route that you can hike, bicycle, or ride horseback. Explore it as far as you wish.

Head via Interstate 75 for Dade Battlefield State Historic Site near Bushnell. Take the FL 48 exit and follow signs. Everyone has heard of Custer's Last Stand, but the Dade Massacre in this lonely pine woods was even more poignant. Major Francis Dade and more than a hundred of his soldiers were bushwhacked by Seminole Indians here in December 1835. So remote was the wilderness where they fell, it was weeks before the outside world learned of the tragedy. See the small museum and a replica of the pitiful pine fort the embattled men tried to erect as the battle raged. The site is open during daylight hours; the visitor center is open daily 9 A.M. to 5 P.M.

Continue north on Interstate 75 to FL 44, which runs west through pretty lake lands to Crystal River State Archaeological Site. Six ceremonial and burial mounds were built here by prehistoric tribes on what is considered to be one of the longest continually occupied sites in North America. Historians believe that as many as seven to eight thousand Indians made pilgrimages here each year to bury their dead.

From Crystal River, a brief jog south on US 19 leads to Homosassa Springs State Wildlife Park. Educational programs here focus on black bear, manatee, alligators, bobcats, and birds. View the springs through an underwater window. If you want to see the mermaid show at Weeki Wachee, it's not far south of here off US 19. One of the state's oldest attractions, it's a beautiful underwater ballet.

Resuming our trip up the Gulf Coast, we continue north on US 19 and turn west on FL 24 toward Cedar Key. Imagine this sleepy hamlet before the Civil War, when it was one of Florida's busiest ports. The state's first railroad ran from here to Fernandina Beach, also a major port. Because of its salt industry, Cedar Key was a Union target during the Civil War, when salt was needed to preserve meat. The town's namesake cedar trees were cut down almost to the last matchstick and made into pencils. A couple of devastating hurricanes, along with the changing whims of industry, almost spelled the death of the little community, which now subsists on tourism. Camp, sightsee, tour the museums, fish, and shop the galleries and boutiques. Return to US 19 on FL 347 through wetlands and along the Suwannee River.

Once back on US 19 continue north with as many side trips as you have time to take. A dozen roads lead west from the highway to dead-end at the Gulf, and they are excellent for wildlife watching or fishing. Beaches and communities are few, however. For example, you might take FL 51 out to Steinhatchee for a look and some fishing, returning to the highway on FL 361. The snowy beaches of the Panhandle await, so don't dally.

Still traveling on US 19, enter Florida's summer playground, where winter is low season and summer is the time for water sports. At Perry, the Tree Capital of the South, visit the forestry museum. It's of interest to any nature lover, and its models of major forest fires make it easier to understand the massive burns that can occur in forests anywhere.

Leave US 19 behind here. US 98 is now the chief route, leading all the way to Pensacola on one of the most scenic drives in the South. For the rest of the journey, you'll never be more than a few footsteps from the Gulf. Take FL 14 off US 98 to Econofina

State Park for excellent fishing as well as the sight of great veils of Spanish moss creating a silver glow in the trees at sunrise and sunset.

Returning to US 98, drive through Newport and then turn left on FL 363 and head south to St. Marks, where seafood is always in season and the famous oyster bars serve raw oysters all winter. Fort San Marcos de Apalachee here was one of the first Spanish outposts along the coast; later, Andrew Jackson rallied his troops here on his way to fight Indians. See the museum and enjoy the wildlife sightings. It's all part of St. Marks National Wildlife Refuge.

Camping is available at Ochlockonee River State Park (850-962-2771), just north of US 98 and south of Sopchoppy on US 319. The park is on the south edge of Apalachicola National Forest, which offers more camping, canoeing, and nature watching if you want to head inland at this point. This trip sticks with the coastal route and its white satin beaches, however. At Eastpoint, take the toll bridge to St. George Island State Park (850-927-2111). This finger of land offers miles of pristine beaches, a full-service campground, and fishing on both the Gulf and the bay.

Relax in a breezy, riverfront setting once fortified by the Spanish. Today the reeds make a good fishing spot for shore birds.

Apalachicola has dozens of historic mansions.

Apalachicola

Continue west on US 98 to Apalachicola, a name that is often paired with oysters, which are harvested here by the ton September through April (it's easy to remember that oysters are harvested only in months containing an R: not May, June, July, or August). The town's first fortunes were made in timber and cotton. The old cotton warehouses can still be seen downtown, and block after block of grand old homes remain from the town's glory days. Few are open to the public; enjoy strolling the streets as you imagine them in another time.

How these same streets must have buzzed with wagons when Apalachicola was a major seaport. How horrifying they must have been when another "yellow jack" epidemic broke out. How frightening they must have been during World War II when ships were regularly torpedoed in the Gulf. In 1942, a British oil tanker was sunk by a German submarine just off Cape San Blas. Volunteers from Apalachicola rushed out in their own boats to pick up survivors, rescuing fourteen of the forty-seven crew members who had been aboard.

Tip:
The dividing line between Eastern and Central time zones is roughly the Apalachicola River, west of Tallahassee. If you have time-sensitive appointments in this area, be sure to verify the zone in which you're traveling.

Dr. John Gorrie, a local physician, invented a primitive cooling machine during a yellow fever epidemic in the 1840s. It was a forerunner of the refrigerators and air conditioners that today make Florida livable in summer. On Gorrie Square, visit the small museum that houses a replica of Gorrie's ice machine as well as a church that was built in the north and transported by riverboat to Apalachicola and reassembled.

Event:
The Apalachicola Seafood Festival in early November features feasting, oyster shucking contest, and the blessing of the fleet.

Shop the old downtown area for antiques and souvenirs. Sail with Apalachicola Eco-Ventures (850-653-2593) up the river into the swamps or across the bay to barrier islands. It's a good chance to see the enormous variety of plant, bird, and fish life in an estuarine environment. Sail on an authentic tall ship, the *Governor Stone*, which is a Gulf Coast schooner that was built in 1877. A project of the Apalachicola Marine Museum, she has been lovingly restored (call 850-653-8700 for more information and hours). Leave Apalachicola on US 98.

Head West

Port St. Joe, 34 miles (54.4 km) from Apalachicola, is barely a blip on today's scene. It was a rich cotton port early in the 1800s, however, when it was the site of the state's first constitutional convention. The majority of the town's population died in a yellow fever epidemic, which was followed by a fire that destroyed much of the town. A hurricane-spawned tidal wave finished the town off, covering much of the ruins in sand. Visit the small museum here.

If you need a place to camp, don't go directly to Port St. Joe; rather, take FL 30, which parallels the shore, then FL 30E out a narrow sand spit to St. Joseph Peninsula State Park (850-227-1327). In busy seasons, it has campfire programs and guided nature walks.

From Port St. Joe, resume course on US 98 to Panama City. The city has amusements and rides and is also the site of St. Andrews State Recreation Area, a 1,260-acre preserve with long fishing piers, a boat ramp, and jetties where you can also fish. Picnic overlooking the Gulf of Mexico or the Grand Lagoon. From here to Destin, stop almost anywhere to hit the beach for a jog, or a game of Frisbee. Play 126 holes of championship golf in this area. Shop quaint art galleries, feast on fresh seafood, pick up seashells and history, and bask in sea breezes. The seascape is an artist's or photographer's dream.

At Point Washington (north off US 98 on FL 395), Eden State Gardens are open daily, 8 A.M. to sundown, and the mansion is open for tours Thursday through Monday, 9 A.M. to 4 P.M. Among the estate's treasures is the largest collection of Louis XVI furniture in any one room in the United States. Return to US 98 to continue the journey.

At Grayton Beach on FL 30A, you'll pass Monet, Monet, a re-creation of Claude Monet's home and garden in Giverny, France. It's open to the public free on Wednesdays. Grayton Beach State Recre-

Sea Dream **was one of the boats that rescued sailors stranded when their ships were torpedoed off Apalachicola by German U-boats.**

Along the way, stop at roadside markers. This one tells the story of a town that once grew up along the coast not far from today's highway. Nothing remains but a cemetery.

ation Area (850-231-4210) is a 356-acre park with camping, surf fishing, a boat ramp on Western Lake, and a white sand beach on the Gulf of Mexico. The park is located on FL 30A, south of US 98. Ask rangers for a map to the self-guided nature trails. When you're ready, continue west on US 98.

Gulf Islands National Seashore

You've seen some breathtaking beaches by now—including some that appear on every top ten list of the world's most beautiful beaches—but it's still impossible to be blasé about this endless strand of sugar sand and the jade-green water that edges it. Gulf Islands National Seashore (south of Pensacola on US 98) covers about 96,000 acres, some of them on offshore islands, some on the mainland, and some next door in Alabama and Mississippi. Most of the services and sightseeing are around Fort Pickens, which has a 200-site campground (850-934-2621). One of a series of brick forts that were built around the Florida coastline after the War of 1812, this brick giant is

filled with dark passages and echoing dungeons. The great war chief Geronimo was imprisoned here.

Headquartering at a campground, explore Gulf Islands National Seashore on day trips. Swim at Johnson Beach on Perdido Key, a 247-acre barrier island. Surf cast for pompano, sea trout, and mackerel. Picnic at Naval Live Oaks, which is off US 98 east of Gulf Breeze. Now part of the national seashore, it is a plantation of live oaks that were planted for use in warships. Long before the oaks matured, iron ships came into use. Historic fortifications on board Pensacola Naval Air Station are also part of the national seashore, and there are rest rooms, a visitor center, displays, and a nature trail at Fort Barrancas on the station.

Ready for some city life? Sightseeing in Pensacola can occupy a couple of pleasant days. Walk, walk, walk. See museums, the old rail depot (now a hotel lobby), art galleries, and a galaxy of old neighborhoods filled with fine mansions.

Pensacola is also the home of the Blue Angels and the world's largest collection of naval war birds at the National Museum of Naval Aviation on board Pensacola Naval Air Station. The museum is southwest of downtown via well-marked routes. Admission is free. If you're an aviation buff, you'll need an entire day to see all the displays indoors and out. If not, give it a couple of hours. There's plenty to entertain both children and adults.

Event:
Pensacola's Blue Angels Air Show is in November.

From Pensacola, Interstate 10 provides clear sailing east and west. If you want only to get back to your starting point in Tampa as quickly as possible, take the interstate at least as far as US 19 east of Tallahassee; then decide whether to retrace your route on US 19 or continue to Interstate 75 for an easy, quick route.

CHAPTER 19

A Louisiana Celebration
Sugar, Cajun Spice, and Everything Nice

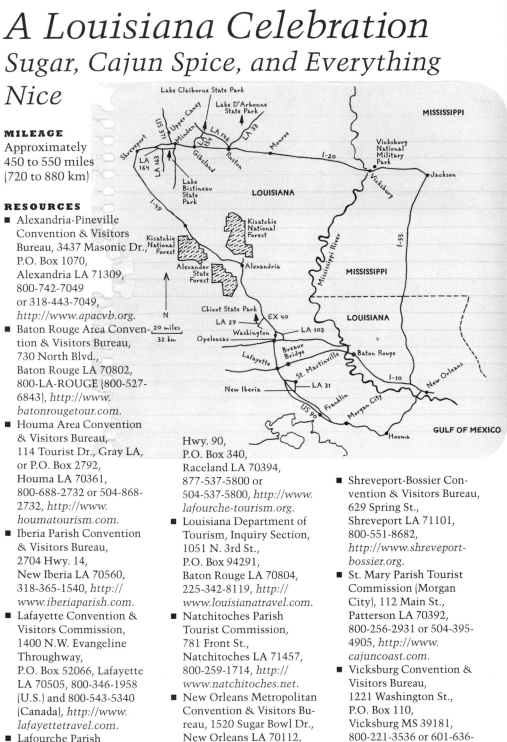

MILEAGE

Approximately
450 to 550 miles
(720 to 880 km)

RESOURCES

- Alexandria-Pineville
  Convention & Visitors
  Bureau, 3437 Masonic Dr.,
  P.O. Box 1070,
  Alexandria LA 71309,
  800-742-7049
  or 318-443-7049,
  http://www.apacvb.org.
- Baton Rouge Area Convention & Visitors Bureau,
  730 North Blvd.,
  Baton Rouge LA 70802,
  800-LA-ROUGE (800-527-
  6843), *http://www.
  batonrougetour.com.*
- Houma Area Convention
  & Visitors Bureau,
  114 Tourist Dr., Gray LA,
  or P.O. Box 2792,
  Houma LA 70361,
  800-688-2732 or 504-868-
  2732, *http://www.
  houmatourism.com.*
- Iberia Parish Convention
  & Visitors Bureau,
  2704 Hwy. 14,
  New Iberia LA 70560,
  318-365-1540, *http://
  www.iberiaparish.com.*
- Lafayette Convention &
  Visitors Commission,
  1400 N.W. Evangeline
  Throughway,
  P.O. Box 52066, Lafayette
  LA 70505, 800-346-1958
  (U.S.) and 800-543-5340
  (Canada), *http://www.
  lafayettetravel.com.*
- Lafourche Parish
  Tourist Commission,
  Louisiana, Hwy. 1 at U.S.

Hwy. 90,
P.O. Box 340,
Raceland LA 70394,
877-537-5800 or
504-537-5800, *http://www.
lafourche-tourism.org.*

- Louisiana Department of
  Tourism, Inquiry Section,
  1051 N. 3rd St.,
  P.O. Box 94291,
  Baton Rouge LA 70804,
  225-342-8119, *http://
  www.louisianatravel.com.*
- Natchitoches Parish
  Tourist Commission,
  781 Front St.,
  Natchitoches LA 71457,
  800-259-1714, *http://
  www.natchitoches.net.*
- New Orleans Metropolitan
  Convention & Visitors Bureau, 1520 Sugar Bowl Dr.,
  New Orleans LA 70112,
  800-672-6124, *http://
  www.neworleanscvb.com.*

- Shreveport-Bossier Con-
  vention & Visitors Bureau,
  629 Spring St.,
  Shreveport LA 71101,
  800-551-8682,
  *http://www.shreveport-
  bossier.org.*
- St. Mary Parish Tourist
  Commission (Morgan
  City), 112 Main St.,
  Patterson LA 70392,
  800-256-2931 or 504-395-
  4905, *http://www.
  cajuncoast.com.*
- Vicksburg Convention &
  Visitors Bureau,
  1221 Washington St.,
  P.O. Box 110,
  Vicksburg MS 39181,
  800-221-3536 or 601-636-
  9421, *http://www.
  vicksburgcvb.org.*

A Gumbo of Fun

Louisiana makes for a magical trip that combines three distinct areas: Cajun country, the exotic French accent of New Orleans, and the old Dixie flavor of the northern half of the state. Nowhere in the nation will you find more succulent, spicy seafood, more jubilant music and dance, or a better nature show. Our trip begins and ends in New Orleans, but we have two options. One ends the trip after a romp across the bayous to see the fabulous bird life. The second option takes us to Baton Rouge, then west again for a northern swing ending in Vicksburg, Mississippi, and then south along the Mississippi River back to the Big Easy.

Coming to Cajun Country

It has been more than three hundred years since its founding in 1699, but Louisiana has never forgotten its French roots. For the RV traveler, this means a spicy feast of festivals, music, people watching, and good times plus a rich and varied nature show in some of the south's most unusual terrain. Don't worry about filling your pantry before this trip. If you love Cajun food, this is the place to eat out three times a day, dance the night away, and then slather a big, puffy buttermilk biscuit with huckleberry jam for a late-night snack.

Our trip begins in New Orleans, one of

For More Information

Louisiana has nine state welcome centers, one at each place an interstate enters the state.

---

the most exciting cities on the planet but also the last place you want to drive an RV. Stay at one of the many area campgrounds where tour buses pick up passengers, such as KOA New Orleans East (800-562-2128) and KOA New Orleans West (800-562-5110). If you want to drive into town, use one of the commercial parking lots along the river.

The Mississippi River is the city's *raison d'être* as well as its leading point of reference. If you come into town from the northeast on Interstate 10, turn south on Canal Street, which takes you to the river between the French Quarter to your left and the central business district to your right. We always start with one or two tours to put us in the Dixieland mood. The St. Charles Street Car Line (504-523-4662) allows hopping on and off at ten points of interest. Gray Line (800-535-7786) offers a Plantation Tour and a Swamp Tour, as well as a Garden District Walking Tour. The steamboat *Natchez* (800-233-2628) does two-hour harbor cruises with jazz by day and dinner-jazz cruises by night. Dinner-jazz cruises are also offered by the *Creole*

The French Quarter in New Orleans is Lousiana's most-visited site.

LOUISIANA TRICENTENNIAL COMMISSION

Queen and the *Cajun Queen* (800-445-4109).

Along the riverfront, which is a non-stop street fair, take the Aquarium/Zoo cruise, see Jacksonville Brewery with its fifty shops and restaurants, have coffee and a beignet in the Cafe du Monde, shop the farmers market, and amble the streets of the French Quarter soaking up local color. The city offers many swamp tours, but you'll have opportunities later to see the outdoors on your own. While you're here, concentrate on attractions found in the Queen City and nowhere else.

When you're ready to venture outside the city, head southwest on US 90 through beautiful bayous, keeping an eye out for bird sightings: acadian flycatchers, kingbirds, woodpeckers, martins and swallows, vultures, and a world of waterfowl and shorebirds. This is the largest wetlands in the United States, a natural wonderland alive with buzzing insects, marine life, beavers, black bears, white-tailed deer, muskrats, and snakes galore. Lowlands sparkle with waters that range from mere puddles to sprawling lakes. They're dotted

Event:
Depending on the dates of Lent, you may be in the area during Mardi Gras in late winter. It's a blowout of epic proportions, not just in New Orleans but almost everywhere in Cajun country.

with islands filled with stands of tupelo, willow, and cypress trees draped in Spanish moss. Waters may be choked with water hyacinth, a beautiful nuisance. Live oaks dominate some landscapes, their trunks twisted and sculpted by the wind. Dozens of bird species make their year-round homes in southern Louisiana. Others—including cattle egrets, ducks, gallinules, geese, and coots—come for the winter.

Most of the sightseeing in the bayous hinges on swamp tours, which is fine with us because nature is always filled with surprises, making every tour different. The Cajun Man's Swamp Cruise (504-868-4625) features Rob Guidry, who is an excellent nature guide and can sing and play a Cajun squeeze box.

You'll have plenty of tours to choose from here, all of them through wetlands alive with birdsong, flopping fish, sunning gators, and swooping waterfowl. Thousands of acres here are under wildlife management, and most of them can be reached only by boat or float plane, so we do recommend taking a tour. Even if you bring your own boat or canoe, which is a good idea on this loop, a local guide is invaluable.

Beautiful Bayou Country

Continuing southwest on US 90, visit Southdown Plantation in Houma. This Victorian manor house filled with history exhibits is open daily except Sunday and Monday. If you happen to be here in October, don't miss the Downtown on the Bayou Festival, which takes over Houma's historic downtown area.

US 90, one of the state's most beautiful

LOUISIANA TRICENTENNIAL COMMISSION

Mardi Gras in New Orleans.

drives, continues to Morgan City, which is mostly surrounded by the 137,000-acre Atchafalaya Wildlife Management Area (318-373-0032) and the 26,000-acre Attakapas Wildlife Management Area (318-948-0255). Both can be accessed by boat only.

For history buffs, Morgan City has the Turn of the Century House downtown. It is furnished to show family life in the early 1900s, and it also has an extensive collection of Mardi Gras costumes. While in this city, also visit the International Petroleum Museum with its oil rig exhibits. It's closed Sunday.

From Morgan City, follow the Old Spanish Trail (US 90 or LA 182) to Franklin, and tour the Grevemberg House Museum in the center of town. A Greek Revival townhouse built before the Civil War, it's filled with period furnishings, toys, and artifacts. Oaklawn Manor is another Greek Revival masterpiece dating to 1837. Both mansions are open every day.

Visit St. Mary's Episcopal Church, built in 1872; Asbury Methodist Church, built in 1838; and the stunning Victorian St. Mary Bank & Trust Building, built in 1898. One of the most picturesque towns in Acadiana, Franklin is surrounded by plantation homes, most of them privately owned and viewable only from the highway. If you're into *Gone with the Wind*–era fantasies, ask locally for maps and take a driving tour of the countryside.

Continue to New Iberia (northwest of Franklin on LA 182), where you'll find America's oldest rice mill, Konriko. Take a guided tour, and shop for Cajun foods and crafts. Also visit the Rip Van Winkle Gardens on Jefferson Island in Lake Peigneur. Something will be in bloom during your visit, even on the coldest winter day. Tour Shadows-on-the-Teche, a historic house and museum on East Main Street.

Avery Island and Tabasco

A side trip takes you to Avery Island, where you can see the 250-acre Jungle Gardens and the world-famous Tabasco Pepper Sauce Factory. From New Iberia, take LA 14 West and LA 329 South. Take the free tour to see how the sauce is made, get a free sample, and shop for Tabasco-related souvenirs.

Take LA 31 north from New Iberia to St. Martinville, home of Catfish Heaven Aqua Farm where you can fish for farm-raised catfish. Nearby, a state commemorative area honors Longfellow and his poem *Evangeline*. Do read the poem while you're here to help you understand how Cajuns came to be. In the little downtown, La Maison Duchamp on Main Street offers guided tours of this 1876 home. On Church Square, Petit Paris Museum features exhibits of many Mardi Gras costumes. Arrange a guided tour of St. Martin de Tours Church (103 Main St.). You'll also pass Evangeline Oak, which is at the bayou end of Port Street and surrounded by a pleasant park. Legend has it that the tree was the meeting place of the real Evangeline and her love, Gabriel. When leaving, travel west on LA 96 and join US 90 into Lafayette.

A Choice of Side Trips

For a scenic side trip, drive northwest from Franklin on US 90 and pick up LA 83 from Sorrell to Cypremort, where LA 319 takes you to Cypremort Point on Vermilion Bay. Picnic, fish, or swim off the manmade beach here.

Another option is to head northwest on LA 182 from Franklin to Baldwin and turn right at the sign to Charenton. In Charenton, the Chitimacha Cultural Center is open daily except Sunday. Exhibits tell the story of the Chitimacha tribe, the only Native American tribe in Louisiana that still dwells on its ancestral lands.

Lafayette

Lafayette is the heart of Acadiana, the place where the three areas of Cajun country—prairie, coastal, and bayou—meet. A good place to begin a visit is at Vermillionville, which is across from the airport on US 90 and has plenty of parking for big rigs. Every day, live Cajun music plays while you im-

LOUISIANA TRICENTENNIAL COMMISSION

Acadian Village, Lafayette.

merse yourself in Cajun sounds, sights, and scents. Twice a day, Cajun and Creole cooking demonstrations are held here. Dine in the plantation-style restaurant, see a

What is a *Cajun*?

Early in the 1600s, French settlers streamed into eastern Canada and, by 1604 (fifteen years before the Mayflower *landed) they had a permanent colony in what is now Nova Scotia. When the French lost that part of Canada to the English, the Acadians—who were French and Catholic—were exiled in 1775 because they wouldn't swear allegiance to the Crown and the Anglican church. Their story is best told in Longfellow's epic poem* Evangeline. *They made their way to the Louisiana Territory, which was French, and in time the name* Acadian *was corrupted to* Cajun.*

The Acadian refugees got a cold reception from Louisiana's French aristocrats, so they scattered into the bayous and settled in several pockets. They had little communication with Anglos or one another. Thus, there is no single Cajun language, music, or culture; instead, there are several. What the groups have in common is a love of tradition, family, mass on Sunday, and the Saturday night fais-do-do. Come on and join the party!

gallery of local arts, shop the bakery, learn Cajun history from guides in traditional dress, and take to the dance floor.

To reach Chretien Point Plantation from Lafayette, drive 5 miles (8 km) west on Interstate 10 to LA 93, then 11 miles (17.6 km) north to Parish Road 356. Head west to Chretien Point Road, then drive north 1 mile (1.6 km). The grand staircase at the Plantation was copied for the film *Gone with the Wind*. Take a boat trip into the swamps to photograph nature scenes and watch for birds. Walk 3.5 miles (5.6 km) of nature trails at Acadian Park (1201 E. Alexander St.), and explore Acadian Village (5 miles/8 km south of Lafayette on US 167), which depicts Cajun life in the nineteenth century.

At the Acadian Culture Center in Jean Lafitte National Park, view a film and displays that help sort out the different colonies of Acadians who settled the bayous, prairie, and coastline. Don't miss the Cathedral of St. John the Evangelist (914 St. John St.), a Dutch Romanesque treasure with a museum, a historic cemetery, and a good gift shop. It's open to tourists on weekdays only. Off US 90, 50 miles (80 km) south of downtown, the city also has a 45-acre zoo with more than 750 rare and exotic animals.

Just east of Lafayette off Interstate 10 at

Breaux Bridge, stop at the visitor center at 314 East Bridge Street. Pick up information about attractions, dance halls, and restaurants here in the Crawfish Capital of the World. Take time to visit Lynch Botanical Gardens and Bird Sanctuary. From Breaux Bridge, head east on Interstate 10—stopping to fish the Atchafalaya River along the way—to Baton Rouge, the state capital.

A Cajun Christmas

The Christmas holidays are celebrated in Catholic Louisiana with more reverence, light, and tradition than almost anywhere else. Early in December, Lafayette holds its Christmas Parade. Mamou holds its parade mid-December, and Carencro's War Veterans Christmas Parade is just before Christmas. Almost every church and museum has candlelight, caroling, special displays, lighted trails, and much more. Of special interest are the Festival of the Bonfires in Gramercy, Cajun Christmas in Lafayette, and the Christmas Festival of Lights in Natchitoches.

Baton Rouge

The glitz of the casinos has eclipsed a lot of Baton Rouge's old French charm, but the timeless nature show plays on in the swamplands. At the BREC Bluebonnet Swamp Nature Center (10503 N. Oak Hill Pkwy.), walk nature trails and view educational exhibits. The nature center is closed Mondays.

By now you know that this isn't a where-to-eat guide, but the Culinary Arts Institute of Louisiana/Caila's Fine Cuisine is a unique chance to dine on gourmet food prepared by student chefs and served at affordable prices. Parking is no problem for an RV. For more information, call 800-927-0839 or 504-343-6233.

While you're in Baton Rouge, visit the Enchanted Mansion Doll Museum (190 Lee Dr.), the Old State Capitol (which dates to 1850 and has a grand view of the river), Magnolia Mound Plantation with its 1790s French Creole home, and the Old Arsenal Museum (Riverside Mall and Spanishtown

Rd.). The old powder magazine here was built in the 1830s. At Interstate 10 and Essen Lane, the Rural Life Museum has more than twenty buildings from the pre-industrial age and 25 acres of gardens filled with greenery and statuary. It's open daily. Seek out the USS *Kidd* on River Road. It's a restored World War II destroyer, museum, veterans memorial, and gift shop.

The Northern Route

From Baton Rouge, it's a short hop back to New Orleans on Interstate 10, but Louisiana isn't finished with you yet. If you have time now or in the future for an entirely different tour, head west from Baton Rouge on US 190 out of Cajun country into a countryside that is more southern, more likely to be Protestant than Catholic, higher and dryer, and spread with great expanses of state parks and national forest land.

Stop at Opelousas to see the Jim Bowie Museum at US 190 and Academy Street. Memorabilia here includes items owned by Jim Bowie, a frontiersman best known for designing the 15-inch (38 cm) Bowie knife that was an all-purpose tool and weapon in early America (the knife is also credited to his brother Rezin Bowie). Nearby, the What Bayou Trading Company is a folk-art gallery housed in an 1850 law office.

Just north of Opelousas on LA 103, Washington is a river town filled with buildings that date to between 1760 and 1835. Drive through, or get out and walk. Continue north on Interstate 49 and take the LA 29 exit; follow signs from here to Chicot State Park. Hike 6,000 acres of woodlands, fish a stocked, 2,000-acre lake, swim, boat, and see 150 species of trees in the Louisiana State Arboretum. Return to Interstate 49 and continue north.

Tip:
Louisiana has superb hunting and fishing. For information on seasons and licenses, contact the Louisiana Department of Wildlife and Fisheries, Information Section, Box 98000, Baton Rouge Louisiana 70898.

Alexandria, the next stop, was the focus of the bitter Red River campaign during the Civil War, which resulted in the burning of the city. Still, some historic highlights remain. Visit Kent Plantation House, a 1796 Creole raised cottage on Bayou Rapides Road off US 165/71. It's open all winter and features open-hearth-cooking demonstrations on Wednesdays.

You're now at the threshold of the 600,000-acre Kisatchie National Forest, where you can hike a 31-mile (49.6 km) trail through pine and hardwoods. Neither the wild azaleas nor the white dogwoods will be in bloom now, but the dogwoods will be covered with bright red berry-like drupes. The forest almost surrounds Alexandria. Its headquarters are at 2500 Shreveport Highway, Pineville (318-445-9396). Camp at KOA Alexandria (800-562-5640 or 318-445-5227), which is on Kincaid Lake, said to be one of the area's best fishing holes. Avid anglers also like Fish 'N Heaven RV Park (318-448-9269), which has several stocked fishing ponds.

Alexander State Forest Wildlife Management Area and Indian Creek Recreation Area are also in this area, covering more than 10,000 acres and offering camping, boating, fishing, and hunting. Continue northwest on Interstate 49 to Natchitoches.

Natchitoches

Can you pronounce *Natchitoches*? As close as we can come is *NACK-a-tush*, but you'll make a new friend if you seek out a friendly native and take a lesson on how to pronounce the name of this town, which is Louisiana's original French colony. The town's name is said to be an Indian word meaning "Place of the Paw-Paw." Folks

have been living here since 1714, when a French trading post was established to trade with the Indians and the Spanish.

Take a walking tour of the historic downtown along the Cane River on Jefferson Street, Front Street, and Second Street, starting at the Bust of St. Denis at the end of Lafayette Street. Here at the information office, you can pick up a free brochure describing the tour. You'll pass the restored Ducournau Square, dating to 1830, the 1870 La Costa Building with its cast-iron balconies, and many other historic sites.

Longleaf Trail

In Natchitoches, you're still surrounded by Kisatchie National Forest, and you're never far from a state park, campground, hiking trail, fishing lake, or picnic area. For an awe-inspiring side trip, take LA 6 west of Natchitoches to the Longleaf Trail National Forest Scenic Byway. Drive 17 miles (27.2 km) of sandstone sculptures, mesas, bluffs, and buttes through some of the state's most dramatic scenery.

Return to the Natchitoches area to visit Magnolia Plantation Home, built in 1753, and Melrose Plantation, which has two homes built in 1796 and 1833 respectively. Both sites are open every afternoon. Tour Beau Fort Plantation, built about 1790, to see the antique furnishings and splendid gardens. Downtown, the Old Courthouse Museum, which was built in 1869, houses historic relics from the parish. Open Tuesday to Saturday, it's the state's only courthouse museum.

See more history just by walking or driving the streets past antebellum homes that are either privately owned or have been turning into bed-and-breakfast inns. Spend pleasant hours strolling the historic downtown to see antique shops, restaurants, and art galleries. The Christmas lights along the Cane River are lit from early December through the New Year. The tradition begins on the first Saturday of December with a parade, fireworks, and a street party. Try to be here then.

Event:
On the first Saturday in January, Natchitoches holds a jazz and R&B festival on four stages along the banks of the Cane River.

Melrose Plantation is a classic example of French Colonial architecture.

Shreveport

The drive northwest on Interstate 49 now takes you to Shreveport, which was named for Henry Shreve, the man who opened the log-jammed Red River to navigation in 1835. As a river town—and later as an oil and gas center—the city thrived. The Ark-La-Tex Antique & Classical Vehicle Museum, housed in an original, 1920 car dealership, has more than fifty vintage vehicles plus fire trucks and firefighting memorabilia. Next door is the Spring Street Historical Museum, so plan several hours at each place.

The sightseeing menu in Shreveport also includes the Meadows Museum of Art, the R. W. Norton Art Gallery with its works on the American West, the Sci-Port Discovery Center with hands-on exhibits for children, the Spring Street Historical Museum, and concerts by the Shreveport Symphony, which are given September through May. See what's playing while you're in the area. Shreveport is also the home of the American Rose Society's own 118-acre garden, a showplace of roses that bloom well into December. Between the late roses and the early bulbs, something will probably be in bloom during your visit.

Stretch your legs in C. Bickham Diskcon Park (70th St.), where you can

hike nature trails in the hush of winter. Northwest of the city on LA 1, Soda Lake Wildlife Management Area covers 1,300 acres. Its observation tower is an ideal place to watch for the flocks of waterfowl that are found here in winter.

The American Rose Center, Shreveport.

Event:

In November, Christmas in Roseland opens in Shreveport.

Eastward Bound

From Shreveport, travel east on Interstate 20 to the Minden area, where you can decide whether to head north to Caney Lakes Recreation Area, which is off LA 159 and part of Kisatchie National Forest, or south to Lake Bistineau State Park, a 750-acre preserve surrounded by pine forest and centered by a sparkling lake. To reach Lake Bistineau, drive 3 miles (4.8 km) south of Minden on US 371, turn right on LA 164 and, in about 5 miles (8 km), turn left on LA 163 toward the park.

Another Season, Another Reason

We've made this a winter trip and bird sightings are abundant now, but consider coming back in spring or fall to drive the Creole Nature National Scenic Byway through what Wildbird magazine calls one of the top forty birding spots in North America: the Mississippi Flyway. Thousands of acres of oak forests form wildlife refuges that are home to more than two million birds, which represent dozens of species including rare and accidental species. The byway is also a route to some of the Gulf's best beaches, campgrounds, launch ramps, and fishing spots. For a map and description, contact the Southwest Louisiana Convention & Visitors Bureau, 1211 North Lakeshore Drive, Lake Charles LA 70601, 800-456-SWLA (800-456-7952) or 318-436-9588.

If you choose Caney Lakes Recreation Area, hike or mountain bike the 7.6-mile (12.2 km) trail that circles Upper Caney Lake. Camping is also available at Lake Claiborne State Park (888-677-2524), which is northeast of Minden a short distance

from the interstate (take the Gibsland exit, LA 154, and go north to LA 146), and also at Lake D'Arbonne State Park at Farmersville (888-677-5200). Take LA 33 northeast from the Ruston exit to reach Lake D'Arbonne. To return, backtrack to Interstate 20 and travel east to Monroe for historic sightseeing.

In Monroe, tour the Biedenharn mansion. The home was built by Joseph Biedenharn, the first person to bottle Coca-Cola. Also on the estate are gardens, a Bible museum, and a conservatory filled with foliage and blooming ixora, bougainvillea, peace lilies, and plumbago. The Biedenharn mansion is open daily except Monday at no charge.

Event:

Each January, the Bagwell Antique Show is held at the Vicksburg Convention Center (1600 Mulberry St.).

See Layton Castle, which is also called Mulberry Grove. It's on the National Register of Historic Properties and is filled with nineteenth-century antiques. Call 318-325-1952 or 318-322-4869 for directions and an appointment. Visit Rebecca's Doll House (4500 Bon Aire Dr.), which contains more than two thousand dolls, and the Louisiana Purchase Gardens and Zoo (Bernstein Park Dr.)—ride the miniature train to see exotic animals in natural habitats, then walk winding paths under moss-draped live oaks.

Nature lovers will enjoy the Ouachita Wildlife Management Area southeast of Monroe off LA 841. The hardwood bottomland forest covers almost 9,000 acres and offers hunting and fishing in season. The Russell Sage Wildlife Management Area on the Bayou Lafourche floodplain, is in two parcels near Monroe. They make up a 17,280-acre wilderness where you can hunt, hike, fish, camp, and train your binoculars on a world of bird life.

Vicksburg, Mississippi

When you're ready to move on, Interstate 20 takes you across the Mississippi River to Vicksburg, Mississippi, one of the nation's most historic and beautiful sightseeing treasures. Stop at the Mississippi Welcome Center near the state border for a wealth of brochures and information. The more you love history, the richer your visit will be—but Vicksburg has something for everyone. Keep an eye out for one of the steam paddle wheelers that ply Ol' Man River. With luck you'll get a glimpse of the *Delta Queen*, *American Queen*, or *Mississippi Queen*, calliopes wheezing as they churn up- or downstream. Local boat excursions are available in town, but these three steamboats take passengers only by the week or longer.

During the Civil War, Vicksburg took weeks of merciless pounding. Union forces knew that defeating Vicksburg was the key to defeating the Confederacy. A surprising number of antebellum mansions survived, however, so spend several days touring them and losing yourself in a Scarlett O'Hara time warp. Like so many other cities along the Mississippi, Vicksburg has been transformed by casino gambling. You'll have your choice of history hunting, gambling and nightlife (some campgrounds run free shuttles to the casinos), or the same hunting, fishing, and hiking that has always been a part of river life.

Warm, sunny days are plentiful here, so spend one of them at Vicksburg National Military Park (US 80 at Interstate 20). The park is quieter in winter, when there are no living history performances and firing of cannon and muskets. This peaceful air makes a visit even more poignant as you ponder the thousands of troops who died here while Union forces fought, foot by foot, toward Confederate strongholds. Take the self-guided tour, which has fifteen stops with signs describing almost to the minute what happened at each point. Tour the USS *Cairo* here, a gunboat that sank in 1862. For more than a century it was preserved deep in the mud of the Yazoo River. When it was finally raised, it yielded a fortune in artifacts frozen in time. The artifacts and the ship itself are a triumph of restoration.

In town and the surrounding area, walk past mansions, stately antebellum churches, and the 1858 Greek Revival courthouse, now a superb museum. See the Biedenharn Candy Shop where Coca-Cola was first bottled (it's a delightful museum), and tour the Waterways Experiment Station of the U.S. Army Corps of Engineers. The station is on Hall's Ferry Road, 2 miles (3.2 km) south of Interstate 20. The whole family will be fascinated by the miniature models of America's major rivers, which are used by the Corps in determining future dams and other waterway management.

The trip at an end, get back on Interstate 20 and turn south at Jackson on Interstate 55, which leads back to New Orleans in a few hours.

The Civil War battlefield at Vicksburg.

CHAPTER 20

Florida to the Tip
Going All the Way South

MILEAGE
Approximately 1,000 miles (1,600 km)

RESOURCES
- Central Florida Visitors & Convention Bureau, P.O. Box 61, Cypress Gardens FL 33884, 800-828-7655 or 863-324-2111, *http://www.cfdc. org/tourism.*
- Convention & Visitors Bureau of Highlands County, 309 S. Circle, P.O. Box 2001, Sebring FL 33871, 800-255-1711 or 863-385-8448, *http://www. sebringflchamber.com.*
- De Soto County Chamber of Commerce, 16 S. Volusia Ave., Arcadia FL 34266, 863-494-4033.
- Greater Miami Convention & Visitors Bureau, 701 Brickell Ave. Suite 2700, Miami FL 33131, 800-933-8448 or 305-539-3000, *http://www. tropicoolmiami.com.*
- Kissimmee–St. Cloud Convention & Visitors Bureau, 1925 E. Irlo Bronson Hwy., Kissimmee FL 34744, 800-327-9159 or 407-847-5000, *http://www. floridakiss.com.*
- Lake Wales Area Chamber of Commerce, 340 W. Central Ave., Lake Wales FL 33853, 863-676-3445, *http://www. lakewaleschamber.com.*
- Monroe County Tourist Development Council for Florida Keys and Key West, 3406 N. Roosevelt Blvd. Suite 201,

Key West FL 33040, 800-FLA-KEYS (800-352-5397) or 305-296-1552, *http:// www.fla-keys.com.*

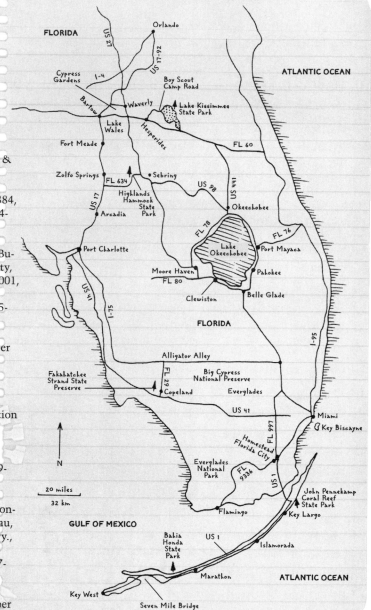

- Orlando–Orange County Convention & Visitors Bureau, 6700 Forum Dr. Suite 100, Orlando FL 32821, 800-551-0181 or 407-363-5872, *http://www.go2orlando.com.*
- Tropical Everglades Visitor Center, 160 U.S. Hwy. 1, Florida City FL 33034, 305-245-9180, *http://www.tropicaleverglades.com.*
- Visit Florida, 661 E. Jefferson St. Suite 300, Tallahassee FL 32301, 888-7FLA-USA (888-735-2872), *http://www.flausa.com.*

Orlando and Theme Park Mania

Walt Disney World is the most-visited tourist attraction in the world, a wonderland of four (soon to be five) major theme parks, three eye-popping water parks, thousands of hotel rooms, hundreds of dining venues, championship golf courses, and its own campground, Fort Wilderness (407-934-7639), complete with petting zoo, heated swimming pools, in-line skating trail, pony rides, nightly Disney movies and campfire program, restaurants, lounge, dinner show, and lake. If the campground is too big to cover on foot, rent a bicycle or a golf cart.

Fort Wilderness offers campsites, including a special section for RV campers with pets, and on-site "lodges" where you can rent a stationary RV with sleeping room for six plus a kitchen and full bath. From your campsite here, ride the free Disney transportation network to Epcot, the Magic Kingdom, Disney-MGM Studios, Typhoon Lagoon, Blizzard Beach, Discovery Island, Downtown Disney for nighttime fun, and hundreds of places to shop and dine. It's the easiest and most economical way to visit Walt Disney World. You just hop on the bus; day-trippers must drive in, pay to park their RVs, and then walk to the tram that takes them to the toll gates.

Once you've had your fill of Disney, you'll find far more economical accommodations at the campgrounds of the Kissimmee area, which is handy to all the other theme parks and sightseeing here. Universal Studios comprises two colossal theme parks and a nighttime entertainment complex. Plan a couple of days at Sea World to see polar bears, penguins, manatees, sharks, and a wealth of other aquatic animals. Sea World also offers a Polynesian luau dinner and show nightly as well as one of the area's best playgrounds for kids. This entire region is filled with thrilling water parks, attractions galore, and a number of shopping-

A visit to Walt Disney World should be part of a Florida vacation. Spend a day at each theme park, starting with the Magic Kingdom and its enchanting Main Street.

dining-entertainment centers, such as Mercado, Church Street Exchange, Downtown Disney, and Pointe Orlando.

Tip:
Our book **Florida Guide** (Open Road Publishing) is not a camping guide, but it is a comprehensive guide to restaurants, sightseeing, tours, fishing guides, water-sports rentals, and much more that cannot be covered here.

If you're not a theme-park fan, the City Beautiful (Orlando) has a rich choice of cultural sightseeing including a Shakespeare Festival, professional opera and ballet companies, symphony, art and history museums, a superb science museum with lots of hands-on fun for children, and the Charles Hosmer Morse Museum of Art, which houses the world's most comprehensive collection of the works of Louis Comfort Tiffany. Another attraction, The *Titanic*: Ship of Dreams, contains dozens of artifacts from the ship, plus memorabilia and a full-size reproduction of the grand staircase.

Take the kids to Green Meadows Petting Farm, Gatorland, and HorseWorld with its petting zoo and pony rides. Take an airboat ride. Canoe the Wekiva River. Go fishing for trophy bass. Go horseback riding at a working cattle ranch. Go northeast on Interstate 4 to Daytona Beach to see the NASCAR displays at Daytona USA, or head out to DeLeon Springs north of DeLand on US 17 to go bird watching at Lake Woodruff Wildlife Preserve. Swim in the sweet waters of Blue Springs, Wekiva Springs, and DeLeon Springs. Blue Springs north of Orlando on US 17/92 in Orange City is the winter home of manatee, who

Cypress Gardens.

come in from the cold in January and February to live in the 72°F waters here.

Heading South

Leaving Orlando westbound on Interstate 4, allow a day or more for Cypress Gardens. Take the US 27 South exit to Waverly. A right turn on FL 540 takes you to one of the Sunshine State's oldest tourist attractions. Cypress Gardens dates to the 1930s, but it's as modern as can be now, offering a couple of rides plus dazzling ice and acrobat shows, good restaurants, a butterfly garden, heart-stopping water-ski shows, and acre after acre of glowing gardens that change with the seasons. Aboard a silent electric boat, float through ancient canals past trees that have been here for centuries. The nature show is so beguiling that many locals buy annual tickets and come back day after day.

Leaving Cypress Gardens, return to US 27 and go south to Lake Wales. Bok Tower Gardens is another botanical showplace and the home of a soaring carillon tower built in the 1920s. The tower's songs peal out throughout the day, and the special concerts held here during the full moon are

Event:
Kissimmee holds a rousing bluegrass festival in March. The Silver Spurs Rodeo, one of the most important rodeos in the East, also plays here this month.

Event:

Cypress Gardens' annual Chrysan-
themum Festival features three
million brilliant mums that don't
fade until the Poinsettia Festival
bursts forth in December. Don't
miss Cypress Gardens' Festival
of Lights, which is part of the
poinsettia spectacular and runs
December through early January.

spellbinding. We'll come back through Lake Wales at the end of our tour.

Continuing south on old US 27, you follow one of the state's oldest trails, the original highway through the belly of the state. Pass timeless villages, and gaze out over trackless miles of scrubland roamed by grazing cattle. Most visitors don't realize that Florida has been a major cattle-raising state for centuries. The scrawny, range-fed beeves you see here will be sent north to be

---

City Lights, Cypress Nights

When Cypress Gardens lights its winter fairyland, all of Polk County follows suit. Each community adopts a theme—such as City of Snowflakes, City of Poinsettias, and City of Mistletoe—and for six weeks puts on a nighttime spectacle that is one of the American Bus Association's Top 100 Events. If you'll be in this area between late November and early January, call ahead for a free "City Lights, Cypress Nights" map (800-828-7655 or 941-298-7565).

The festival routes range from only a few blocks in Frostproof to extensive grids of streets in Fort Meade, Haines City, and Eagle Lake. Other communities that participate are Auburndale, Bartow, Davenport, Dundee, Lake Alfred, Lake Wales, Lakeland, Mulberry, Polk City, and Winter Haven. Make the circuits in your RV at your own pace. The route can be done in one night, but it's better to break it up into two or three evenings—plus an entire day and evening at Cypress Gardens to see the poinsettias as well as the lights.

---

fattened on grain before they arrive at the supermarket.

If you're an auto racing fan, plan to arrive in Sebring in March when fifty thousand fans attend the twelve-hour race (call 863-655-1442 or 863-385-8448 for more information). Sebring is also home to Highlands Hammock State Park (2½ miles west of Sebring on FL 634), one of the state's original four state parks established in the 1930s. Thanks to the foresight of early environmentalists, ancient hardwoods and even older cypress trees survive here. Camp in the shade of live oak trees. In season, a tram takes you around the park's eight trails. Get off anywhere you like and hike back. Along the way, watch for whitetail deer, bald eagles, armadillos, and wild hogs. In the lakes and wetlands, keep an eye out for alligators and otters. Trees are alive with songbirds and wild orchids, while raptors swoop overhead. Wear mosquito repellent.

PHOTO BY CARRIE CANFIELD, COURTESY OF FLORIDA STATE PARKS

Highlands Hammock State Park.

Lake Okeechobee

What is the second-largest natural lake in the United States? This is a trick question because—except for Lake Michigan—the Great Lakes are partly in Canada. That leaves Lake Okeechobee, which is totally within the United States, to claim second-biggest status. It's a major recreation resource with legendary fishing, plenty of camping areas and picnic sites, and a sprinkling of communities that time forgot. It is also part of the Okeechobee Waterway that runs from the Atlantic Ocean to the Gulf of Mexico.

When you reach the point where US 27 crosses Fisheating Creek, be sure to pull over and get out the cameras. In season, for as far as the eye can see, fields are blanketed with black-eyed susans in riotous bloom. Locals fish in the creek under a sky filled with puffy clouds. A light breeze blows, sunshine gilds the wildflowers, and cattle graze in the midst of all the splendor. The scene is unforgettable.

Florida Parks with RV Camping

Bahia Honda State Park, 305-872-2353
Biscayne National Park, 305-230-7275
Everglades National Park, 305-242-7700
John Pennekamp Coral Reef State Park,
305-451-1202
Lake Kissimmee State Park, 863-696-1112

If you have an extra day or two, drive around Lake Okeechobee for a trip through history. This enormous saucer once caught all the water that drained from the 3,000-square-mile (7,770 sq. km) Kissimmee River Basin and expelled it into the Everglades. Woods and waters leapt with fish, a lavish supermarket for prehistoric Indian tribes. When these tribes vanished, they left a network of canals. Early Spanish explorers noted the lake's location, but even as late as the Seminole War era of the 1830s, the region was still known in Washington only as terra incognita. Eventually soldiers were sent to build forts in an unforgiving wilderness, and today we can still see the blazes they left on cypress trees.

After the Civil War, settlers began arriving by boat to farm, fish, and hunt alligator. Lakeport, now just a speck on the map, was a flourishing settlement of Belgian and Polish immigrants until it was wiped out in a 1926 hurricane. At Moore Haven, which is on US 27, you can launch a boat, fish, take shots of the stately old courthouse, and visit a small museum with displays depicting the same 1926 hurricane, in which two hundred people drowned here. Continue on US 27 to Clewiston.

The "sweetest little town in America," Clewiston has an excellent museum with relics from the Seminole and sugar eras, plus memorabilia from the early 1940s when British pilots trained near here. The Union Jack still flies over a British-owned cemetery where British dead are buried. Continue on US 27 to the Bolles Hotel at Lake Harbor, where eager land speculators stood on the roof of the hotel, looked out over the lake, and bought submerged land on the promise that it would be drained. The project was doomed by the hurricanes of 1926 and 1928, followed by the stock market crash of 1929. At Belle Glade, a sculpture remembers the two thousand people who drowned in a 1928 hurricane.

From Belle Glade, US 441 leads north along the dike to Pahokee with its rows of royal palms. The town was settled after World War I in a feverish grab for the rich swamplands. Remnants from its glory days include a grand bank (circa 1922) and an abandoned Art Deco–era school. Stately homes situated along the road once were on the lake; today they overlook only the stark, 42-foot (12.8 m) tall Herbert Hoover

The Everglades can be explored by boat, canoe, footpaths, and boardwalks.

Dike, which was built after the disastrous 1926 and 1928 hurricanes.

At Port Mayaca, still on US 441, fish the St. Lucie canal for freshwater and saltwater species. From here follow US 441 to the community of Okeechobee with its regal courthouse and a KOA campground (800-562-7748) that has a nine-hole golf course, planned activities, tennis courts, and a waterfront restaurant.

The best sightseeing on the lake is at the thirty-nine free parks along the way that are marked "Dike Access." Most have picnic tables, rest rooms, and launch ramps; some have campgrounds, marinas, and other facilities as well as historic markers or displays related to the lake's booms and busts. Stop at as many as you can. From Port Mayaca, FL 76 takes you to Interstate 95 or the Florida Turnpike for the plunge southward.

If you choose not to circle Lake Okeechobee and stay on US 27 instead, cross Interstate 75 (also called Alligator Alley), which cuts through the heart of the Everglades and Big Cypress National Preserve, and continue southeast into the outskirts of the megalopolis that is Fort Lauderdale and Miami. The best route to Homestead from here is to take FL 997, which takes off US 27 to the right about 20 miles (32 km) south of Interstate 75, and follow signs.

Tropics Bound

Suddenly the air is warmer and sweeter. You're now in the tropics, where fruits and tender vegetation thrive in frostless winters. Stop at roadside stands to buy tomatoes and strawberries in February and to sample exotic star fruit, blood oranges, and sweet, yellow, juicy Key limes.

To be honest, the next hour or so of driving time through the congestion of the Miami area won't be a day at the beach. You're heading for Homestead, where you can continue down US 1 to the Florida Keys or to Florida City, which is the gateway to Everglades National Park. (We visit the national park on the way back north.) This is the time to see Miami, especially if you have a tow car and can leave your RV in a campground in the suburbs. The city is

---

Key Lime Pie

There are as many recipes for "real" Key lime pie as there are Conchs, which is what Keys natives call themselves. Some insist that the crust be pastry, while others call for a graham-cracker crust. Some say that meringue is traditional, while others argue for whipped cream. The one thing everyone agrees on is that Key limes, which are yellow, should not be confused with larger, green Persian limes. Here's how the pie is made chez Groene—a tart pie that throws together in seconds in any RV galley. (From Janet Groene, Cooking Aboard Your RV, *see appendix.)*

1 *graham-cracker piecrust*
1 *can sweetened condensed (not evaporated) milk (such as Eagle Brand)*
   Juice of three to four Key limes
   Whipped cream

Have the piecrust ready. Empty the condensed milk into a medium bowl. Using a balloon whisk, quickly stir in the lime juice to the desired tartness, and immediately transfer the filling to the crust. The lime juice causes the milk to set.

Chill, cut, and serve with whipped cream.

---

tough going for a motor home, but we've done it. Stay with US 27, and rely on signage, local maps obtained ahead of time, and your own list of must-see sites.

On the plus side, Miami Beach has the largest neighborhood of art deco buildings in the world. In South Beach, also known as SoBe, walk streets lost in a time warp of gaudy hotels and apartment buildings, street cafés, and shops tended by a Babel of nationalities. Public access to the beach itself is abundant. If you have a small motor home or a tow car, use one of the metered parking lots. Miami Seaquarium on the Rickenbacker Causeway is a 38-acre marine attraction where you can see a killer whale, sea lions, and "Flipper."

On the Rickenbacker Causeway, travel to Bill Baggs Cape Florida Recreational Area on the southern tip of Key Biscayne,

Event:

Calle Ocho's Carnival Miami—a nine-day Hispanic Festival along twenty-three blocks of Miami's 8th Street—is held in March. It's a fabulous street party, but don't go in your RV. Use public transportation.

which has a historic lighthouse, ranger-guided nature walks, and one of the most picturesque beaches on the planet. The beach is a wide span of sugar sands fringed with palms on one side and washed on the other by clear jade waters. The original lighthouse was destroyed during the Seminole Indian Wars in 1836; the current tower was completed in 1846.

On the west side of Dade County, handy to your route to the Keys, visit a Miccosukee Indian village with crafts demonstrations, a museum showing the history of the tribe, and airboat rides. Boats that "fly" over water, land, and swamp are the only way to skim the variety of terrain in the "river of grass" that is the Everglades. Despite the fearsome noise, we still saw a world of wildlife on our airboat ride.

Miami's MetroZoo at 12400 SW 152nd Street is a 290-acre cageless park where animals wander in natural habitats. Also west of the city are Monkey Jungle (14805 SW 216th St.) and Parrot Jungle and Gardens (11000 SW 57th Ave.). Both are oldies but goodies in a steamy, tropical setting of vines, thick vegetation, nattering wildlife, and exotic blooms. Each is worth several hours.

To us, the best part of driving US 1 through the Florida Keys is the drive itself, but don't expect to win any popularity contests. For long miles at a stretch the highway has no passing lanes, so drivers get exasperated when they can't get around an RV. This is the time to dust off all your best driving manners. Use signals faithfully. If you can't pass quickly, don't hog the passing lane. If a long line forms behind you, pull over and let the cars pass while you

enjoy the views. In many places where there is nothing but shining water on both sides of the road and the shallows are alive with wading birds, it's one of the best nature shows in the state. Let the rest of the world speed past while you enjoy it.

Addresses on US 1, which is also called the Overseas Highway, are given in mile markers (MMs), which indicate the distance from Key West. John Pennekamp Coral Reef State Park at MM 102.5 has a section of living reef plus artificial reefs created from sunken ships. Take a guided snorkel or scuba tour through an underwater wonderland to see a different show every day: brilliant reef fish; entire gardens made of sponges, brilliant coral, and sea fans that dance in the current; living shells including emperor helmets and big horse conchs; and all the other denizens of the reef from barracuda and shark to moray eels and Florida lobster. This is also the home of the underwater bronze statue Christ of the Deep. Above the surface take a canoe safari among tangled mangrove roots, ride a glass-bottom boat over the reef, and browse the

Cape Florida Light, Bill Baggs Cape Florida Recreational Area.

visitor center with its educational displays on reefs and the sea.

Theater of the Sea (in Islamorada at MM 84.5) has continuous shows starring sea creatures, a Swim with the Dolphins program, and a four-hour snorkel cruise. At MM 50 in Marathon, visit Tropical Crane Point Hammock to explore a 64-acre native hammock. See shipwreck artifacts, an authentic Conch house, and a children's museum with hands-on exhibits. At MM 78.5 you'll be able to see Indian Key on the ocean side. It's accessible only by boat, but nearby marinas run charters out to one of the most interesting archaeological digs in the South.

Jacob Hausman—one of the many adventurers who made a living along this coast by salvaging the many ships that wrecked on the reefs just offshore—made Indian Key his headquarters. Soon the island was a thriving community with a hotel, warehouses, and homes for as many as seventy permanent residents. (The exact total isn't known because slaves were sometimes counted as chattel instead of people). In 1840 during the Second Seminole War, the entire settlement was burned to the ground by Indians. Seven people were slain. Hausman survived, but was later buried on the island. View fascinating excavations that give a clear picture of the thriving community that once was.

We never drive this highway without thinking of the price paid for building it. It all began during the railroad era, when Henry Flagler extended his rails all the way to Key West. Until then, Key West was a shipping crossroads with closer cultural and economic ties to Cuba and the Bahamas than to the United States. (Many of the mansions you'll see here were built in the Bahamas, disassembled, and shipped here for reassembly.) Battling storms, tropical diseases, bugs and heat, rail workers spent eight years and lost seven hundred men building an Overseas Railroad over miles of causeways and across bridges as long as 7 miles (11.2 km).

Once the railroad was built, traders and settlers could go all the way to Key West by rail and then take a ferry for the short trip to Havana. Settlements grew up all along the line. Then in 1935, a devastating hurricane rampaged across the rail bed. Entire locomotives were washed away, and people in passenger cars perished by the dozens. The lifeline was broken, and the Keys were islands once again. It wasn't until 1938 that a decision was made to use Flagler's strong foundations to build a highway. The railroad was gone forever.

One of the original railroad's engineering marvels, Seven Mile Bridge has been upgraded many times since Flagler's day. It is

Event:

The Miami International Boat Show held mid-February in Miami Beach is the second largest in the world. This maritime blockbuster is a must for anyone who boats or fishes as well as for RVers who want to shop for gear or space-saving ideas. We park our RV in one of the satellite parking lots and ride a free shuttle bus among the show's several venues.

still an exciting drive that offers a sailor's view of nothing but water for miles around. At the eastern end of the bridge, visit Pigeon Key, where you can still see buildings used by the original rail crews. Lower Matecumbe Key (at MM 77.5) is your jumping-off point for trips to Indian Key and Lignumvitae Key, which is named for a rare tree with wood as hard as a rock. Before harvesting of the tree was stopped for preservation, it was used for cutless bearings and other boat-building components. Take a nature walk on the island to see lignum vitae, mangroves, poisonwood, and gumbo limbo trees. The woods and waters are alive with birds, and you'll also see a stone wall that was built long ago for reasons nobody remembers.

Competition for campsites at Bahia Honda State Park (MM 37) is fierce. If you can't get a campsite in the park itself, stay in the area and visit the park as a day-tripper. The beach here is one of the best in the Keys. The park also forms the edge of the National Key Deer Refuge. With luck you'll see one of the miniature deer, which grow to only about 30 inches in height. Take a boat from Big Pine Key (MM 29) to Looe Key National Marine Sanctuary, where you can dive or snorkel along a 5-mile (8 km) beach.

Continuing south, consider lunching at Little Palm Island Resort, which is reached by boat from Little Torch Key. There's ample parking at Little Torch Key for most rigs. Prices are outlandish, but the food is outstanding and the setting—once Harry Truman's private fish camp—is as exotic as a South Seas atoll.

Key West

Continue island-hopping on roads and bridges until you reach Key West, a unique mix of the Caribbean, San Francisco, Fire Island, and Margaritaville. At one time it was the richest community in the United States, thanks to goods-laden ships that sank on its reefs, forming a veritable Sam's Club for professional shipwreck salvors. Entire homes were built and furnished by the booty. By the Depression years of the 1920s and 1930s, however, Key West was one of the country's poorest communities. A lighthouse had been built, so ships no longer wrecked on the reefs.

The keys run almost due west, which could account for the name of the island, but the name is also said to derive from another source. Spanish explorers called it Cayo Hueso, Key of Bones, because of the skeletons they found here. To English ears, the name could have sounded like Key West.

A good choice of campgrounds exists throughout the lower Keys and on Key West itself, but this area is not a place for driving and rubbernecking. Walk the downtown area, and get around most of the island by bicycle. Start by taking one of the tram tours to get your bearings. The narratives are delightful.

To visit all the sightseeing treasures of Key West can take several days. Visit the forts, Truman's Little White House, and old mansions, including one where Ernest Hemingway lived and wrote and another where John James Audubon spent a few weeks while researching tropical birds. Walk narrow streets past "shotgun" houses, "eyebrow" porches, elaborate grillwork, and rooftop "scuttles." Show up at Mallory Square at Sunset (the locals spell it with a capital S). Marvel at the natural spectacle as the sun sinks into a molten gold sea, often with a foreground of a tall ship under sail. Mallory Square is also a freak show, a fascinating bazaar, and the best place to get up close and personal with the natives.

Pubs stay open into the wee hours, and pub-crawling is the local religion. While some spots seem to be straight out of a

If You Have a Pet

Pets have long been barred from Florida state parks. In recent years, however, they have been allowed at some state campgrounds on an experimental basis. This program could be expanded, altered, or discontinued at any time, so it's best to ask about pet policies when making reservations. Pets are welcome at almost all KOA campgrounds and at many other private camps. Check ahead.

Hemingway book or a Jimmy Buffett song, many are just the same tourist-trap gin mills you'd find anywhere. *Caveat emptor.* Dining is another story. It's almost impossible to get a bad meal in Key West, whether a cheap bowl of black beans and rice or the most divine gourmet dinner in an upscale restaurant. The seafood is fresh, the chefs talented, and the competition fierce.

Climb the lighthouse and visit its museum. Browse art galleries and kinky shops. Get a pair of handmade sandals. See the treasure trove at Mel Fisher's Maritime Museum. And don't miss the Key West Cemetery with its quirky grave markers. Locals are characters until they die—and then some. Go swimming, diving, snorkeling, fishing, and sailing. We spent two entire winters in Key West and never ran out of things to do.

The road stops here, but the Keys continue another 70 miles (112 km) out to sea, through the Marquesas to the Dry Tortugas. If you want to camp overnight there, take a boat or seaplane that will land you and all your gear. You must take everything you'll need including water. You can also make it a day trip. Bring water, snorkel gear, and a picnic. Dive and snorkel the clearest waters this side of the Bahamas. Tour the rambling brick fort, a masonry masterpiece of cool tunnels and dark dungeons. Dr. Samuel Mudd was imprisoned here as a suspected conspirator in the assassination of Abraham Lincoln (he was later pardoned). Bush Key near Fort Jefferson, a bird-watcher's mecca, is one of the world's major nesting grounds for sooty terns. Here you'll see massive frigate birds, brown noddy terns, and hosts of other seabirds.

Returning north from Key West on US 1 you'll retrace your original route, so this is your chance to do and see the things that were closed or rained out on the way down. When you get back to the mainland, head for Everglades National Park on FL 9336 out of Florida City. (Or, if you wish to shorten the trip, continue north to US 41, known locally as Tamiami Trail, which leads west through the heart of the Everglades into Big Cypress National Preserve.)

More of the Everglades

An entire lifetime could be spent studying the unique ecosystem that is the Florida Everglades. Compared to mountains, canyons, and towering redwoods found in the national parks in the West, the Everglades seem lifeless, flat, and colorless. Only when you listen for their whispered secrets can you feel the drama of the life cycles played out here. Alligators watch silently, sometimes invisibly, as you hike the hammocks. Insects sing with a constant buzz. Eagles and osprey float overhead, swoop down to pounce, and soar skyward again with a slithering snake or hapless squirrel in a talon or beak. Wild orchids

bloom in trees. Coon oysters cling to the tangled roots of mangrove forests. Even in winter, mosquitoes are ferocious, and in summer they drive all humans away. Wear a high-powered repellent.

Start your Everglades National Park visit at the Main Visitor Center (just follow the signs); then 2 miles (3.2 km) later visit the Royal Palm Visitor Center. For a short visit, choose an easy hike or two. For a longer stay, hike all the trails, take a canoe safari, rent a boat, or just fish all day every day. The road ends at Flamingo. For all its sunny silence, this park has unique dangers. Consult a tide chart, and file a float plan. Ask the advice of park rangers. And never, never feed any wildlife—especially alligators.

Returning to Homestead and heading west on US 41, enter the Everglades again at Shark Valley, where a tram takes you through alligator-infested waters and sloughs alive with birds, leaping fish, otters, and crocodiles.

Continue west on US 41 to Big Cypress National Preserve, which is more of the same scenery but enhanced by the enormous bald cypress trees, some of which are one thousand years old. Before these trees were protected, they were hauled out of Florida by the thousands to make lumber that termites wouldn't eat and fungus wouldn't rot. Coffins, boats, and many of Florida's early mansions were built from heart cypress and pecky cypress that can never be harvested again. Just north of Big Cypress, Corkscrew Swamp Sanctuary is another stand of bald cypress. View it from the boardwalk.

From US 41, take FL 29 north to Copeland and Fakahatchee Strand State Pre-

Event:
In February, the Everglades Seafood Festival in Everglades City serves up more than 3,000 pounds of local seafood along with swamp parties and Native American song and crafts.

serve, the world's only stand of cypress mixed with royal palm. It also has one of the largest displays of wild orchids in the nation. This isn't a trip to be hurried. Sunrises and sunsets occur in God's good time. Birds take flight. The water's surface is broken by the eyes of a hungry gator. A blue heron picks its way along the shallows, ducks its head, and comes up with a silvery fish. Look high in the trees where snails lay their eggs, anhingas spread their wings, osprey nests grow to 9 feet (2.7 m) across, and snowy egrets preen prettily. Blink and you might miss a Florida panther. Only a few dozen survive here in the most remote areas of the Everglades. Return to US 41 to continue your trip.

From US 41 it's an easy hop to Interstate 75, which could take you back north all the way to the Midwest. To continue our recommended route, however, take Interstate 75 and exit north at Port Charlotte on US 17, which runs through farmlands and old cow towns. Arcadia, still looking much as it did in its 1920s heyday, has a rousing rodeo in March. Continue through Zolfo Springs, Fort Meade, and Bartow; from Bartow, follow FL 60 east to Lake Wales, where one more sightseeing bonanza awaits. You have driven through cow country, and you've seen the vastness of Florida's swamps, scrub and prairie. Now visit Lake Kissimmee State Park to meet the men who tamed these lands.

From Lake Wales, travel east on FL 60 to Hesperides while watching for Boy Scout Camp Road, which takes off north. Follow signs to Lake Kissimmee State Park. Camp, fish, picnic, launch a boat, and disappear into an 1872 cow camp. It's run by one or two cow hunters who are dressed in homespun and are packing braided whips that

run 30 feet (9.1 m) long and longer. Don't say "cowboy" or you'll be set straight. In the old South, *boy* was an insulting term. Using special dogs and specially bred horses brought over by the Spanish, these cow hunters use their whips to "pop" cattle out of the scrub.

Ask the cow hunters here anything that happened after President Grant was in the White House, and they are lost. They do know their cow hunting, though, and they'll

> **Event:**
> In January, the annual Florida Citrus Festival and the Polk County Fair in Winter Haven combine to make an eleven-day celebration of rides, contests, feasting, and fun.

tell you about fevers and agues, the problem with wild boars, the meals they make out of grits and bacon, and the reason they cut one tine off their three-tine forks. A fork looks too much like a devil's trident, they figure, and out here you can't take any chances.

Unlike the thundering cattle roundups that took place in the West, Florida cattle had to be herded more carefully through swamps and forests filled with rattlesnakes, sinkholes, and saw grass. Eventually the cattle would reach the Gulf of Mexico, where they would be sold for Spanish gold and shipped to Havana. There isn't a zipper, a radio antenna, or a soda bottle in camp. Coffee cooks over an open fire. The shelter is a chickee hut with plaited roofing, and the beds are covered in rough, wool army blankets. At the end of your visit, walk the long pathway back to the parking lot. Only then are you back in the present.

From here, you're only an hour from Orlando and your starting point. Retrace your route to US 27, and then jump back on Interstate 4.

> **Event:**
> Arcadia holds its All-Florida Championship Rodeo, an old-fashioned classic ridin' and ropin' contest, in March. The De Soto County Fair also runs here this month.

Appendix:
Resources

BOOKS

Bridges, Fraser. *Natural Places of the Gulf Coast from Florida to Texas: A Traveler's Guide to the Culture, Spirit, and Ecology of Scenic Destinations*. Rocklin CA: Prima Publishing, 1997.

Brooke, Steven. *The Majesty of Natchez*. Gretna LA: Pelican Publishing, 1999.

Curran, Jan D. *The Appalachian Trail, a Journey of Discovery*. Moore Haven FL: Rainbow Books, 1991. See also Jan D. Curran, *The Appalachian Trail: How to Prepare for It and Hike It* (Highland City FL: Rainbow Books, 1995). Even if you'll be hiking only portions of the trail, these books are invaluable as guides, sources of background information, and armchair reading.

Dunbar, David. *The Outdoor Traveler's Guide to Canada*. New York: Stewart, Tabori & Chang, n.d.

Farrant, Don W. *The Lure and Lore of the Golden Isles: The Magical Heritage of Georgia's Outerbanks*. Nashville: Rutledge Hill Press, 1993.

Folwell, Elizabeth, with Neal S. Burdick. *The Adirondack Book*, 3rd ed. Lee MA: Berkshire House Publishers, 1998.

Good, Merle, and Phyllis Good. *Twenty Most Asked Questions about the Amish and Mennonites*. Lancaster PA: Good Books, 1979.

Groene, Janet. *Cooking Aboard Your RV*. Camden ME: Ragged Mountain Press, 1993.

Groene, Janet. *Florida Guide*. New York: Open Road Publishing, 2000.

Groene, Janet, and Gordon Groene. *Country Roads of Ohio*. Chicago: Country Roads Press, 1999,

Groene, Janet, and Gordon Groene. *Living Aboard Your RV: A Guide to the Fulltime Life on Wheels*. 2nd ed. Camden ME: Ragged Mountain Press, 1993.

Groene, Janet, and Gordon Groene. *Natural Wonders of Georgia: A Guide to Parks, Preserves, and Wild Places*. Oaks PA: Country Roads Press, 1997.

Groene, Janet, and Gordon Groene. *Natural Wonders of Ohio: Exploring Wild and Scenic Places*. Oaks PA: Country Roads Press, 1998.

Hirtz, Rob. *North Carolina Handbook: From the Great Smoky Mountains to the Outer Banks*. Chico CA: Moon Travel Handbooks, 1999.

Houk, Rose. *Great Smoky Mountains National Park*. Boston: Houghton Mifflin, 1993. This is a natural history guide to the national park.

Hunter, Dave. *Along the Interstate*. Mississakga ON: Mile Oak Publishing, annual publication. Editions cover major interstates and give locations of restaurants, service stations, and other facilities at each exit.

Jones, John Oliver. *U.S. Outdoor Atlas and Recreation Guide: Maps and Charts for All 50 States*. Boston: Houghton Mifflin, 1994. This is a barebones listing of places to hike, fish, bicycle, camp, view wildlife, boat, and so forth in the United States.

Knapp-Sawyer, Kem, editor. *Pennsylvania Dutch: The Amish and the Mennonites*. Carlisle MA: Discovery Enterprises, 1997.

Kraybill, Donald B. *The Puzzles of Amish Life*. Intercourse PA: Good Books, 1990.

Kuhns, Oscar. *The German and Swiss Settlements of Colonial Pennsylvania: A Study of the So-Called Pennsylvania Dutch*. Ann Arbor MI: Gryphon Books, 1971.

Lashomb, Audrey. *Going Home*. Clayton NY: Grindstone Press, 1998. This poignant memoir captures the flavor of the Thousand Islands of the St. Lawrence River.

McClure, Deneen. *The Florida Dog Lover's Companion*. San Francisco: Foghorn Press, 1996. This is an invaluable guide to pet-friendly campgrounds, beaches, restaurants, and other sites. The company also publishes dog lover's guides for other areas, including Boston, Washington DC, and Atlanta. See also Heather MacLean Walters, *Take Your Pet Too! Fun Things To Do* (Chester NJ: M.C.E. Publishing, 1996). Note that some other books on traveling with pets list only motels and hotels, so they aren't useful for RV travel.

Miller, Levi. *Our People: The Amish and Mennonites of Ohio*. Scottdale PA: Herald Press, 1983.

Price, Eugenia. *Maria*. Franklin TN: Providence House Publishers, 1999. See also any other fiction books by Eugenia Price that are set in the southeastern states.

Rafferty, Robert. *Frommer's America's 100 Best-Loved State Parks*. Currently out of print. This is a nice addition to any RV library.

Reader's Digest Association. *America from the Road*. Pleasantville NY: Reader's Digest Association, 1982.

Reader's Digest Association. *See the USA the Easy Way: 136 Loop Tours to 1,200 Great Places*. Pleasantville NY: Reader's Digest Books, 1995.

Rogers, Barbara Radcliffe, and Stillman Rogers. *New Hampshire Off the Beaten Path*. 2nd ed. Old Saybrook CT: Globe Pequot Press, 1995.

Scott, David Logan. *Guide to the National Park Areas: Eastern States*. 5th ed. Old Saybrook CT: Globe Pequot Press, 1998.

Sentell, Lee. *The Best of Alabama: A Guide to Attractions, Restaurants, Lodging, and Events*. Currently out of print.

Smith, Patrick D. *A Land Remembered*. Sarasota FL:

Pineapple Press, 1998. This is a fictional history of Florida.

Smithsonian Guides to Historic America are published by Stewart, Tabori & Chang in editions for Virginia and the Capital Region, Southern New England, the Mid-Atlantic States, Northern New England, the Deep South, the Carolinas and the Appalachian States, and the Great Lakes.

Sternberg, Mary Ann. *The Pelican Guide to Louisiana*. Gretna LA: Pelican Publishing, 1993.

Stigleman, Michelle. *Wheelchairs on the Go: A Guide to*

Accessible Fun on Florida's Gulf Coast. Clearwater FL: Access Guide Publishing (888-245-7300), 1998.

Summerlin, Cathy, and Vernon Summerlin. *Highroad Guide to the Tennessee Mountains*. Marietta, GA: Longstreet, 1998.

Travel Centers and Truckstops. Norcross GA: Interstate America, annual publication. This is a guide to more than 5,000 truckstops in the United States and Canada where RVers can find service, fuel, meals, overnight parking, and other conveniences.

MAPS AND OTHER

Delorme Mapping Company, P.O. Box 298, Freeport ME 04032. This company publishes detailed maps of every state. Most editions are geocoded for use with GPS.

National Park Service campground reservations, 800-365-2267. (Also, <*http://www.recreation.gov*> is a database of all federal recreation areas. A visit to this website is a must for anyone who camps, hunts, fishes, hikes, or visits historic sites.)

Index

Numbers in **bold** refer to pages with illustrations